CHARLES DICKENS AS EDITOR

CHARLES DICKENS AS EDITOR

BEING LETTERS WRITTEN BY HIM TO
WILLIAM HENRY WILLS
HIS SUB-EDITOR

SELECTED AND EDITED
BY
R. C. LEHMANN

WITH PORTRAITS

HASKELL HOUSE PUBLISHERS Ltd.
Publishers of Scarce Scholarly Books
NEW YORK, N. Y. 10012
1972

HASKELL HOUSE PUBLISHERS Ltd.
Publishers of Scarce Scholarly Books
280 LAFAYETTE STREET
NEW YORK, N. Y. 10012

Library of Congress Cataloging in Publication Data

Dickens, Charles, 1812-1870.
   Charles Dickens as editor, being letters written by him to William Henry Wills, his sub-editor.

   Reprint of the 1912 ed.
   I. Wills, William Henry, 1810-1880.
II. Lehmann, Rudolph Chambers, 1856-1929, ed.
PR4581.A4W5 1972   823'.8   73-38842
ISBN 0-8383-1393-0

Printed in the United States of America

PREFACE.

The letters printed in this volume were written by Charles Dickens to my great-uncle, William Henry Wills, who first became closely connected with him at the time of the foundation of the *Daily News* in 1846, and was afterwards for nearly twenty years his sub-editor on *Household Words* and *All the Year Round*. With the exception of a certain number (relatively small) which have already appeared in whole or in part in the three volumes of the " Letters of Charles Dickens" published by Miss Hogarth and Miss Dickens in 1880 and 1882 these letters are new.* They were carefully preserved by Wills, and at his death passed to his widow. She left them to her niece, Lady Priestley, from whose eldest son, my cousin Mr. R. C. Priestley, they have now come to me. I desire to express my warm thanks to Miss Hogarth and Mr. H. F. Dickens, K.C., for their permission to publish this selection from the 450 letters in my possession.

It may be said of these letters that their effect is to concentrate the light upon one side of Dickens's manifold and unceasing activities. They show him as an editor, ardent, but patient; sometimes impulsive, but always immovably steadfast in the execution of his purpose; firm in his grasp of principles, but resolutely careful in every detail which might serve to carry those principles into execution; himself an indefatigable worker, and not content with anything short of hard and honest work on the part of his fellow

---

* I ought, perhaps, to add that two were printed by me in " Memories of Half a Century."

labourers; generously warm in his gratitude for good service loyally rendered, but merciless to sham, slovenliness or incapacity; always devoted to good causes and perfectly fearless in his efforts to promote them. He had a consuming desire to do whatever he undertook as thoroughly as it was capable of being done, and his performance rarely fell short of his desire. This is no small thing to say when all that he did in addition to his editorial work is remembered. Indeed, one cannot conceive him as ever taking any real rest. He speaks of himself in one of his letters as " Coming off his back (and the grass) " in order to consider some business matter, but even in that position he was, I am sure, devising new plans and novel methods for giving effect to them. In a letter of June 6th, 1867, he says, " I shall never rest much while my faculties last, and (if I know myself) have a certain something in me that would still be active in rusting and corroding me if I flattered myself that it was in repose."

In regard to his relations with Wills these letters form a very remarkable record, for they show how a mere official connection, involving at first a little friction, gradually developed into a perfect confidence and a warm and enduring friendship. Wills did not hesitate, when the occasion, as he thought, arose, to tender advice which ran counter to Dickens's own inclinations—not a light matter with a man who held and expressed his inclinations so strongly as Dickens. He did this notably when Dickens was debating with himself the question of going to America (see letter of June 6th, 1867, and the note to the letter of September 24th of the same year), and neither on that occasion nor on any other was their friendship clouded for a moment. I may be pardoned, perhaps, for devoting a few pages to the career of this friend of Dickens :—

William Henry Wills was born in Plymouth on January 13th, 1810. His father had been at one time wealthy, his business being that of a ship-owner and prize agent. No doubt the close of the great war with France had a depressing effect upon his undertakings. At any rate he suffered misfortunes and lost the greater part of his money. Towards the end of 1819 or the beginning of 1820 he transferred himself and his family to London. Many years afterwards Wills described his journey to London (" Forty Years in London," *All the Year Round*, April 8th, 1865) :—

"My mother," he writes, "brought me from the West of England in the middle of the severe winter during which the present century glided out of its teens. At that time stage-coach travelling was one of the loudest boasts of this modest country. Peers horsed, and baronets drove, the 'crack' conveyances of that day. Yet we were a week on the road in the mail, having been snowed up at a village on the edge of Salisbury Plain ; our guard perishing in a gallant attempt to push on with the mail-bags on the back of one of the leaders. How well I remember the hasty dinners at the great inns we stopped at on the road ; all alike !— the long table, the big joints, the invariable pigeon pie, the selfish scrambling of the passengers to get their full three-and-sixpence-worth tucked in in time for the warning notes of the guard's horn ; the tin, thin tripod plate-warmer at the fire, the nimble waiters in white cotton stockings and pumps, who were constantly wiping plates with napkins whipped in and out of the side-pockets of their natty striped jackets. Then once more inside the coach, don't I gasp at the recollection of the smell— like bad nuts—occasioned by four human beings performing asphyxia upon themselves from prudent dread of 'the night air' ; the word ventilation having been at that time hardly invented ? I shiver to think of the cold blast that woke us two or three times each night when a change of coachman forced shilling subscriptions at the open door from each passenger, and shall I ever forget the awe with which I regarded, during that tedious journey, the helpful good-natured fellow-traveller—a real live Londoner—who told us, modestly, as if it were a mere commonplace, that he had actually, spoken with the Lord Mayor of the City of London, face to face? Every word he dropped about London was caught in my eager ear as greedily as gold let fall into a miser's purse: How that trees could actually be seen even in the City; how that there were one thousand hackney-coaches allowed by government —no more and no less; how that the cries of London were attuned by Act of Parliament, and that milk and mackerel were the only articles permitted to be cried on Sundays, because of their perishable nature; how that crossing-sweepers disguised themselves as noblemen after business hours, married rich wives whom they maintained splendidly in suburban palaces, ignorant of their profession, and went to town and returned home each day with the punctuality of bank-clerks, changing their clothes on the way to and fro; how that public opinion fell crushingly upon any person who dared to light fires or wear a great-coat until the fifth of November, however soon the winter may set in before the great bonfire day; how that nobody could appear out of mourning in Lent, nor face the world pleasantly at Easter without bran new clothes; how every country visitor was bound, within the first week of his sojourn in London to ascend St. Paul's and to the top of the Monument, to inspect the water-works at London Bridge, the lions in the Tower, Mr. Crosse's menagerie at Exeter Change, Miss Linwood's Exhibition in Leicester Square, and Mrs. Salmon's shilling wax-works in Fleet Street. They must also wait in the narrow part of the same thoroughfare to see the hour struck on the big bells of St. Dunstan's Church by the iron giants. All these ideas, with others derived from a fat little green volume in vogue before the word 'Hand-book' had been imported from Germany, and known as 'Leigh's Picture of London,' filled the childish imagination with a wonder and impatience that became almost insupportable as the stages towards the metropolis diminished. In the hazy twilight of morning congealed breath was wiped from the windows; and a huge lump of the mist, densified into shape dimly in the distance, was pointed out as Windsor Castle. Then came tearful stories of a blind old king, sometimes bemoaning his mental eclipse, sometimes flinging his coat over his shoulder and crying old clothes round a padded room.

"By-and-by, bright, sunshiny, breezy morning. What enormous draft-horses, and what little houses! Surely this can't be London! Not quite; only Hammersmith.

"Out of the bewildering excitement of being actually in London, and the distracting succession of new objects passed by, and passing us, only two recollections can be revived, at this very long distance of time, from the scene at the White Horse Cellar, Piccadilly; first, the endless succession of old clothes-men; second, the number and perseverance of hawkers of pale, sour, cold-looking oranges, which made even my young teeth chatter to behold. The sound of 'Ole Clo!' 'Ole Clo!' 'Old Clo!' never left the ear an instant's respite: an endless procession of Jews with empty black bags under their arms, walking rapidly, uttering exactly the same sound, but on different notes. That was no time to ask questions, and story-book lore supplied the childish notion that they were all wicked wandering Jews, bound to let the world know they were duly performing their penance by incessantly exclaiming 'Ole Clo!' as watchmen cried the hour in the night. The prodigious number of these candidates for cast clothing is not so wonderful when we remember that the poor could get at that time nothing else to wear. Amongst the great benefits conferred by machinery and free trade on the present generation is cheap new clothing, and the extinction of a race of disreputable hawkers.

"We start for the City. What a glory of shops on both sides of the way! A street full of scaffolding—half-built Regent Street; Charing Cross; the statue of a man on horseback close to the gates of the King's stables; Temple Bar; St. Paul's. At length St. Martins-le-Grand—a 'cheat,' I thought; for, being then a squalid-looking lane, it was the reverse of grand, no removal of the Post Office from the ample premises in Lombard Street being then dreamt of. Finally, the yard of the Bull and Mouth Inn, up a narrow turning. Here my father had lived for three days, expecting us every minute, and was in the coffee-room with groups of other persons waiting for friends from all parts of the country, discussing chances and possibilities of their having perished in the snow, like the mail guard. No post letters could precede us, and the joy of that meeting, now nearly half a century old, swells my heart, even as I write these words."

The family made their home in Somers Town, and there, at "The Polygon," in the middle of Clarendon Square, Wills was put to school with "a genteel old lady, professing in her prospectuses the strictest exclusion of the sons of tradesmen." Of the immediately succeeding stages of Wills's history I have no accurate details. He tells us in the article from which I have quoted that, after leaving school, he had to take the walk to the Strand every day. In the sketch of his life, which appears in the "Dictionary of National Biography," it is stated that at his father's death the support of the family devolved upon Wills, and it is added that he became a journalist and contributed to periodicals. I know he did not go to a university, and I think it is likely that, having been placed in some office (whether mercantile or journalistic I cannot say), he was gradually drawn into the vocation of literature. I suppose he bombarded editors in the usual way. He is known to have contributed to the *Penny* and *Saturday Magazines*. At any rate the first letter in this book shows that in 1837 he had sent two contributions to Dickens, then editor of *Bentley's Miscellany*, that one of these was accepted, and that further contributions were invited. After this the first authentic news I can obtain of him is that he had made a sufficient literary reputation to warrant his being asked to join the enterprising company of those who, under Landells, Henry Mayhew and Mark Lemon, were in 1841 engaged in founding *Punch*. From the first he was a member of the literary staff of that paper, he is believed to have helped in the drafting of its prospectus, and he is known to have contributed to its first number. Many years ago he himself showed me the early volumes of *Punch* in which he had marked his own contributions, and I can remember that the epigram on Lord Cardigan ("The Blackballed of the United Service Club") was amongst them. He became the dramatic critic of the paper, and his contributions in prose and verse, though latterly in decreasing quantities, seem to have continued until 1848.

In the meantime, however (in 1842), he had gone to Edinburgh, having been appointed assistant editor of *Chambers's Journal*. I have a copy of a letter written by him to William Chambers in Edinburgh, on November 4th, 1842, in which he says: "I cheerfully accept your offer of the situation of literary assistant in your office at £300 per ann. . . . Before taking a long farewell of London I have arrangements to make which will occupy me at least a week; so that I shall not have the pleasure of meeting you in Edinburgh till about the 12th inst." This position he retained for three years, but his literary connection with the journal, though interrupted for a time, was resumed again, for the records of the publishing office show that in 1849, when he was in London, he was a pretty regular contributor and was receiving the handsome remuneration of £10 a week for his articles. In 1845, I think—I am sorry I cannot fix the date with any greater precision—he married Janet, the sister of William and Robert Chambers.

Towards the end of 1845 he was back in London to take part in another journalistic venture. The *Daily News* was in process of establishment under the editorship of Dickens, and Wills was appointed a member (probably the chief) of the sub-editorial staff and secretary to the editor. The first number appeared on January 21st, 1846, but in less than three weeks Dickens resigned his editorship to John Forster, who continued to hold it during the greater part of what he himself describes as " that weary, anxious, laborious year." Wills remained on the paper. and must have proved his ability to the new editor's satisfaction, for it was Forster who, when *Household Words* was established, suggested to Dickens that Wills should be his assistant. " There remained," says Forster (" Life," II., 422), " only a title and an assistant editor : and I am happy now to remember that for the latter important duty Mr. Wills was chosen at my suggestion.

He discharged its duties with admirable patience and ability for twenty years, and Dickens's later life had no more intimate friend." When, in 1859, *Household Words* gave way to *All the Year Round*, Wills went on as "sub-editor" to the new publication.

From the moment of his appointment on *Household Words* Wills was drawn more and more closely within the orbit of Dickens. The letters in this book sufficiently show that Dickens, in spite of all his other work and his frequent absences abroad, kept a very close hold on all that concerned his weekly journal. Wills, however, was his *alter ego*, and a large part of the heavy burden of work and responsibility fell on his shoulders. The letters themselves prove how generously Dickens appreciated his sub-editor's work. Their pages are brightened by frequent expressions of confidence, regard and affection.*

Wills was secretary to the Guild of Literature and Art, and at the end of 1851 he accompanied Dickens during a part of the theatrical tour undertaken for the benefit of that institution. So far as I can discover, there was only one other piece of "outside" work that Wills took, and that was when, in 1855, at Dickens's recommendation, he accepted the position of almoner-secretary to Miss Coutts (afterwards the Baroness Burdett-Coutts).

Wills, though his opportunities for indulging his tastes had been few, had always had a great liking for country life and, in particular, for the sport of fox-hunting, of which, like John Leech, he was an ardent follower. In 1867 he decided to move his

---

* I refer particularly to December 14th, 1853; October 27th, 1854; February 15th, 1856; January 2nd, 1862; April 5th, 1862; May 20th, 1864; and November 3rd, 1867 (in the Introduction to that year).

headquarters from London into Hertfordshire, having taken a pleasant house named "Sherrards," near Welwyn. Here he was able to hunt to his heart's content with the Hertfordshire hounds. He was an absolutely fearless rider, and his preference was for large and powerful horses, to the control of which his muscular strength—for he was very thin and slightly built—was not always quite adequate. His thinness, indeed, was the constant object of his friends' chaff. One story related how someone, noticing his absence from a gathering and asking where he was, had been advised to look for him in the flute-case and had found him snugly tucked up there. Another told how an absent-minded old lady, sitting next him at dinner, had mistaken his leg for the leg of her chair and had curled her own leg comfortably round it. As to his mounts, I remember that on one occasion I rode on a pleasure jaunt with him, and I noticed, at first with some surprise, that his horse, a great bony animal with a Roman nose, would suddenly put its head down between its knees and, without any previous consultation with its rider, go off for a hundred yards or so at a gallop, thereupon calmly resuming its solemn walk. This happened over and over again, but it provoked no comment from my uncle, who thoroughly enjoyed his outing. In 1868, while Dickens was in America, Wills did, however, meet with a bad accident in the hunting-field. He was thrown on his head and was for some time in great danger, and even after he had recovered he felt the effects of the concussion. In the following year he decided to retire from active journalistic work, being then in his sixtieth year.

He settled down very comfortably at "Sherrards" and took his part in the life of the country-side. He became a member of the Committee of the Hunt, was appointed a magistrate, and elected Chairman of the Board of Guardians. He survived his great friend and chieftain more than ten years, and died on September 1st, 1880.

In 1850 he edited "Sir Roger de Coverley, by the Spectator." In 1861 he published "Old Leaves Gathered from *Household Words*," a collection of his contributions, affectionately inscribed "To The Other Hand, whose masterly touches gave to the Old Leaves here freshly gathered their brightest tints." In the same year he published an anthology entitled "Poets' Wit and Humour," with illustrations. This contained two specimens from his own pen. He also published, under the title of "Light and Dark," a selection from his articles in *Chambers's Journal*.

Mrs. Wills survived her husband for twelve years. Dickens had a great regard for her and much appreciated her delightful qualities—her wit, her humour, her gift for the telling of a Scotch story or the singing of a Scotch song. One of her sayings is recorded by Mr. Spielmann in his "History of *Punch*":—how she had noticed that those who advocated the rights of women were generally the left of men. Of a small and spindle-shanked boy relation in a Highland suit, she remarked that his legs, no doubt, would be better in the breech than in the observance.

After her husband's death Mrs. Wills came to London, and died there on October 24th, 1892.

I have prefixed introductions to the letters of each year, not with any intention of giving an exhaustive

PREFACE. xv

account of Dickens's life, but solely for the purpose of explaining the story of the letters and making clear the allusions they contain. In order to carry out this purpose more fully I have also added footnotes wherever it seemed desirable.

For the identification of the authors of contributions to *Household Words* I have availed myself of the Office Book of that journal. This book, which is now in my possession, was kept and posted up week by week by my uncle. In one column he wrote the name of the author, in another the title of the article, in a third its length in columns, in a fourth the amount paid for it, while in a fifth he showed in what manner and when the payment was made. This book covers every issue of *Household Words*. Unfortunately no such book is available for *All the Year Round*.

I have referred frequently to Forster's " Life of Charles Dickens " in three volumes and to the " Letters of Charles Dickens " published (also in three volumes) by Miss Hogarth and Miss Dickens. In referring to the former I have used the word " Life " (*e.g.*, " Life," II., 190); for the latter I have used the term " Letters " (*e.g.*, " Letters," III., 137). In the " Letters " I have been able to note a few minor inaccuracies in regard to dates, and a few cases in which by an error due, doubtless, to confusion in a great mass of loose sheets, a paragraph from one letter has been incorporated into another of a different date.

Wills's letters, five of which (to Dickens) will be found in the course of this book, while parts of a few others have been quoted, are taken from an old MS. book in which Wills entered copies of some of his letters.

The photographs reproduced in this book are from a collection formerly in the possession of Dudley Costello, one of the actors in the " Guild " performances of 1851, and a contributor to *Household Words*.

R. C. L.

January, 1912.

CONTENTS.

	PAGE
PREFACE	v

BENTLEY'S MISCELLANY—
1837—1845 3

THE DAILY NEWS—
1846—1849 9

HOUSEHOLD WORDS—
1850 19
1851 44
1852 76
1853 96
1854 121
1855 157
1856 192
1857 225
1858 238

ALL THE YEAR ROUND—
1859 261
1860 276
1861 283
1862 301
1863 321
1864 331
1865 340
1866 347
1867 353
1868 377
1869 389
1870 394

INDEX 397

PORTRAITS.

CHARLES DICKENS . . . . *Frontispiece*

WILLIAM HENRY WILLS . . . . *To face p.* 4

WILKIE COLLINS . . . . ,, 96

WILLIAM MAKEPEACE THACKERAY . . . . . ,, 176

I
BENTLEY'S MISCELLANY

1837.

DICKENS was editor of *Bentley's Miscellany* from January, 1837, for two years. In a letter to Mr. W. L. Sammins ("Letters," III., 12), dated January 31st, 1839, he speaks of himself as being "no longer its editor." His successor was Harrison Ainsworth.

The original of the following letter, the first written by Dickens to Wills, is undated and is written on black-edged paper. Wills has added to it this pencil note: "Date probably 1837. Mourning for Mary Hogarth, his sister-in-law, who died in his house May 7th. The 'first great grief of his life.'" This letter, therefore, in which Dickens proposes to insert Wills's "little poetic tale" in the July number, must have been written after May 7th, but before the middle of June, when the July number would presumably be made up. At this time "Pickwick" was still running in monthly parts, and "Oliver Twist," begun in January of this year, was continuing its appearance in *Bentley's Miscellany*.

48, DOUGHTY STREET, MECKLENBURGH SQUARE,
Wednesday Morning.

Mr. Dickens presents his compliments to Mr. W. H. Wills, and begs to apologise to him for the delay which has occurred in returning the inclosed paper, which has been quite accidental. Mr. Dickens would have accepted it with much pleasure, had not so many papers founded on the same idea (translations and otherwise) appeared in our periodical Literature of late years. It is curious that he has by him at this moment no less than three which have been offered for the *Miscellany*, and the main feature of each of which, is, the very same delusion that Mr. Wills describes.

The little poetic tale pleases Mr. Dickens very much, and he proposes to insert it in the July Number. He will be happy at all times to pay the promptest attention to anything Mr. Wills may send him.

For the next eight years I find no letters, and I assume that Wills did not become actually acquainted with Dickens until he met him in 1845—1846 in connection with the establishment and issue of the *Daily News*.

I append a short summary of the chief events in Dickens's literary career during these years:—

1838.

"Oliver Twist," which ran in *Bentley's Miscellany* during 1837 and this year, was published in three volumes.

Nine monthly parts of "Nicholas Nickleby" appeared, April to December.

1839.

Monthly parts of "Nicholas Nickleby" appeared from January to October. The book was published complete in October.

1840 and 1841.

"Master Humphrey's Clock," containing "The Old Curiosity Shop" and "Barnaby Rudge," ran in eighty-eight weekly parts.

(In 1841 Wills helped to found *Punch* and became a member of its staff.)

1842.

Dickens went to America in January and returned home in July. The "American Notes" were published.

(Wills went to Edinburgh to help in editing *Chambers's Journal*.)

1843.

Twelve monthly parts of "Martin Chuzzlewit" were issued from January to December.

1844.

"Martin Chuzzlewit" continued to run in monthly parts until July, when the complete volume was published.

In the summer Dickens went to Italy, returning to England for a short visit towards the end of the year. "The Chimes" published.

1845.

Dickens returned to Italy, coming back to England in June.

(Wills returned to London to join the staff of the *Daily News*.)

II
THE DAILY NEWS

1846.

In this year Dickens, who during the autumn of the previous year had been actively engaged in preparations for the establishment of the *Daily News*, became its first editor. Wills was at this time, and had been since its foundation in 1841, a member of the staff of *Punch*. He was appointed a member of the sub-editorial staff of the *Daily News* and secretary to Dickens. The first number of the *Daily News* was issued on January 21st, its price being 5*d*. Dickens resigned his editorship on February 9th, after a tenure of less than three weeks, and went abroad.

Clarkson Stanfield, R.A. (1794—1867), who is mentioned in the letter of March 2nd, as wishing to become a subscriber to the *Daily News*, was one of Dickens's best friends and his frequent assistant in his theatrical enterprises. Before becoming distinguished as a marine painter, he had been in the Navy and had served as a sailor on the same ship on which Douglas Jerrold was a midshipman. Subsequently he became a theatrical scene-painter. In 1832 he founded the Society of British Artists in conjunction with David Roberts and others.

The letter of April 22nd refers to the following account in the *Daily News* of April 7th of the first dinner of the General Theatrical Fund, held under the chairmanship of Dickens on the previous evening ("Life," II., 195) :—

GENERAL THEATRICAL FUND.

Last evening the first dinner, and the seventh anniversary of the establishment of the General Theatrical Fund was celebrated at the London Tavern. Charles Dickens, Esq. presiding.

After the usual loyal and preliminary toasts, the Chairman, in proposing "Prosperity to the General Theatrical Fund," explained its objects. The theatrical funds already in existence—those attached to Drury Lane and Covent Garden Theatres, which only extend their benefits to persons having long engagements at those theatres. But it was now nearly impossible to comply with the conditions for sharing the advantages of those funds. Covent Garden is, in a dramatic point of view, a vision of the past ; and as to Drury Lane, it is so exclusively devoted to opera and ballet, that the statue of Shakspeare which is placed on its portico serves as emphatically to mark Shakspeare's tomb as that at Stratford-on-Avon. The life of the country performer, who has not been able to command a high position, is not passed on a bed of roses, but of very artificial flowers, indeed. He who often gives away magnificent fortunes has to exist upon fifteen shillings per week. Yet it is good to know, that for the seven years during which the fund has existed, the members have, despite all their struggles, paid up their subscriptions. These are especially the class of performers who stand in need of such a fund as the one whose anniversary is now being kept. When they have passed from before the glittering row of lights, let us aid them in retiring to comfort, and, if possible, sufficiency. Having taught many a wholesome lesson, and beguiled us of many a pleasing smile, they have been our benefactors and friends, let us not therefore forget them in their old age.

The Hon. FITZHARDING BERKELEY, M.P., proposed the "Health of the Chairman," which was drunk with great enthusiasm.

Mr. C. DICKENS felt deeply grateful for the manner in which the toast had been received, the more so as he felt a great interest in the association.

The chairman having sat down,

Mr. CULLENFORD, the Secretary of the Society, read a list of subscriptions, amongst which were the Hon. F. Berkeley, 5*l.*; the Hon. Dr. Hope, 10*l.*; Sir Bellingham Graham, 10*l.*; Luke Hansard, Esq., 25*l.*; B. B. Cabbell, Esq., 21*l.*; James Strutt, Esq., 10*l.*; T. P. Cooke, Esq., 5*l.*; D. W. Osbaldiston, Esq., 5*l.*, besides many others.

The CHAIRMAN next proposed the health of Mr. B. Webster, but that gentleman being absent, Mr. Douglas Jerrold having been called on returned thanks.

Mr. DICKENS then proposed the health of Mr. J. B. Buckstone, the Treasurer of the fund, the solvency of which had, he was happy to say, not been at all impaired by the treasurer having of late been constantly asking a great many persons to "Lend him Five Shillings."

Mr. BUCKSTONE, in returning thanks, adverted to the advantages of the society. To the other theatrical funds no individuals, even though they were attached to the two large houses, could share their benefits, if they were dancers or pantomimists, whilst the length of time required to elapse before the regular performer could become eligible for the fund, made him eligible for the workhouse. The General Theatrical Fund, however, provided for all sorts and conditions of actors, provided they shall have paid their subscriptions during seven years. But for this institution, where could the decayed English performer turn for support? Nowhere but to the General Theatrical Fund, and the treasurer hoped that, by the liberality of the public, the demands of the fund would never exceed the means of meeting them.

Several toasts were drunk, the whole under the experienced generalship of the well-known O'Toole. The meeting separated at a convivial hour, after enjoying an excellent dinner.

Between the speeches several musical performances were given by the Misses Rainsforth, Williams, M. Williams, Kate Loder, and Madame Albertazzi, Mr. Godefroid elicited great applause by his performance on the harp, and Mr. Hobbs by his clear and agreeable singing.

OFFICES OF THE *DAILY NEWS*,
WHITEFRIARS,
Tuesday Night.

(Date added in pencil by W. H. W., 4*th Feb*., 1846).

MY DEAR MR. WILLS:—I dine out to-morrow (Wednesday) and next day (Thursday) and shall not be here either evening until rather late. Will you have the goodness to let the Sub Editors know this—and as I shall not wish to be detained here unnecessarily, to ask them to have ready for me anything (*if* anything) requiring my attention.

You may tell them at the same time, if you please,

that I shall not be here, generally, on Sunday nights; and that I shall always wish to let them know of the general arrangements for Sunday nights, on Fridays before I go away.

Faithfully yours always,
CHARLES DICKENS.

DEVONSHIRE TERRACE,
Sixteenth February, 1846.

MY DEAR MR. WILLS :—I miss you a great deal more than I miss the Paper.

May I ask you to reply to all strange letters coming to the office addressed personally to me, that my connection with the *D.N.* does not extend to the consideration or settlement of such matters, and that I have forwarded the letter to the Editor—dating, in all such cases, from *here*. I have sent this answer to all the enclosed documents that I have marked with a X.

Among them, is an uncrossed epistle from one Mrs. ——, referring to a first letter which I have *not* received. Do you know what it is about? If she wants money, I do not like her style of correspondence at all, and would rather plead (as well I may) the immense number of similar appeals.

Always believe me,

(The signature has been cut off).

DEVONSHIRE TERRACE,
Eighteenth February, 1846.

MY DEAR MR. WILLS :—I have written to Howitt, and to Mr. Manly, and to Reynard the Fox. I think the pamphlet by the latter gentleman had better "be dealt with," favourably, " on the premises."

Do look at the enclosed from Mrs. What's-her-name. For a surprising audacity, it is remarkable even to me, who am positively bullied, and all but beaten, by these people. I wish you would do me the favour to write to her (in your own name and from your own address) stating that you answered her letter as you did, because if I were the wealthiest nobleman in England I could not keep pace with one-twentieth part of the demands upon me—and because you saw no internal evidence in her application to induce you to single it out for any especial notice. That the tone of this letter renders you exceedingly glad you did so; and that you decline, for me, holding any correspondence with her. Something to that effect, after what flourish your nature will.

Faithfully yours always,
C. D.

Devonshire Terrace,
  Monday Morning, Second March, 1846.

My Dear Mr. Wills:—I really don't know what to say, about the New Brunswicker. The idea *will* obtrude itself on my mind that he had no business to come here on such an expedition; and that it is a piece of the wild conceit for which his countrymen are so remarkable; and that I can hardly afford to be steward to such adventurers. On the other hand, your description of him pleases me. Then that purse which I never could keep shut in my life makes mouths at me, saying "See how empty I am!" Then I fill it; and it looks very rich indeed.

I think the best way is, to say, that if you think you can do him any *permanent* good with five pounds (that is, get him home again) I will give you the money. But I should be very much indisposed to give it him, merely to linger on here about town for a little time, and then be hard up again.

As to employment, I do in my soul believe that if I were Lord Chancellor of England, I should have been aground long ago, for the patronage of a messenger's place.

Say all that is civil for me to the proprietor of the *Illustrated London News*, who really seems to be very liberal. "Other engagements," &c., &c., "prevent me from entertaining," &c., &c.

Faithfully yours ever,
C. D.

Will you tell the publisher to cause to be sent to Clarkson Stanfield, Esquire, R.A., 48, Mornington Place, Hampstead Road, a complete set of the *D.N.* to this time—and to be regularly continued. He wishes to be a Subscriber.

Devonshire Terrace,
Fourth March, 1846.

My Dear Mr. Wills:—I assure you I am very truly and unaffectedly sensible of your earnest friendliness—and in proof of my feeling its worth, I shall unhesitatingly trouble you sometimes, in the fullest reliance on your meaning what you say.

The letter from Nelson Square is a very manly and touching one. But I am more helpless in such a case as that, than in any other: having really fewer means of helping such a gentleman to employment, than I have of firing off the Guns in the Tower. Such appeals come to me here in scores upon scores.

The letter from Little White Lion Street does not impress me favourably. It is not written in a simple and truthful manner—I am afraid. And Mr. Thomas Cooper is *not* a good reference. Moreover, I think it probable that the writer may have deserted some pursuit for which he is qualified, for vague and less laborious strivings which he has no pretensions to make. However, I will certainly act on your impression of him, whatever it may be.

And if you could explain to the gentleman in Nelson Square, that I am not evading his request, but that I do not know of anything to which I can recommend him, it would be a great relief to me.

I trust the new Printer *is* a Tartar; and I hope to God he will so proclaim and assert his Tartar breeding as to excommunicate —— from the "chapel" over which he presides.

Tell Powell (with my regards) that he needn't "deal with" the American notices of the Cricket. I never read one word of their abuse, and I should think it base to read their praises. It is something to know that one is righted so soon; and knowing that, I can afford to know no more.

Ever faithfully yours,
C. D.

DEVONSHIRE TERRACE,
Twenty-second April, 1846.

MY DEAR WILLS:—I meant to have written to you long ago, to tell you in reference to the Theatrical Dinner, that I am sure you wrote the account in a spirit of regard for me: and that I care a great deal more for that, than for any number of columns of any number of newspapers, and rate it much higher. Do not think I say so the less heartily, because I say it after some delay.

     Faithfully yours,
       Charles Dickens.

After this there is another gap of three years in the correspondence except for one unimportant letter of June, 1847.

1847.

"Dombey," which had started in the previous October, ran in monthly parts all through this year.

1848.

"Dombey" continued to run till April, when it was published in book-form.

"The Haunted Man" was published at Christmas.

1849.

"David Copperfield" started in May and ran through the year in monthly parts.

III
HOUSEHOLD WORDS

1850.

THIS year saw the establishment of *Household Words*, a project which had for some time occupied Dickens's attention. A copy of the agreement made between Charles Dickens, William Bradbury, Frederick Mullett Evans, John Forster, and William Henry Wills is among Wills's papers. It is dated March 28th, and its stipulations are briefly to the following effect:—

(1) The aforesaid parties are to be joint proprietors of the periodical in the following proportions both as to sharing the profits and as to paying the losses:—
  (*a*) Dickens one half share;
  (*b*) Bradbury and Evans one quarter share;
  (*c*) Forster one eighth share;
  (*d*) Wills one eighth share.
(2) Dickens is to be editor at a salary of £500 a year, with an additional sum to be paid for any literary articles he may contribute. This to be in addition to his share of profits.
(3) Bradbury and Evans are to be printers and publishers and managers of the Commercial Department.
(4) In consideration of his eighth share Forster is from time to time to contribute literary articles to the periodical without any additional remuneration.
(5) In consideration of his eighth share Wills is to act as sub-editor at a remuneration of £8 a week to be paid weekly in addition to his share of profits. He can withdraw on giving twelve months' notice, and full power is given to Dickens to dismiss him on giving him six months' notice or an equivalent amount of salary.

The first number of *Household Words* is dated Saturday, March 30th, 1850. It should be noted that, though every number bore date a Saturday, it was actually issued to the public on the previous Wednesday, like *Punch* during a considerable part of its career. The price was 2d.

Writing to Mrs. Gaskell on January 31st ("Letters," I., 216), Dickens describes the characters and aim of his proposed "new cheap weekly journal of general literature. . . . No writer's name," he says, "will be used, neither my own, nor any other; every paper will be published without any signature, and all will seem to express the general mind and purpose of the journal, which is the raising up of those that are down, and the general improvement of our social condition."

During a large part of this year Dickens was also working at "David Copperfield," which he finished in October.

Horne, who is mentioned in two of the letters this year, was Richard Henry (afterwards Hengist) Horne (1803—1884), the author of "Orion," an epic poem which he published in 1843 at the price of a farthing. His life was an adventurous and a pugnacious one. He was now on the staff of *Household Words*, and Wills considered that his salary was too high for the work he actually performed. The letter of August 16th from Dickens to Wills is the only one in the course of the whole correspondence that shows any serious difference between the two men. In 1852 Horne went with William Howitt to Australia, and on his return in 1869 he substituted Hengist for Henry as his second name.

Morley, referred to in the letter of December 12th, was Henry Morley (1822—1894), a very busy and useful member of the *Household Words* staff. Later on he edited several literary series. From 1865 to 1889 he was Professor of Literature at King's College, London.

Miss Martineau, whose story is mentioned in the letter of March 29th, was Harriet Martineau (1802—

1876), novelist, story-writer, political-economist, historian, writer on religion, journalist (she was a regular contributor to the *Daily News* from 1852 to 1866), and condenser of Comte's " Positive Philosophy." James Payn, who knew her and liked her, gives a very pleasant account of her (and her celebrated ear-trumpet) in his " Literary Recollections." In 1856 there came a rupture between her and Dickens, the causes of which are explained in the introduction to the letters of that year.

The following suggestions for the title of the new weekly are in Dickens's handwriting on two slips of paper :—

>The Hearth.
>The Forge.
>The Crucible.
>The Anvil of the Time.
>Charles Dickens's Own.
>Seasonable Leaves.
>Evergreen Leaves.
>Home.
>Home-Music.
>Change.
>Time and Tide.
>Twopence.
>English Bells.
>Weekly Bells.
>The Rocket.
>Good Humour.

Thus at the glowing FORGE of life our actions must be wrought;
Thus on its sounding anvil shaped
Each burning deed and thought.—*Longfellow.*

THE FORGE,
A WEEKLY JOURNAL,
CONDUCTED BY CHARLES DICKENS.

DEVONSHIRE TERRACE,
Twenty-second January, 1850.

MY DEAR WILLS:—I have fully discussed the matter with Bradbury and Evans, on which we spoke to-day. We have concluded to make you the offer (which I hope may be satisfactory) of Eight Pounds a week absolutely, and one eighth share in all the profits of the work, as well as of any other works that we may publish in connexion with it.

If you can let me know your decision on this proposal before we meet on Thursday it may facilitate our business. Faithfully yours always,
CHARLES DICKENS.

DEVONSHIRE TERRACE,
Monday, Eleventh February, 1850.

MY DEAR WILLS:—I send the book. I observe (in reference to something you said on Saturday night) that Chambers' use the single inverted comma for quotations, and I think its adoption by us decidedly objectionable on that account. There is nothing I am more desirous to avoid, than imitation.
Faithfully always,
C. D.

HOUSEHOLD WORDS OFFICE.
A Weekly Journal conducted by Charles Dickens.
No. 16, WELLINGTON STREET NORTH, STRAND,
Twenty-eighth February, 1850.

MY DEAR WILLS:—I think the addresses I enclose in this, the best. I would certainly give all these in the article. If you have a *fac-simile* of any, I recommend Valparaiso.*

---

* An allusion to an article, entitled "Valentine's Day at the Post Office" in the first number of *Household Words*. It was written by Wills, with

There are several letters and proffered articles, waiting your attention here. I have put them in the right hand drawer of your table.

We must have a great reform in the printing arrangements, without which it will be quite impossible to go on. *I have not yet seen one line in proof.* The consequence will be that I shall be worried and fretted to death by being overwhelmed with proofs, when I am turning to Copperfield—that I shall not have leisure to look at them as carefully as I would—that the public is not more at sea than I am, as to what we are doing—and that I *cannot*, with my occupations, do work in this way. I get into a state of irritation quite incompatible with it.

Mrs. Crowe's* story I have read. It is horribly dismal; but with an alteration in that part about the sister's madness (which must not on any account remain) I should not be afraid of it. I could alter it myself in ten minutes. This, too, is in your drawer here.

A great part of Mrs. Gaskell's story† has come in. It is very good, but long. It will require to be printed either in three or in four numbers.

I have written two articles—the opening one, and another—and sent them to Mr. Stacey. I suppose I might almost as profitably have put them on the top of the theatre opposite.

At 3 on Saturday.

Faithfully always,

C. D.

touches from Dickens's hand. The *fac-simile* address given was "For George Miller, boy on board *H.M.S. Amphirtrite, Voillop a Rayzor,* or *Ellesware.*"

* Mrs. Catherine Crowe, authoress of "The Night Side of Nature." The story referred to was "Loaded Dice," which appeared in *Household Words* of April 20th following.

† "Lizzie Leigh" appeared in the first three numbers of *Household Words*.

DEVONSHIRE TERRACE,
Sixth March, 1850.

My Dear Wills:—I should wish Hogarth to see that article before it is used. Will you see him, and set him to work on something else? He has nothing in hand now. And will you name to me, certain days and hours when you can always be found in Wellington Street. So that I may know, for my own guidance, and that of any one whom I may want to send to you.

I have given Greening a little article of my own, called "A Bundle of Emigrants' Letters,"* introducing some five or six originals, which are extremely good.

I don't feel your objection to "Lizzie Leigh" so much, for this reason. She had seen and watched Susan, before she deserted the child; and she has yet to give her own account of that transaction.

To-morrow I am going to Brighton (148, King's Road), whence I shall come up, of course, for Saturday. I should like to have a proof of the Funeral article sent down to me. I understood it to be quite arranged that we were only to make up *one* number at this next meeting. Will you tell them to have the fire lighted at the office, at 10 on Saturday?

Ever faithfully,
C. D.

I understand my father went on like the Steam Leg (oratorically speaking) at your dinner.

---

* This article appeared in the first number of *Household Words*. It was written in support of a scheme, propounded by Mrs. Chisholm, for the establishment of "A Family Colonisation Loan Society." Its authorship is attributed in the Office Book to Dickens and Mrs. Chisholm, the latter having probably contributed the letters contained in it.

Brighton, 148, King's Road,
Tuesday Night, Twelfth March, 1850.

My Dear Wills:—My objection to entering into the Sunday business* is, that whatever we state, is *sure* to be contradicted; and I observed Rowland Hill to be a very cautious and reserved man, whom I should strongly doubt as to his backing qualities in such a case. If the passage stand at all, I should wish it to stand as I have altered it. But I should be glad if you would show it to Forster, as a casting opinion. We will abide by his black or white ball.

I have made a correction or two in my part of the Post Office article. I still observe the top heavy " Household Words " in the title. The title of " The Amusements of the People " † has to be altered as I have marked it. I would as soon have my hair cut off, as an intolerable Scotch shortness put into my titles by the elision of little words. " The Seasons " wants a little punctuation. Will the " Incident in the Life of Madlle. Clairon " go into those two pages? I fear not, but one article would be *infinitely better,* I am quite certain, than two or three short ones. If it will go in, in with it.

I shall be back, please God, by dinner time tomorrow week. I will be ready for Smithfield, either on the following Monday morning at 4, or on any other morning you may arrange for.

Would it do, to make up No. 2 on Wednesday the

---

* Probably the question of the Sunday delivery of letters. There is no allusion to it in the article, " Valentine's Day at the Post Office " (by Wills and Dickens), which appeared in the first number.

† By Dickens, in the first number. Another article with the same title followed in No. 3. Sixteen years afterwards the scheme of these articles was taken up again (presumably by Dickens) in *All the Year Round,* of June 16th, June 30th, July 7th, and July 21st, 1866. These four articles, however, are not included amongst the miscellanies from *All the Year Round* in Vol. 36 of " The National Edition " of Dickens's Works.

20th instead of Saturday? If so, it would be an immense convenience to me. But if it be distinctly necessary to make it up on Saturday, say so by return, and I am to be relied on. Don't fail in this.

Supposing you had a place for the Household Narrative,* and we could come distinctly to the understanding of it, I should incline to Forster's opinion. But I apprehended, last Saturday, that neither was your plan sufficiently matured, nor were the materials for its execution sufficiently considered (as to assistance and so forth) to admit of our beginning now, otherwise than short-sightedly—say with a blindness of one eye.

Thanks for the prison facts.

Faithfully always,
C. D.

Devonshire Terrace,
Twenty-ninth March, 1850.

My Dear Wills :—I have sent a note to you, just now, in Wellington Street. I suppose you'll get it before you get this?

I really can't *promise* to be comic. Indeed your note puts me out a little, for I had just sat down to begin "It will last my time." I will shake my head a little, and see if I can shake a more comic substitute out of it.

The first part of Miss Martineau's † story is in Greening's hands. It is heavy.

---

* This was an allusion to a proposal to publish at the end of every month "A Household Narrative of Current Events," at the price of 2*d.*, as a Supplement to *Household Words*. The first narrative was accordingly published at the end of April.

† "Sickness and Health," by Miss Martineau, ran through four numbers of *Household Words*, from May 25th to June 15th.

As to *two* comic articles, or two any sort of articles, out of me, that's the intensest extreme of nogoism.

Faithfully,
C. D.

[In " Letters," I., 221, this letter, owing to the obscurity of the handwriting, is wrongly dated *July* 27th. The "Model Paper" was an article, by Dickens, entitled, "The Ghost of Art," which appeared in *Household Words*, July 27th. See also "Life," II., 452, note, where Forster gives a letter from Dickens to himself dated Paris, *June* 24th. In that letter Dickens states his intention of going to the Français on Wednesday, for "Rachel's last performance before she goes to London."]

HOTEL WINDSOR, PARIS,
Thursday, June Twenty-seventh, 1850
(*after Post-time*).

MY DEAR WILLS :—I send you the Model paper, with a good title. Its place in the No. we can discuss when I come home. I have had much ado to get to work; the heat here being so intense that I can do nothing but lie on the bare floor all day. I never felt it anything like so hot, in Italy.

I am afraid this will floor the Whelks* ideas, as far as Paris is concerned. There is nothing doing at the Theatres, and the atmosphere is so horribly oppressive there, that one can hardly endure it. I came out of the Français last night, half dead. I am writing at this moment with nothing on but a shirt and pair of white trousers, and have been sitting four

---

* In "The Amusements of the People" (by Dickens, in the first and third numbers of *Household Words*) Joe Whelks was the character whom the writer followed to various places of popular entertainment.

hours at this paper, but am as faint with the heat as if I had been at some tremendous gymnastics. And yet we had a thunderstorm last night!

I hope we are doing pretty well in Wellington Street? My anxiety makes me feel as if I had been away a year. I hope to be home on Tuesday evening or night at latest. I have picked up a very curious book of French statistics that will suit us—and an odd proposal for a company connected with the gambling in California—of which you will also be able to make something.

I can correct the proof of this paper when I come home. You will see in the proof that I speak of forty associates belonging to the Royal Academy. I am not sure that their constitution includes so many— and I don't like to ask Maclise, lest we should stumble on any point of difference.

I saw a certain "Lord Spleen" mentioned in a playbill yesterday, and will look after that distinguished English nobleman to-night, if possible. Rachel played last night for the last time before going to London, and has not so much in her as some of our friends suppose.

Poole* is staggering about like a bad automaton, and the English people are perpetually squeezing themselves into courtyards, doorways, blind alleys, closed edifices, and other places where they have no sort of business. The French people, as usual, are making as much noise as possible about everything that is of no importance, but seem (as far as one can judge) pretty quiet and good-humoured. They made a mighty hallaballoo at the Theatre last night, when

---

* John Poole, the dramatic author, then residing in Paris. Dickens, in the course of this year, obtained for him a Civil List pension of £100 a year, Dickens being appointed trustee and sending it to him every quarter.

Brutus (the play was "Lucretia") declaimed about Liberty.

Ever faithfully,
C. D.

Devonshire Terrace,
Twelfth July, 1850.
Friday.

My Dear Wills:—I observe a report in *The Times* this morning of a most intolerably asinine speech about Smithfield,* made in the Common Council by one Taylor. It would be a good beginning of our Playing at Parliament. If you will look to the other papers, and send me the best report, or a collation of the greatest absurdities enunciated by this wiseacre, I will try to make something of it—in any case, to enshrine it in a chip, but perhaps to do something better.

Ever faithfully,
C. D.

Devonshire Terrace,
Twelfth July, 1850.

My Dear Wills:—You remember, I suppose, that the statement in question is NOT OURS? It is in the records of that Establishment which is described, and is—I am quite certain—unmitigated gammon. I must consider whether it is worth while to alter the

---

* A strong attack on the organisation and methods of the Smithfield Cattle Market and on the treatment of cattle there was published in *Household Words* of May 4th this year. It was written by Wills, with touches from Dickens's hand. The subject was again referred to in a "Chip" (Chips were a collection, under one heading, of short articles) in the issue of July 13th. I do not think Dickens wrote anything further on the matter.

making up by putting it in again; but in future don't touch my articles without first consulting me.*

I wonder you think "A Night with the Detective Police" would do for a title!† After all those nights with Burns, and the Industrious Fleas, and Heaven knows what else!! I don't think there could be a worse one within the range of the human understanding.

Will have another night, certainly, I suppose Forster has corrected my Detective proof? I think the Bank Note‡ *very good indeed.* Do the Hippopotamus.§ Do Swinging the Ship.‖

Faithfully always,
C. D.

Yes, to Mason. I have learned to be suspicious, in spite of myself, of all such things.

[Wills to Dickens. In answer to the preceding letter. From Wills's "Letter Book."]

ATHOLL COTTAGE,
Twelfth July, 1850.

MY DEAR DICKENS:—I hope you will understand what I endeavour always to intimate:—that when I make an objection to *any* article I do it suggestively. I am exceeding jealous of anything appearing which might have the remotest tendency to damage the

---

* This referred, as the subjoined reply from Wills shows, to an article in the issue of June 22nd, entitled "The Devil's Acre," written by Alexander Mackay. I presume Dickens wished to make some statement in a subsequent number casting doubt on it. It described some reformatory schools in Westminster.

† The title chosen was "A Detective Police Party," *Household Words,* July 27th and August 10th. The articles were by Dickens.

‡ "Review of a Popular Publication," by Wills, *Household Words,* July 27th.

§ "The Hippopotamus," by R. H. Horne, *Household Words,* August 3rd.

‖ "Swinging the Ship," by F. K. Hunt, *Household Words,* July 27th.

name which appears at the top of each page; and which is responsible for every word printed below it, unless the contrary be specifically stated. The story at p. 300 [of Vol. I. of *Household Words*] although said to be derived from the Institution, is adapted by the editor; it is not quoted from the *Master's Record* (like a former one), but is set forth editorially; and if the editor doubted its truth the statement ought to have been accompanied with that doubt. If it be contradicted afterwards without excuse or explanation confidence would be commonly shaken in his other statements.

I ordered the passage to remain in type: because it is more easy to expunge a few lines from another article, when a passage is required to be inserted, than to add matter when one has to be taken out. I did not suppose you would wish me to consult you upon so simple a matter of mechanical convenience. As your injunction is strong as to this I must mention that in Eike's Case I have added that he was "accused" of stealing the debentures instead of that he actually stole them* and struck out that Field said " he is sure to be transported." Eike is just now *sub judice* and, besides the manifest injustice of these passages, he would have a good case against us in his defence.†

Now for the third count. The title for the Detective article I merely submitted, as usual as a "mild suggestion," for I think it useless to hint what may strike me as a defect without indicating a remedy. I said " A Night with the Detectives " was

---

* In "A Detective Police Party," *Household Words*, July 27th (Vol. I., p. 413).
† In the article as it appeared in *Household Words*, Wills's emendations were maintained.

the best title I could think of. I still think it is better than "The Detectives" merely, though certainly not *the* title; but I am *sure* it is not the worst one within the range of human understanding. Forgive me for claiming for my worst suggestion a *locus* within that pale. . . .

Lots of articles have come in. We have now enough for a number and a half. I have wrought so hard and anxiously lately that I am a little done up. If possible I shall rush off to-morrow night all the way to Walthamstow till Thursday. On Tuesday I shall be in Wellington Street and will have letters, etc., brought to me every night. My address is at W. S. Orr, Esq., Church Hill, Walthamstow.

W. H. WILLS.

DEVONSHIRE TERRACE,
Ninth August, 1850.

MY DEAR WILLS:—I shall be obliged to you if you will write to this man, and tell him that what he asks, I never do—firstly, because I have no kind of connexion with any manager or theatre; secondly, because I am asked to read so many manuscripts, that compliance is impossible, or I should have no other occupation or relaxation in the world.

A foreign gentleman—with a beard—name unknown, but signing himself "A Fellow Man," and dating from nowhere—declined, twice yesterday, to leave this house for any less consideration than the insignificant one of "twenty pounds." I have had a policeman waiting for him all day.

Faithfully always,
C. D.

DEVONSHIRE TERRACE,
Tenth August, 1850.

My Dear Wills:—I have written to Horne. The idea is a good one. The execution the main thing.

My travels are chiefly old, and I have none of those books. But I have told him you will get them.

I will consider about Port Natal. I think I *do* know somebody—but he might lie, or favour lies.

The New Zealand sketch is exactly the kind of thing that weighs upon my mind, frightfully. I don't know where to put it. I haven't the courage to destroy it—and it reappears awfully, every now and then, like an evidence of crime.

I send you a communication from one of our innumerable starvers.

Ever yours,
C. D.

DEVONSHIRE TERRACE,
Wednesday, Fourteenth August, 1850.

My Dear Wills:—I have gone down to Maidenhead this afternoon. Will you come, to make up, AT 10 TO-MORROW MORNING, before I begin a good day's work.

You will find, on this paper, two proofs, in which I have made some alterations. "Evil is Wrought,"* I have touched at the end. It left off with a disagreeable impression as to the feeling between the sisters. Mr. —— I have shorn of his humour in the emetical line, and also of his account of a calm—which is less correct than I hope his other facts are. I have seen

---

* "Evil is Wrought by Want of Thought," by Coventry Patmore, appeared in *Household Words,* September 14th.

D.E.

a calm on the Atlantic, three or four days long, when the ship had no more motion than this table.

Faithfully ever,
C. D.

Devonshire Terrace,
Sixteenth August, 1850.

My Dear Wills :—I will not enter on that question of comparison which you raise in your note, because I do not think my doing so would at all facilitate or soften our business.

I have not the least intention, at present, of making any change in Horne's engagement. I think (as you know) highly of his abilities, and I have always seen him most willing and anxious to work. If, on its being distinctly shewn to him what he is required to do, it should appear, either that he dislikes doing it, or cannot do it, the case would be different. But I do not feel that it would become me to assume any such thing from your premises.

If you will write me such a letter as I can put before him, distinctly stating what assistance you require from him, which you have not, I will write to him immediately, and enclose that communication. And I have no doubt the matter will be easily arranged.

But you must excuse my saying that I think you are hardly so disposed to accommodate matters with Horne (and never have been) as it would be pleasant and advantageous for all of us that you should be.

I send you an " Illustration of Cheapness," * and some papers you left here yesterday.

---

* A series of articles appeared under this title. They were by Charles Knight.

Mrs. Dickens being happily confined,* I go to Broadstairs this afternoon. My address there, is Fort House.

Ever faithfully yours,
CHARLES DICKENS.

[Wills to Dickens. In answer to the preceding letter. From Wills's "Letter Book."]

HOUSEHOLD WORDS OFFICE,
Seventeenth August, 1850.

MY DEAR DICKENS:—Your letter gives me both surprise and pain. There is nothing to "soften." What I have proved is merely a matter of business calculation, and should be discussed as such.

It was my duty to show you that Horne's articles had cost us something like £8 apiece, even when his other services are taken into account. If you believe the work [i.e., Household Words] can afford such terms I have nothing more to say on that head, but I cannot afford to make up, as I have been obliged to do, his deficiency of service by extra services of my own. The limit for the cost of contributions is £16 per average week. Unless I write as much as I have done and more than I can promise myself to write for the future, it is impossible to adhere to that limit until Horne's engagement is modified.

I feel that you mistake me, but have no fear that by and bye you will [not] unreservedly understand that in all I do I aim at one only object:—the welfare and success of the property in which we have embarked. Anything I perceive which tends to

---

* Dickens's third daughter, Dora Annie. She died suddenly on April 14th, 1851, and the news was brought to Dickens while he was presiding at the dinner of the General Theatrical Fund at the "London" Tavern

impede that success no personal considerations prevent me from pointing out. Personally I have a liking for Horne which (personally) is growing upon me, but officially I cannot be satisfied with any man who does not, I conceive, come forward with his *quid pro quo*. Indeed I quite agree with you that if it were put to him from the computations I have given you that he is receiving some £5 · 5 for what other contributors are not paid half that sum for he would be as ready as anyone to acknowledge that it is a great injustice not only to me (who have to bear the brunt of all deficiencies) but to every contributor to the work, and would be as ready to discuss any more equitable arrangement as I am.

It is not for me, however, to urge such a point to him, and for that reason I placed data in your hands to make some such communication. I have nothing special to suggest. All I wish is that Horne should mitigate my occasional agonies for articles by writing more articles—by, in short giving five guineas' worth of services per week in exchange for £5 : 5 : 0. His three months' engagement terminates tomorrow.*

Yours, &c., &c.,
W. H. WILLS.

BROADSTAIRS,
Nineteenth August, 1850.

MY DEAR WILLS :—Yes—very gently—as to Miss Martineau. And say I want to cut the end of Woodruffe.† (I have no proof.)

---

* A letter in Wills's "Letter Book" of March 5th, 1851, shows that Wills returned to the charge and again pressed this matter on Dickens's attention. What happened I do not know. Horne went to Australia in 1852.

† Miss Martineau's story, "The Home of Woodruffe," appeared in *Household Words*, from August 24th to September 7th.

What shall we do about the making up? What Mrs. Micawber calls "the unconscious stranger" has so put me out, that I can't leave here before Friday, clearly.

In great haste,
Faithfully always,
C. D.

BROADSTAIRS,
Wednesday Night, Twenty-first August, 1850.

MY DEAR WILLS:—I have cut Woodruffe as scientifically as I can, and I don't think Miss Martineau would exactly know where.

The "Illustrations of Cheapness" having become known to our readers, I think I would put the Steel Pen first. It has an Educational reference—is very good—and I think upon the whole might exchange places with the Forgery chapters to advantage, as we have already had the Bank first, in a former No.

Of course they have NOT sent me the Forgery Proofs.*

The contents otherwise, are very fair, I think. Of course I proceed on the idea that you have not found any new first article.

If I have a favorable day's work to-morrow (it may be a wayward one, as I am particularly ready to do it, and have considered it a long time) I shall be at the office all day on Friday. Also, I shall be happy to have Downing Bruce to dinner on Friday at 6. That subject should be *nailed*. Have a roast loin of mutton for one thing. We had nothing to cut and come again at, last time.

* Two chapters on "Bank Note Forgeries," by Wills, with touches by Dickens, *Household Words*, September 7th and 21st.

I received both the letters you mention. Ask Forster to dine on Friday.

What do you and Mrs. Wills say to coming down about to-morrow week—as soon as you have got that week's number off your hands?

I enclose a note, which I don't understand. What on earth does the man mean, by returning an incivility?

Faithfully always,
C. D.

BROADSTAIRS, KENT,
Twenty-seventh August, 1850.

MY DEAR WILLS :—I enclose you some papers I have received in connexion with the *H. W.* Among them, a letter from Horne, in answer to one from me, pointing out to him the heads of your statement. You will see that he is willing and anxious to do anything, and to render you assistance in any way in which you will allow yourself to be assisted.

I have been in a kind of prostrated condition, as to any power of thinking about anything, since I finished my last Copperfield. Consequently, what I am to do for *H. W.* is still a sheet of blank paper. I suppose (like Mr. Micawber) that Something will turn up.

When I know, for certain, on what day I shall be in town, I will write to you again—probably by to-morrow's Post. You remain in the same mind about Saturday?

Always faithfully yours,
C. D.

BROADSTAIRS,
Thursday, Twenty-ninth August, 1850.

MY DEAR WILLS :—I send you the best *résumé* my used-up-ed-ness will yield, of the three best Police stories.* Will you please look carefully at the Proof, and be particular with the turned comma in the Dialogue.

Stanfield being here, I shall come to town on Saturday Morning, and be at the *H. W.* at 11 o'clock, to dispatch all needful business. I purpose returning by the Boat on *Sunday Morning.* Is there anything in the Presbyterian way, to prevent you and Mrs. Wills coming back with me? If so, and you would prefer preceding me by a train on Saturday afternoon, write to that effect (to my little housekeeper Miss Hogarth) by return, and she will expect you.

In haste,
Always faithfully,
C. D.

BROADSTAIRS,
Sunday, Eighth September, 1850.

MY DEAR WILLS:—I send you the beginning of our joint article† on Cumming Bruce's theme. I have endeavoured to make it picturesque, and to leave the ground open for you. I return your notes. You are wrong about the £45 in a day. I have stated it as I understood the fact to have been.

I don't like the name I have given the subject. What do you think of " The Fate of Wills, in England " instead ? Or something of that sort? If you will send the proof to me when you have done I will try to put a few lines at the end, so as to wind up with an effect. I think we shall make a great hit with the subject.

* "Three 'Detective' Anecdotes," by Dickens, *Household Words*, September 14th.
† "The Doom of English Wills," by C. D. and W. H. W., *Household Words*, September 28th, October 5th, November 2nd, 16th (Chip), and 23rd.

The "Diplomacy," splendid. I should like to begin that with a sketch of an aristocratic attaché and so forth. I know the reality very well, having seen a good deal of it abroad.

Horne spoke to me—wrote to me, I mean—about the "Steam Plough";* and I meant to have called your attention to it, but forgot it. You have done quite right.

The parcel is a clean set of curtains for the office windows, when wanted, and the glass-cloths we bought.

Will you tell Vale to receive and pay for two dozen champagne and two dozen claret? They will come in cases, and had better be put in the top room.

The 14th of October, *impossible*. I am afraid I shall not be available for the 26th either, having made a pledge to Bulwer. But the event *may* not come off. I can't say, yet.

Looking back to your letter, I observe that you speak of my letting you have "the first article." You understood, I suppose, that we agreed I should send you the opening of the first article for you to go on with?

I am very glad to hear of the Edinburgh man again.

Faithfully always,
C. D.

Even Paxton must be second-fiddle to the Ecclesiastical subject, in case you do perceive there, a divided duty. Remember me to him, with congratulations.

---

* An article by Horne in the issue of September 21st.

BROADSTAIRS,
Friday, September Seventeenth, 1850.

MY DEAR WILLS:—I am extremely sorry to hear about your brain—but if you suppose that our Number went down, because the Illustration was first, and wouldn't have gone down if the Forgery had been first, I think the disease must be, the gigantic strength of your imagination.

You'll find Broadstairs do you more good, than anything could.

I am in that tremendous paroxysm of Copperfield—having my most powerful effect in all the Story on the Anvil—that you might as well ask me to manufacture a Cannon seventy-four pounder, as to finish the Turtle, or do the Junk, or do anything NOW. But I will be at the office, please God, at eleven on *Friday Morning;* and if we have, as I fear we must have, in default of anything else, the second Will article in the No. I will write the introduction then and there. I have arranged to go over the asylum for Idiots, that day, which ought to afford a fine description.

I will look over "Hints on Emergencies,"* with the view you suggest, *if* it comes.

You may tell Mr. Field that the only word in that passage which he did *not* use, is "slow" as applied to "Justices." I put that in, to express what his manner expressed.† But that if he means to say he didn't mention about "while they were looking over the

---

* By Wills and Dr. Stone, October 5th.
† The allusion is to Inspector Field, of the Detective Police, who had supplied Dickens with material for his "Three 'Detective' Anecdotes" in *Household Words,* September 14th. The passage to which the Inspector appears to have objected is at the end of the second "Anecdote":—"Well, if you'll believe me, while them slow Justices were looking over the Acts of Parliament to see what they could do to him, I'm blowed if he didn't cut out of the dock before their faces."

Acts of Parliament," he means to say the thing which is not. Lemon's recollection, and Leech's, be my judge! There would be no objection to a facetious chip about the "slow," but what Mr. Field did say shall not be unsaid—can't be.

I enclose you, from a correspondent, a Post Office order for a Sovereign in favor of that Westminster Reclamatory Institution whereof we have treated. Also a communication from Mr. ——, another name for Blight, and Locust.

Ever faithfully,
C. D.

DEVONSHIRE TERRACE,
Thursday, Twelfth December, 1850.

MY DEAR WILLS:—This proof of Morley's, when corrected, will require to be very carefully looked to. I had better go over it myself. I can't make out whether he means Mr. Buster to be actually a prize-fighter, or a person in the position of a gentleman with prize-fighting tastes. I have adopted the latter hypothesis, as involving less inconsistency and incongruity.*

Mrs. Gaskell's story,† I enclose, with two or three slight corrections. The name I have given it, expresses it better than any other I can think of. Withal, it is not a common name. The story is very clever—I think the best thing of hers I have seen, not excepting Mary Barton—and if it had ended happily (which is the whole meaning of it) would have been a great success. As it is, it had better go into the next No., but will not do much, and will link itself

---

* "Mr. Bendigo Buster on our National Defences against Education," by Morley and Dickens, *Household Words*, December 28th.
† "The Hearty John Middleton," *Household Words*, December 28th.

painfully, with the girl who fell down at the Well, and the child who tumbled down stairs. I wish to Heaven her people would keep a little firmer on their legs!

Ever faithfully,
C. D.

DEVONSHIRE TERRACE,
Saturday, Fourteenth December, 1850.

MY DEAR WILLS:—I heard something last night, which makes me averse to reviving the Good Hippopotamus."* I must therefore trouble you to take out that article after all, and put in another chip.

I could not think of making so important an alteration in Mrs. Gaskell's story without her consent. It must therefore stand as it is.

I forgot to tell you yesterday that Egg† proposes to meet us at the Blackwall Railway *at* 3 *on Monday* to go down (by appointment with the Proprietors) to those Plate Glass Works. He says the visit will occupy some three hours. Therefore our friend H[ousehold] W[ords] must improvise a city dinner afterwards. I shall be at the office on Monday, between 12 and 1.

I have taken out the cripple in the Railway paper, because he has hobbled bodily out of Head's book.

There are a few alterations elsewhere.

Ever yours,
C. D.

* By Dickens, *Household Words*, October 12th.
† Augustus Egg, A.R.A. (afterwards R.A.), the painter of historical pictures. He and Wilkie Collins went with Dickens on a tour through Switzerland and Italy in 1853.

1851.

During this year Dickens's time and his energies were largely absorbed by the Guild of Literature and Art, in the foundation of which he took a leading share. Lytton, then Sir Edward Bulwer Lytton, wrote a comedy in five acts, "Not So Bad As We Seem; or, Many Sides to a Character," for the performances to be given in aid of the institution. The first performance took place on May 16th, by permission of the Duke of Devonshire, at Devonshire House. Wills, to whom Dickens offered a small part, did not act, but he became the Secretary of the scheme, and later in the year, when Dickens took his company into the provinces, he sometimes went with them. The following advertisement of the project was published in the daily papers of the time:—

GUILD of LITERATURE and ART: to encourage life assurance and other provident habits among authors and artists; to render such assistance to both as shall never compromise their independence; and to found a new Institution where honourable rest from arduous labour shall still be associated with the discharge of congenial duties. To bring this project into general notice, and to form the commencement of the necessary funds, Sir Edward Bulwer Lytton, one of its originators, has written and presented to his fellow-labourers in the cause, a New Comedy in Five Acts. It will be produced under the management of Mr. Charles Dickens, in a theatre constructed for the purpose; and will be performed by Mr. Robert Bell, Mr. Wilkie Collins, Mr. Dudley Costello, Mr. Peter Cunningham, Mr. Charles Dickens, Mr. Augustus Egg, A.R.A., Mr. John Forster, Mr. R. H. Horne, Mr. Douglas Jerrold, Mr. Charles Knight, Mr. Mark Lemon, Mr. J. Westland Marston, Mr. Frank Stone, Mr. John Tenniel, Mr. F. W. Topham, and others. Portions of the scenery have been presented by Mr. Absolon, Mr. Thomas Grieve, Mr. Lewis

Haghe, and Mr. Telbin. The first representation of the Comedy, which is entitled "Not So Bad As We Seem; or, Many Sides to a Character," will take place at Devonshire House, on Friday, 16th May, before Her Majesty the Queen, and His Royal Highness the Prince Albert. Ladies and gentlemen wishing tickets for the performance at Devonshire House, price £5 each—this sum being regarded as a contribution in support of the design—will, on a written application to his Grace the Duke of Devonshire, at Devonshire House, receive a voucher for the same, exchangeable at Mr. Mitchell's library, 33, Old Bond-street. Prospectuses of the scheme can be had after Thursday, on application, at the office of the Guild, Wellington-chambers, 10, Lancaster-place, Strand; of Mr. Mitchel, 33, Old Bond-street; Messrs. Ebers, 27, Old Bond-street; Mr. Hookham, 15, Old Bond-street; and Mr. Sams, 1, St. James's-street.

WILLIAM HENRY WILLS, Hon. Sec.

Though launched under these brilliant auspices the institution never attained any great success.

In March Mrs. Dickens was at Malvern, and Dickens too was sometimes there, though his headquarters remained in London.

Dickens's father, John Dickens, died on March 31st, and his daughter, Dora Annie, on April 14th. From May to November Dickens was at Fort House, Broadstairs.

In the letter of March 29th there is an allusion to a paper contributed by E. C. Grenville Murray. In the following year this writer began his brilliant series of articles in *Household Words*, entitled "The Roving Englishman," and went on with them until 1856. Some of them were published as a book in 1854. He was a natural son of the second Duke of Buckingham and Chandos. Entering the Diplomatic Service under the protection of Lord Palmerston, he was appointed an attaché at Vienna in 1851; was transferred to Constantinople (after a short interval at Hanover) in 1852; quarrelled with the ambassador, Sir Stratford Canning, whom he afterwards ridiculed as Sir Hector Stubble; and in 1855 was sent to Odessa as British

Consul-General. Thence, after some disagreeable controversies, he returned to England in 1868. In 1869 he started the *Queen's Messenger*, the first "Society" journal published in this country. On June 22nd, 1869, he was horsewhipped in St. James's Street by Lord Carrington on account of some reflections on Lord Carrington's father. He prosecuted Lord Carrington, who was convicted, but only ordered to come up for judgment when called up. Thereupon Grenville Murray was himself prosecuted for perjury in having on oath denied the authorship of the article in dispute. He was remanded on bail, but did not appear again, having fled to Paris. He continued to write, and helped Edmund Yates to found the *World* in 1874. He died at Passy in 1881.

Charles Knight, mentioned in the letter of April 20th, was an intimate friend of Dickens, and was at this time contributing a series of papers under the title of "Shadows" to *Household Words*. As publisher, author and editor he was equally well known. His most popular compilations were "Half Hours with the Best Authors," "Half Hours of English History," and "Half Hours with the Best Letter-Writers." He died in 1873, at the age of 82.

In the letter of August 13th occurs the first mention of George Augustus Sala, then a young man of twenty-three. He was never one of Dickens's close friends, but until 1856 he was a fairly regular contributor to *Household Words*, and Dickens had a considerable admiration for much of his work. In April, 1856, Dickens sent him to Russia to write descriptive articles for *Household Words*. He returned in September, when a disagreement with Dickens as to the republication of his articles in volume form led to Sala's withdrawal from *Household Words*. He renewed his connection with the paper two years later and contributed many articles to its successor, *All the Year Round*. His association with the *Daily Telegraph* began in 1857, and for many years his well-known style—Matthew Arnold whetted his satire on it in "Friendship's Garland"—lent colour and animation to the columns of that paper. He founded and edited two monthly magazines, *The Train* (January, 1856) and *Temple Bar* (December, 1860), Edmund Yates being associated with him on both publications. He died in 1895.

DEVONSHIRE TERRACE,
Monday, Tenth February, 1851.

MY DEAR WILLS:—There is a small part in Bulwer's comedy—but very good, what there is—not much—my servant, who opens the play—which I should be very glad if you would like to do.

Pray understand that there is no end of men who would do it, and that if you have the least objection to the trouble, I don't make this the expression of a wish even. Otherwise, I should like you to be in the scheme, which is a very great and important one, and which cannot have too many men who are steadily—not flightily, like some of our friends—in earnest, and who are not to be lightly discouraged.

If you do the part, I should like to have a talk with you about the secretarial duties. They must be performed by some one, I clearly see, and will require good business direction. I should like to put some young fellow to whom such work, and its remuneration would be an object, under your eye, if we could find one entire and perfect chrysolite anywhere.

Let me know whether I am to rate you on the ship's books, or not. If yes, consider yourself "called" to the Reading (by Macready) at Forster's rooms on Wednesday, the 19th at 3.

And in the meantime you shall have a proof of the plan.

Ever yours,
C. D.

[Wills to Dickens. In answer to the preceding letter. From Wills's "Letter Book."]

Household Words Office,
Twelfth February, 1851.

My Dear Dickens:—I have considered your letter well over, and think it better that I should not take a part in the play. I will not bore you with all my reasons against it. One will suffice, for that is a strong one:—there will be, as I understand, not a few provincial performances; and under present arrangements I think it would be extremely inexpedient for us both to be absent from *Household Words* together and so often as the performances will require.

It is no affectation to say that this is a great sacrifice of pleasure to me, for I should enjoy the fun of acting and the greater glorification of being one of the *corps dramatique;* and, as you know, the smaller the part the better I should like it.

I shall, however, feel very great disappointment indeed if any disinclination to act in the play (brought about chiefly by business considerations) deprive me of the privilege of giving any help in my power to the general scheme. It is one I have long wished to see brought forward, and I have felt a very great interest in it from the moment you mentioned it. If I can be of any service in the way you suggest in your letter, or in any of the business generalities or details of the project I will give my services zealously.

I do hope, therefore, that ridding you of a bad actor will not bar me out from all the co-operation I can give to the other parts of the scheme.

W. H. W.

[The day of the month is not given, but the reference to the cabmen disposes me to attribute the following letter to March 27th (see next letter, and that of March 29th)].

Devonshire Terrace,
Thursday Morning.

My Dear Wills :—I think it not unlikely that Horne may unintentionally commit us to some mistake on the Series question, without careful revision.

Will you show Henry Austin* the proof, and read it with him? We shall then be quite safe.

The cabmen I shall expect to-morrow.

Mr. Sloman, and also Pitt the scene painter, are instructed that you will fork out from time to time as they require money for their work. You will receive a certain list of properties to-day, which please put in your letter to me to-night. I think Pitt had better have rehearsal notices, in order that he may know where to find us.

In case my poor father should take any bad turn, and they should want me hurriedly, I have given my mother a paper, which in that case she would send to you. It contains a memorandum of the best way of

---

* Henry Austin was Dickens's brother-in-law, and intimate friend. He was secretary to the Sanitary Commission ; he died in 1861.

sending a messenger down to Malvern. I saw him last night, and he was then doing quite well.

Ever faithfully,
C. D.

GREAT MALVERN,
Twenty-eighth March, 1851.
Friday.

MY DEAR WILLS:—I will read the Execution Paper by young Dumas, this evening. I am not able to do so before post-time (early here) having an arrear of letters to get through, but I will return it by the *morning* post to-morrow, in case you should desire to know what I think about it at the office to-morrow afternoon. Generally, I don't like, for such a purpose, descriptions of executions—and that kind of Frenchman is not likely to enlighten one's mind about them. But we shall see.

I find in the letter of yours which I missed when I came up, a begging letter (about the twentieth from the same hand) signed Thomas Lewis. I can't make out whether the man's mad or only an unusual vagabond. I merely mention him as a caution to you not to give him anything.

The cabs I will do what I can for, tomorrow.

Ever faithfully,
C. D.

GREAT MALVERN,
Friday Night, Twenty-eighth March, 1851.

MY DEAR WILLS:—I don't like young Dumas' paper at all. Nothing can justify such a subject, but some exceedingly vigorous treatment of it—and this is in the last degree flat and poor. Add to the nature of the thing itself, that it is a translation from a French newspaper, and it is yet more objectionable. I am quite clear against it.

I send a paper by Chesterton which has not much in it, but which, called

"Coolness among Thieves "*

—and altered by the softening of some of his hardest words and finest writing, will—do. I can't say more for it.

Ever faithfully,
C. D.

GREAT MALVERN,
Saturday, Twenty-ninth March, 1851.

MY DEAR WILLS :—I find there is no day-post *from* here, so you will only get the rejected Guillotine paper with this.

Enclosed, the cab paper. I have done what I can with it, but it is a poor opportunity. I hope the information generally, is more correct than that appertaining to Paris, as I found it.†

I think I shall come to town on Monday, and be at the office in good time on Tuesday morning.

I keep this note open until the arrival of to-morrow's Post. But I must not forget to say that you exercised the soundest possible discretion in the matter of Chambers, and that I think very well of him indeed, for his wholesome view of the subject.

Sunday.

I am coming up this afternoon, with the view of dashing over to Bulwer's somehow or other, to confer with him upon some points in reference to which he

---

* It appeared in the number of May 17th.
† " Common Sense on Wheels," by Dickens, Wills and E. C. Grenville Murray, *Household Words,* April 12th.

is in sudden agonies. In good time on Tuesday, I shall see you at the office.

Ever faithfully,
C. D.

GREAT MALVERN,
Monday, Seventh April, 1851.

MY DEAR WILLS:—Don't you think it will be best for us to breakfast together—with a general view to H. W.— on Wednesday morning? Will you breakfast with me in Devonshire Terrace at 10 ? I shall see you to-morrow night of course, but I send this note in case I should otherwise interfere with your arrangements.

I shall also want to take counsel with you about my prospective occupation of the two back rooms in Wellington Street, with iron bedsteads, during the Expositional absence of myself and family. I have an idea (if the Broadstairs people be not made, Expositionally, more than usually sharkish) of taking the Fort House from May to October. And in that case I shall want occasionally to make my tent comfortable at the office.

Faithfully ever,
C. D.

DEVONSHIRE TERRACE,
—I write it naturally—meaning
GREAT MALVERN,
Sunday, Thirteenth April, 1851.

MY DEAR WILLS:—I enclose you the Police Article. I have cut down the number of cases, to save tediousness. Two drunken men, for example, could scarcely have been done with. It occurs to me that I have not described the cells. But I had better "put in that," and any other line or so that occurs to me, when I get the proof. For the present slips are horribly mauled. I have done all I could—sat at it nine hours without stirring—and hope it will come out well.*

I preside at the Fund Dinner tomorrow. I suppose you don't go. Will you breakfast with me again, on Tuesday morning, to talk over things in general?

Ever faithfully,
C. D.

DEVONSHIRE TERRACE,
Sunday, Twentieth April, 1851.

MY DEAR WILLS:—Charles Knight left the enclosed here, to-day.

I am taking Mrs. Dickens out, under a variety of pretences. I make one now, that I am not decided whether to go to Wellington Street for our barrack quarters, or to Lancaster Place. Will you instruct Johnson to be at the latter Chambers to morrow (Monday) at a quarter past 4, and wait till I come? I will show them to her. We are going to look at Stone's house just before.

Ever faithfully,
C. D.

H. W.
Wednesday Evening, Fourteenth May, 1851.

MY DEAR WILLS:—Thornton asked for you here, at 5. I sent word through Mr. Holdsworth that you would be at Devonshire House after 7, and could

---

* "The Metropolitan Protectives," by Dickens and Wills, *Household Words*, April 26th. This article is republished by Wills in his "Old Leaves," it being, however, indicated that Dickens had a part in it.

be seen on demand. You had best instruct the Devonshire House servants, accordingly, on receipt of this.

I have had it in my mind to say to you—and may as well do it now, as at another time—that if your removal really should have put you out for a hundred pounds or so, and you would prefer to borrow where you can certainly incur no obligation rather than where you possibly might incur one without meaning it—I shall be truly pleased to become your banker.

Ever faithfully,
C. D.

[The following letter is wrongly dated by Dickens "Thursday, Twenty-ninth *March*." (1) It is written on black-edged paper, and must, therefore, have been subsequent to March 31st, when John Dickens died; (2) Dickens did not go to Broadstairs till May; (3) on March 29th, which was a Saturday, Dickens was at Malvern (see previous letter of that date).]

BROADSTAIRS,
Thursday, Twenty-ninth [*May*], 1851.

MY DEAR WILLS :—I think we shall now have a very good article. I have two requests to make in connexion with the enclosed copy. First, that you will severely reprove the Whitefriars people in my name, for having the negligence to send me yesterday the uncorrected proof after all. Secondly that you will very carefully correct the proof of the new matter, and, if you have any doubt, refer to the manuscript.

The cheques I enclose, signed.

This is all I have to say about *Household Words*.

Guild.

I enclose a Memorandum for Foster, the Property man.

Will you ask at Simpson's what they will put on a plain cold supper *upstairs in their own place,* for, on the next Play night at about 12, running the chance of the number who may come, and of what each man may order to drink for himself? I would merely have cold joints, lobsters, salad, and plenty of clean ice. Perhaps there might be one hot dish, as broiled bones. But I would have only one, and I would have it cheap.

Then I think Johnson might send round this to the company.

Notice.

There will be a plain cold supper ready at Mr. Simpson's, the Albion, by Drury Lane Theatre, after the Farce on Tuesday, at   per head; not including wine, spirits, or beer, which each gentleman will order for himself.

I hope to begin the Police Article tomorrow. I have gone to Epsom very freshly. Weather beautiful. Wife not so well.

Faithfully ever,
C. D.

Broadstairs,
Thirtieth May, 1851.
Friday.

My Dear Wills:—Since you feel that objection, *perhaps* it will be best to alter the heading of the advertisement. But it did not occur to me when I saw it in *The Times* yesterday. I thought it well placed, and very good.

Of course I shall not answer the begging letter enclosed. If you should receive another from the same man, I should like the Mendicity Society to have them.

Have you heard from Land?

Don't you think some one should supply refreshments—as tea, coffee, soda water, and ices—at Hanover Square, for the audience if they choose, as at other places of entertainment.

If the house should be *bad* on Monday Morning, I would immediately issue, per Johnson, four tickets to every member of the Company. I would also send four to Stanfield, The Green Hill, Hampstead, four to Roberts, 7, Fitzroy Street, Fitzroy Square, four to Austin, Board of Health, four to Beard (Private) Herald Office. It is most important that we should be full, whatever we do, and these would all be safe. Perhaps you will confer with Mark,* according to circumstances.

I have begun the Night article, and hope to bring it up with me, finished.

Ever faithfully,
C. D.

BROADSTAIRS, KENT,
Fourth July, 1851.

MY DEAR WILLS:—The enclosed will do. I have written to the Author, accepting it. It wants a few new paragraphs, and the omission of a familiar slang phrase here and there.

Paxton suggested to me, through Evans, a good

---

* Mark Lemon, one of the founders of *Punch* and its first editor. He and Dickens were great friends.

subject. Ice, and why should its use be confined to great towns.* How useful to the Farmer, for his butter and so forth—how easily an ice-house constructed—and why *don't* he construct one, and have it filled on odd winter's days when his men are lounging about the stable door.

Baines. Don't forget Baines.

I am astonished to find that I had put the letter about my poor father's bill, into my dispatch box. I must have taken it out of the drawer, specially, but I have not the least remembrance of having done so. I enclose it, but suppose the bill will probably have been paid from the Memorandum left at the *D. N.* office.

Will you kindly read the enclosed and see the man? I have communicated with him before, and (if I remember right) given him money. The books he speaks of are bad, but it seems an affecting history, and I should be glad to give him £5 or so, if you thought it would do him real service.

Will you, further, send Callaghan† to Reeves the Stationers in Cheapside for two red solid blotters, *folio size*, which Mark [Lemon] will bring me down if Callaghan will leave them addressed to me, to his care, in the course of the day at the Bedford.

Will you, further, ask Charles Knight if he remembers the address of the agent to be communicated with about the two new houses on Hampstead Heath—he gave me an advertisement during the Play, which I mislaid for want of a pocket—and, if he does, will you write a note to the man in my

---

* An article on this subject, by Morley and Wills, appeared in *Household Words* on August 16th.

† Callaghan was the attendant at the *Household Words* office.

name, asking extent of accommodation, and purchase-particulars.

I think this is trouble enough, for one note!

Ever faithfully,
C. D.

BROADSTAIRS,
Friday Morning. In bed.

[No further date, but it was probably July 11th.]

MY DEAR WILLS:—I am laid up with a most severe cold, and pains all over me. I received yesterday, only the enclosed bit of proof, instead of the whole. The morning's post is not come in when I send this. I suppose it will bring the rest.

I wish Hannay* would not imitate Carlyle. Pray take some of the innumerable dashes out of his article—and for God's sake don't leave in anything about such a man believing in himself—which he has no right to do and which would by inference justify almost anything. Yankee does not mean American but New England merely, I think.

" In the name of the prophet—Smith!"†

would be a better title.

Faithfully ever,
C. D.

BROADSTAIRS, KENT,
Sixteenth July, 1851.

MY DEAR WILLS:—The cheque you have to pay to my account for the Greenwich dinner, is £12. 10. 6.

The enclosed note and *its* enclosed papers are from

---

* James Hannay (1827—1873), the novelist and essayist.

† An account of Mormonism and its prophet, Joseph Smith, by Wills and Hannay. It appeared in *Household Words*, July 19th.

Lady Grey (Lord Grey's wife). I have written to her. Can you make a chip out of them, and correct our orthography of the place?

You know that I have no faith in advertising beyond a certain reasonable extent. I think it a popular delusion altogether. But I do not desire to stand in the way of what you and Evans may concur in deeming a business idea. And if the expense would be advisable, the Household Narrative decision given, I think it is little less advisable, the decision not given. Therefore you had better summon the Lincolnian Mammoth* to a meeting at 3 on Saturday, and Evans too, if he be come back. We will then decide what shall be done, and have it done immediately.

Guild.

Miss Boyle† changes her mind, and wants a family ticket. I have therefore directed her to burn the one you have sent her. Will you tell Johnson to send her a family ticket, for 3 places together near the Stage, to 3 *Hamilton Place, Piccadilly*, instead?

In writing to Ireland, I would propound two questions—what is the best time (if any) before Christmas? What is the best time after Christmas?

I have a letter from Bulwer this morning, in which he expresses a great solicitude that in case of the house being very good on Monday, there should be (with a view to the effect upon the Provinces) another last night—but only if the house should decidedly seem to justify it. Will you take counsel and confidence with Mitchell upon this? If it were decided to be done, I would give it out at the end of the

* John Forster, who lived in Lincoln's Inn.
† The Hon. Mary Boyle, an intimate friend of Dickens, and an occasional contributor to *Household Words*.

Comedy. Or can Mitchell suggest any other place in London where we could make *one dash?*

Have Lady Bulwer looked after. A last chance might stimulate her Ladyship to desperate action.

Faithfully always,
C. D.

The meeting with a view to the Country, Monday the 28th, at 4 *exactly.*

Of course they are to be called to Rehearsal on the stage, next Monday at 12.

BROADSTAIRS, KENT,
Seventeenth July, 1851.

MY DEAR WILLS :—You cannot have remarked it—but I spoke to you, before leaving, about those parcels. It is all right. They were to go to their respective addresses.

I am glad of Brockedon's note. He knows a good deal about some curious places—is very ingenious—and may be very useful.

A Name for the Custom-House article? Hum! Let me see.

What do you say to—

The Great House of Detention.
The Castle of Giant Despair.
The Dull End of the Broad Arrow.
Her Majesty's only Disagreeable Customs.
*The Great Bar in the Harbour of London.**

They are all pretty good.

Faithfully ever,
C. D.

---

* This was the title eventually chosen for the article, which was by Wills. It appeared in *Household Words* on July 26th.

BROADSTAIRS, KENT,
Sunday, Twenty-seventh July, 1851.

H. W.

MY DEAR WILLS:—I am sorry the Brockedon business (though almost unavoidable) should have arisen. I have written to the wrathful being, with a view to mollification.

Bamford (returned herewith) won't do. "The Right One" * poor—but I think just passable.

I enclose you another Shadow from Charles Knight. Have it put in type at once, and send him a proof. I have suggested to him some slight alterations in the beginning—of a tense here and there—which will make it more fanciful. He can easily make them in the proof. They are a mere nothing.

I send the "History of England" †—with a very pretty bit in it, describing the drowning of the son of Henry the First. Proof to me for correction.

Also a proof of that whole No. *I have had none whatever, of next Wednesday's No.*

I am glad you like the Watering Place so much. It pleased me exceedingly.

How about Hannay and the Dreadnought? I am in correspondence with Horne, about some articles that I think he will do very well indeed. Have you told Morley about the Phantom Ship?

I should like a day or so to consider about the advertising. In the meantime go on as at present, and don't alter the arrangement. *Why is it not (as agreed) across the page in the Examiner?* It is not unwise, I suppose, to speak of those matters in the

---

* It appeared on August 9th.
† The "Child's History of England," by Dickens, was appearing in *Household Words*.

Row??? I don't wonder at *Punch* falling; for anything so bad, I suppose, never was done. But *H. W.* really is so good, that it is hardly a parallel case. Never mind. We must stand to our guns in the most indomitable manner, and make it better yet. I have always had an instinctive feeling against the Exhibition, of a faint, inexplicable sort. I have a great confidence in its being a correct one somehow or other—perhaps it was a foreshadowing of its bewilderment of the public. My apprehension—and prediction—is, that they will come out of it at last, with that feeling of boredom and lassitude (to say nothing of having spent their money) that the reaction will not be as wholesome and vigorous and quick, as folks expect.

When do you go to Paris? I can't remember. And by what train? And when do you come back? Grammar-school paper returned herewith.

Guild.

Of course Costello's * idea about postponing the next night is simply frenzy.

What I want to be able to do at the meeting is to be able to say, "At such a time I propose such a trip—at such another time such another trip—at such another time, such another. Derby? Have you made any enquiries about Derby—say, for April? Paxton † is the man.

Keep in view the making of the house on Monday night by the Company, if need for it.

---

* Dudley Costello was one of the actors in the Guild performances and a contributor to *Household Words*.

† Sir Joseph Paxton, the creator of the Crystal Palace, was the Duke of Devonshire's agent and chief gardener at Chatsworth.

General Botheration.

It is impossible to go on with that unfortunate Mr. ——. I met him in the street the last time I was in town, and told him that if I could ever give him anything to do, I would. But that I saw no means or opening.

Pray explain to him that his condition can have nothing to do with him in the character of a contributor as between us and the public—that whatever goes into the Journal goes in for its own sake, and not through any interest of any sort—otherwise I should make contributors of a legion of clients, including all my poor relations.

I think this is all at present.

Ever faithfully,
C. D.

P.S. To my large letter.

Don't lose sight of the "Playing at Parliament." I don't see why you took out that allusion to the Hôtel de Londres (in the Chamounix paper), as it is a most respectable house; and the non-gaming house certainly deserves a lift against the gaming house. It was not quite judicious. What about *Ice?* It won't do so well by and by.

BROADSTAIRS,
Wednesday night, Thirtieth July, 1851.

MY DEAR WILLS :—I went over to Dover—having no other trip on hand—to see you. Was at the railway this morning. But could hear nothing of the train you mention in your note. It is no matter. I had nothing of any moment to say—merely wished to pat you on the back.

I have gone through the No. since returning

home. Again I observe one or two of the articles in a very slovenly state, both as to the Queen's English and pointing. I have not had time to set them quite right. I wish you would look at the proof I have sent Greening, to understand what I mean.

The notion I think of trying with Horne is a kind of adaptation of an old idea I once had (when I was making my name) of a fanciful and picturesque " Beauties of England and Wales." For I never look at the grimgriffinhoof " Beauties " without thinking what might be done. I have not told Horne what my general idea is—I have a notion that it might be made a tremendous card for us—but I have proposed to him to come down with me to Chatham after the next play (on my way back) and take certain bits of the Dockyard and fortifications.* Don't you think a Series of Places, *well* chosen, and described *well*, with their peculiarities and popularities thoroughly seized, would be a very promising Series ? And one that people would be particularly likely to identify with me ?

In haste to save the Post.

Ever faithfully,
C. D.

If I found the Chatham paper come out well, I would cast about for a way of making a splash with it, as a new branch of the *H. W.* Tree.

BROADSTAIRS,
Sunday, Tenth August, 1851.

MY DEAR WILLS :—I send you two slight notes for corrections in proofs I have been reading. †

---

* "One Man in a Dockyard," by Dickens and Horne, appeared in *Household Words*, September 6th of this year. I cannot find, however, that the subject was pursued as Dickens suggests.

† For *Household Words*, August 23rd, in which number the articles

In Hannay's "Dreadnought," for Yankees read Americans.

In the "May Festival" of Miss Howitt (very good) for the Lord's love don't let us have any allusion to the Great Exhibition. Make the first sentence the first paragraph, and then go on with the second paragraph as it stands. Also substitute names for those initial letters, Mr. G. and the like.

I don't know what to write about, in the absence of your Paris-trip notes, but I think of a paper on "Whole Hogs"—Peace Society, Temperance Do., and Vegetarians—all of whom have lately been making stupendous fools of themselves.

Faithfully ever,
C. D.

Broadstairs, Kent,
Thirteenth August, 1851.

My Dear Wills:—I have written to the Author of the "Key of the Street," accepting his paper. It is a very remarkable piece of description, and (although there is little fancy in it) exceedingly superior to the usual run of such writing. I have delicately altered it myself, so as to leave no offence in it whatever. If the young man can write, generally, as well as that, he will be an acquisition to us. I think it quite good enough for a first article—but we will not put it first, for fear we should spoil him in the beginning. It is sure to tell. Will you send him a Proof? George A. Sala, 17, Upper Wellington Street.*

---

mentioned, as well as an article by Dickens entitled "Whole Hogs," appeared. Dickens used that term to imply misdirected effort inspired by wrong-headed zeal (see letter of September 25th, 1854).
  * The article appeared September 6th.

I expect the proof of "Whole Hogs" to-morrow morning, and will send it back by return.

I am now going at once to do the "Flight to France." I think I shall call it merely "A Flight"*—which will be a good name for a fanciful paper. Let me have your notes by return. Don't fail.

Can you give me any facts about Waste of money at Chatham? If so—do.

Miss Martineau all right. Send Howitt † his proof to correct.

You will find (I think) that my other half's invitation refers to next month—when I hope you will be better able to accept it.

Guild.

Lemon will look into all those matters.

Myself.

I wish, when you can, you would take an opportunity of seeing our friend the Registrar of Merchant Seamen, and ask him from me whether he is ever acquainted with the individual characters of Australian Emigrant Ships and their Discipline, and could say to me, (this is with a view to Miss Coutts's Home) such a Ship going to sail at such a time, is a good one—Captain may be trusted. If he has such means of knowledge, and would favour me by communicating them (of course in confidence) he could render me just the help we want and do a great deal of good.

Will you send Callaghan twice a week to Devon-

---

* It appeared August 30th.

† William Howitt (1792—1879), poet, novelist and descriptive writer, mainly in collaboration with his wife, Mary Howitt. He went to Australia with R. H. Horne in 1852.

shire Terrace to see whether there are in the [? any] letters in the hall or in the garden letter box.

Ever faithfully,
C. D.
Broadstairs, Kent,
Twenty-Second August, 1851.
Friday.

My Dear Wills:—I want the enclosed change made in the "Work of the World." *

The introduction to "Soldiers' Wives" † must be entirely re-written, and should be a plain and earnest representation of an obvious impropriety. Pray take out of the correspondent's part the message about "quivering at the smell of gin"—which makes *me* shudder from head to foot, in its unspeakable badness.

"The Whitsuntide Festival" is so horribly maudlin and washy, that nothing can be done with it.

I want a great paper done, on the distribution of Titles in England. It would be a very remarkable thing to take the list of the House of Peers, the list of Baronets and Knights, and (without personality) divide the more recent titles into classes and ascertain what they were given *for*. How many chemists, how many men of Science, how many writers, how many aldermen.

How much intellect represented.

How much imagination.

How much learning.

How much expression of the great progress of the country. How much of Railway construction, of Electric Telegraph discovery, of improvements in machinery, of any sort of contribution to the happiness

---

* By Morley, *Household Words,* September 13th.
† *Household Words,* September 6th (chip).

of mankind. How much soldiering. How much Law.

I think this well done, would make a prodigious impression. And if you can get a powerful array of the facts together, plainly stated for my use, *I* will do the Paper, and (I feel confident) with great advantage to us, and to the question.

What is Brown's address? Is he Commodore or what? Tell me and I will write to him.

Ever faithfully,
C. D.

Broadstairs, Kent,
Monday, September Sixth, 1851.

My Dear Wills:—Let me have a note of what you propose for the next No.—reserving the "History of England" for the No. afterwards. Let us have the best Nos. now, that we possibly can have. Also let me see a made-up Proof.

Morley's "Gold" * requires looking over, for a little carelessness here and there—the repetition of buts and howevers, &c.

In Horne's "Ballooning," † always insert "Mr." before "Green." Also insert "Mr." before "Poole," and call him the well-known Author. At the end of the third paragraph from the commencement, instead of "fanatical sentence was carried into execution," read "Sentence of the Holy Catholic Church was carried into Christian execution."

I think of deciding to return to town on the 20th —perhaps remaining a week or so at the office, before I remove my furniture, and restore the Second Floor

---

* *Household Words*, October 18th.
† *Household Words*, October 25th.

room. Therefore, any time after that, (you getting up in the meanwhile all the preliminary part of the subject) you may appoint with the Pawnbroker. On Saturday the 25th we had better dine at the office— with Morley, Horne, and (I suppose) Forster—to decide upon the form and idea of the Christmas No. I think it would be well to let Morley and Horne know beforehand what we are going to meet for ; as they might then have some suggestion to make. On second thoughts Monday the 27th might be better. The Saturday might be required for the Pawnbroker.

In " The London Tavern," * *dele* " the actor," after " Mr. Macready."

I wish Forster to try the marking of the Extracts. I write to him to that effect, and inform him that you will let him know *when* it must always be done.

Guild.

I return Proofs of the bills, now to be referred to Mr. Chute.

Will you write Webster a note, asking for Miss Young and Mr. and Mrs. Coe on the Monday, Tuesday, and Wednesday ?

I have not yet got Coe's Property List, and consequently cannot instruct Mr. Chute, as to the Furniture we shall want hired.

I have written to the Secretary of the Great Western.

Nathan's bill, I will look over and refer to Mark.

Personal.

I have told the Gardener to see you, and you will explain to him exactly what I want done at Tavistock

---

* By Hannay and Wills, *Household Words*, October 18th.

House. He will then make an estimate of the probable cost, and send it to me. On a separate piece of paper, I make a rough plan, which I hope you may comprehend without difficulty.

Faithfully always,
C. D.

I have told the Gardener, in writing to him for his estimate, that *punctuality and dispatch* are conditions on which I always insist. Will you bear testimony to him that I usually am in earnest on these heads?

BROADSTAIRS,
Twenty-seventh September, 1851.

MY DEAR WILLS:—I send this by Topping who comes to town, partly for *H. W.* and partly for me, and whose costs and charges I shall divide between the two concerned.

I have gone through Mr. Sala's paper, and have cut a great deal out, and made it compact and telling. I wish you would see him and tell him that I have kept it as close as I could to his title—not because the omitted parts were bad (indeed they are very good) but because they refer to used-up aspects of the subject. It had better go into the next No.*

There is nobody about us whom we can use, in his way, more advantageously than this young man. It will be exceedingly desirable to set him on some subjects. I will endeavour to think of a few, suited to him. Suggest to him Saturday night in London, or London Markets—Newport Market, Tottenham Court Road, Whitechapel Road (where there are the most extraordinary men holding forth on Saturday night

---

* "The Foreign Invasion," by Sala, appeared October 11th.

about Corn Plaister—the most extraordinary things sold, near Whitechapel workhouse—the strangest Shows—and the wildest cheap Johns)—the New Cut, &c., &c., &c. I think he would make a capital paper out of it.

I enclose a curious chip from Peter Cunningham.

Also a note and cutting from Jerrold. You might get hold of the man. Mr. Sala would do *him* capitally. Scott of the *Advertiser* will give you any information that he possesses, if you ask in my name.

I want Miss Jewsbury's * *paper.* I must read it myself, and write to her.

Topping returns early to-morrow morning. If he should not find you when he brings this, he shall arrange with Callaghan that he will call at the office for anything you have to send, *to-morrow morning at* 8.

I have not thought of anything yet. But I hope to cudgel something out of myself yet.

Faithfully always,
C. D.

BROADSTAIRS, KENT,
Monday, Twenty-ninth September, 1851.

MY DEAR WILLS :—The " sparkling " Muse has not been at all propitious. I didn't like " Rising with the Subject "—put it away. Began another paper called the " Steam Soliloquy "—didn't like that either, and put it away too. To-day I have begun another, called " Our School " †—like that better, but don't know when I may be able to finish it—doubt doing so, tomorrow, for next No.—can't say—may be—may not.

---

* Miss Geraldine Endsor Jewsbury (1812—1880), the friend of Mrs. Carlyle. The paper referred to was probably " A Curious Page of Family History," in *Household Words* of December 6th.

† *Household Words*, October 11th.

I have had such an affectionate note of invitation from the Duke [of Devonshire], that I can't help running down to Chatsworth howsoever short the time I can spare for the purpose. I shall go down on Thursday, and return on Saturday. If you have no engagement in the way, let us dine at the office *at ½ past 5 on Wednesday next*—the day after tomorrow. We can dine, arrange the No. and break up the meeting, in two or three hours. I shall want the evening after 9 o'clock and cannot make any other appointment.

The Guild matters we will dispose of on Wednesday.

The paper you mention, is (as I told you, but you have forgotten) in the left hand drawer of my writing table at the office. The case has been examined, but no such note can be found here.

Faithfully ever,
C. D.

Broadstairs, Kent,
Thursday, Ninth October, 1851.

My Dear Wills:—Perhaps you will answer the enclosed letters. To Miss Bunbury, I should be inclined to say that we don't want her papers, and that I cannot undertake the responsibility of mediating in such a matter with any other Editor. Mr. Keith you will perhaps appoint to see yourself. If his proposal involves my sitting to anybody, acceptance is quite out of the question.

Market Gardens near London, is a fine subject. Chadwick can open the way to a first-rate Market Gardener, if you will consult him in my name. This is another subject you might get ready by the time of my return.

I purpose being at the office between 1 and 2 on Saturday. If Erasmus Wilson * should call, will you see him? I understand he has something to communicate.

Mrs. ——'s story will be very good now, I think. It would be as easy (almost) to write one, as I found it to get point and terseness out of such an infernal hash.

I think I have no more to say, today—except that the Gardener has sent a very business-like, prompt, plain, and not unreasonable estimate.

Ever faithfully,
C. D.

BROADSTAIRS,
Thursday, Sixteenth October, 1851.

MY DEAR WILLS:—I send the proof of "The Child's History" by the cheap train.

I have been looking over the back Numbers. Wherever they fail, it is in wanting elegance of fancy. They lapse too much into a dreary, arithmetical, Cocker-cum-Walkingame dustyness that is powerfully depressing.

Faithfully always,
C. D.

[Wills to Dickens. Answer to the preceding letter. From Wills's "Letter Book."]

Seventeenth October, 1851.

MY DEAR DICKENS:—The only fair way of judging of the contents of *Household Words* is, I think, to

---

* Afterwards Sir Erasmus Wilson (1809—1884), dermatologist, Egyptologist and philanthropist. He brought Cleopatra's Needle to England at a cost of £10,000.

compare them with those of other publications of its class. From such a comparison we come out brilliantly in the very excellence which you say we want—fancy. It is universally acknowledged that subjects of an uninviting nature are treated—as a rule—in *Household Words* in a more playful, ingenious and readable manner than similar subjects have been hitherto presented in other weekly periodicals; but to such a rule there must necessarily be large exceptions in all works which demand a certain space to be filled by a certain time every week. No one, not even yourself (as you said the other day) * can sparkle to order, especially writers who have only an occasional sparkle in them. As to the " Elegance of Fancy " you desiderate, that, I apprehend, is simply impossible as the prevailing characteristic of twenty-four pages of print published fifty-two times a year. Elegance of fancy cannot be thrown broadcast over such an acreage of letter-press; although, happily for *Household Words* (and for *Household Words* alone) it can be *sprinkled* over its pages. If you could regularly see and go over each sheet before it is put to press there would be a very thick sprinkling of the excellence in which you say *Household Words* is deficient. When the number *has* had the benefit of your revision the touches you have given to it have improved it to a degree that has seemed to me marvellous. I was delighted with your proposal of coming from Broadstairs every Wednesday, to give a finishing touch, for a reason personal to myself. It would be most gratifying to me if my own judgment could be brought to some corrective test. I should go on with more confidence because with less uncertainty. I

---

* See, *ante*, letter of September 29th.

have my own notions of what such a publication as *Household Words* should be; and, although I have good reason to suppose from the latitude of confidence you give me, that my notions square with your own generally, yet I cannot (less perhaps than many other men) be *always* right; and it would lift a great weight of responsibility from me if everything which passes into the columns of *Household Words* had the systematic benefit of another judgment before publication.

Believe me ever faithfully yours,
W. H. WILLS.

TAVISTOCK HOUSE,
Eighth December, 1851.

MY DEAR WILLS:—I can't begin the Xmas article and am going out to walk, after vain trials.*

I send you some papers that I have, and the book from Willis's (did you pay for it?) out of which I think Morley can make a good article as to the Science of our ancestors. I don't agree with you about Law's article. Reading it this morning before going to return it, I thought it sensible and useful and quite in our way. I send it to you with a new name, to be set up.

It seems to me that what the Xmas No. wants, is something with no detail in it, but a tender fancy that shall hit a great many people. This is what I am trying for. If I can get it, it will not be lengthy.

I am much obliged to you for the Chancery information. I had got to that Number of Solicitors—by a sort of instinct I suppose—but had modestly limited my costs to from forty to fifty thousand pounds.

---

* Dickens's contribution to the Christmas number this year was the article entitled "What Christmas Is As We Grow Older."

I have not received a proof of Sydney's article intact and uncut. Let me have it.

Faithfully always,
C. D.

Thursday Night, Tenth December, 1851.

"You are quite right my Dear Wills" (as a friend of ours would say) * about St. Michael's Mount. I had associated with the place in Cornwall, for which I have a romantic tenderness, another little historical passage—and so firmly settled in my own mind that this passage occurred there, that I take it very ill it didn't. Your suggestion fired (in half an hour) a train of damp gunpowder, which blew my belief to shivers.

Ever faithfully,
C. D.

1852.

The provincial performances of Lytton's comedy on behalf of the Guild of Literature and Art continued this year, Dickens being still the master-spirit. Three summer months he spent at Dover, and then crossed the Channel on a short visit to Boulogne. This was a very strenuous year for him. He was busy with "Bleak House"; was dictating "The Child's History," which was continuing in *Household Words;* and was both editing that journal and writing various articles for it.

---

* Who this friend was I cannot say with certainty, but I incline (and Mr. H. F. Dickens, K.C., agrees with me) to think it was John Forster. He appears to have used this "My Dear" style of allocution. See the letter of April 24th, 1854. Dickens quotes these words again in the letter of August 12th, 1852.

In the first letter (February 28th), he refers to some suggestion which had been made to him to stand for Parliament. Such proposals were more than once repeated, but he never seriously entertained them (see "Life," III., 460).

The "dear friend," to whose death he refers in the letter of August 1st, was Mr. R. Watson, of Rockingham Castle, Northants. Dickens had first met him and his wife at Lausanne in 1846, and a very warm friendship had sprung up between them.

TAVISTOCK HOUSE,
Twenty-eighth February, 1852.

MY DEAR WILLS :—These people have really managed the expenses most admirably, and deserve our best consideration.

I immediately replied to the enclosed about the Light Buoys. I wish you would go down, see the nature of the thing, and make an appointment for Horne, unless it seems to you something that you and I could decidedly do better together. If Horne does it, tell him that the question of the Trinity House, or the Corporation, has no need to be touched at all— that we want a piece of good description.

Miss Zornlevin, or whatever her name is—have you asked about her? Miss Coutts* is coming here this evening, and I should like to be able to give her some information, or Miss N.'s address, or something.

In the Parliamentary matter—it is impossible that I could go into it with the new book in hand. If I had only *H. W.* I might possibly make the dash,

---

* Afterwards the Baroness Burdett-Coutts. Dickens had a high regard for her, and often helped her in her charitable undertakings.

but I should be worried to death if I did it now. And I don't know but I am far more useful (and certainly far more happy) in my own sphere of service than among the bellowers and prosers of St. Stephen's.

Ever faithfully,
C. D.

TAVISTOCK HOUSE,
Saturday, Thirteenth March, 1852.

MY DEAR WILLS:—I am happy to say that Mrs. Dickens is just confined with a brilliant boy of unheard-of dimensions,* and is wonderfully well.

Will you send Callaghan round with the enclosed, and give him the money to pay for their insertion.

And don't you think Horne and Morley had best dine with us on Thursday, with a view to the possible collision of ideas?

Ever faithfully,
C. D.

[To the above letter Wills has added the following note:—

" FAME !

" When John † (Callaghan didn't go) called with the notice at the *Morning Advertiser* office, pointing out that no newspaper ever charged Mr. Charles Dickens for inserting such announcements, the clerk replied, 'Charles Dickens?—Charles Dickens? *What house does he keep?*' "]

---

* His seventh son and last child, Edward Bulwer Lytton Dickens. He was nicknamed " Plornish " or " the Plornishghenter."

† John was Dickens's servant. His name occurs frequently in the letters.

TAVISTOCK HOUSE,
Twenty-ninth April, 1852.

MY DEAR WILLS :—We forgot to speak, yesterday, about the begging letters. I send with this a black surtout. That and £2 will be sufficient, I think, for the Rathbone Place man.

£2 for Macpherson, the orphan.

£1 for the Needlewoman.

And after this, I really must pull up. For I have no funds but my own in hand or in reversion; and I get these letters by hundreds—not counting those that *you* get.

Ever faithfully,
C. D.

TAVISTOCK HOUSE,
Third June, 1852.

MY DEAR WILLS :—A hasty note, for I have been at work the whole day, and am (for my sins) engaged to dine with ——.

H. W.

I went over the proof. I could not conceive what " Hope, An Epigram,"* meant, and I declare to you I have not the least idea now! Having nothing to put in its place, I could not disturb the Make-up by taking it out.

GUILD.

You are doing nobly!!! The York idea is a most admirable one, and will keep us quite right in any case. We must get at least another Thousand Pounds clear.

---

* This appeared in *Household Words*, June 12th, but no name is attached to it in the office book.

HORNE'S DINNER.*

We shall be 10, I think. Coote is coming as a guest—and a piano. I would on no account introduce strangers—such as Mr. Hunt—with so small a party. I know it would never do: most especially with Horne, under the circumstances. I have made a tardy exception in favor of Evans as one of the Proprietors of *H. W.*

Place the Albion—*our* Albion—time 6 for ½ past.

Again let me sound the loud timbrel in your Guild praises.

Ever faithfully,
C. D.

I am not quite sure of your Cork calculations. We will discuss before I answer the letter.

Field† I postponed until next Wednesday. It was of little use after all, my going alone—and horribly boreing.

DOVER,
Thursday, Twenty-Ninth July, 1852.

MY DEAR WILLS:—Miss Coutts writes me this morning, that she will willingly assist this case if it should turn out to be perfectly genuine. Will you, on receipt of this, write a letter to the applicant, stating that you are in my confidence, and making an appointment with him—not delaying it, as the matter seems to press. The thing is, to have such proofs and references and documents or something, from him, as shall render deception perfectly *impossible*. The thing to be said to him, is, that the case is beyond my

---

* Probably a dinner given to Horne before his departure for Australia.

† Inspector Field, of the Detective Police. See letters of September 17th, 1850, *note.*

means, but that I have an affluent and generous friend to whom I think I can recommend it usefully, if it be thoroughly proved. Bear in mind that he may be a begging letter writer of the worst suit.

If you will send me your account of him by any convenient means you like, I will lose no time in communicating with Miss Coutts again. But we must be thoroughly sure of the facts before I can take any money from her.

The Sunderland bill (if we play there) and likewise the Liverpool bill, I must see a proof of before they are issued. Two parts will have to be changed in each.

Ever faithfully,
C. D.

10, CAMDEN CRESCENT, DOVER,
Sunday, First August, 1852.

MY DEAR WILLS:—You have anticipated how deeply grieved I have been by the loss of my dear friend.* I had heard from Mrs. Watson's brother of his lying at the point of death, before it was mentioned in the paper. He dined with us this day three weeks, full of projects for future happiness in the house where we have been so merry, and which is now so desolate. I loved him in my heart, as one of the truest and most affectionate of men.

I am very much obliged to you for taking so much trouble about that afflicted clergyman. I have now reported favorably of his case, and have no doubt that you may make a final appointment with him at the office, for Wednesday afternoon.

* See Introduction to this year.

H. W.

I thought our "Honourable Friend"* would be a success. It seems to be making a great noise.

I don't agree with you as to the "Angel" sketch, which is very curious and good. I have accepted it by itself, but *not* as one of a series.

The Liverpool bill I have altered. As to Sunderland (supposing that performance to come off) Costello will write to you directly (at my request) to say if he can play there. If yes, the bill will require no alteration. If no, then Coe for Lord Loftus in that bill (Smart, Mr. Miller), and Stone for Mr. Nightingale.

I shall be glad to know as soon as possible about Sunderland, with a view to Lord Carlisle.

Ever faithfully yours,

C. D.

[The first paragraph of the following letter is printed in "Letters," III., 137, as the first paragraph of a letter dated "1, Junction Parade, Brighton, Thursday night, 4th March, 1853." The rest of the letter there printed is taken from one written on the *tenth* March, 1853 (*vid. post*).]

10, CAMDEN CRESCENT, DOVER,
Twelfth August, 1852, *Thursday*.

H. W.

MY DEAR WILLS :—I am sorry, but Brutus sacrifices unborn children of his own as well as those of other people—the "Sorrows of Childhood," long in type and long a mere mysterious name, must come out. The paper really is, like the celebrated ambassadorial appointment, "too bad."

* By Dickens, *Household Words*, July 31st.

Sitting down this morning to Morley's "Boys to Mend,"* I couldn't take to it on the short notice, and thought of the enclosed instead. You shall have the rest (about three slips) by tomorrow's post.

I will also go over the No. and send it at the same time.

That Hop subject of last year. Is Sala in town? He might do it very well, if he be. The time is coming on again. If he be not in town, could Thomas† be got up to it?

GUILD.

I am delighted to hear such cheering accounts.

After reading the enclosed letter from Coote, will you instruct Johnson to get the music mentioned in it, and take it down when we all go.

You are "*quite* right my dear Wills," ‡ about Sloman and his extra man.

ASPECTS OF NATURE.

We have had a tremendous sea here—steam packets in the harbour, frantic, and dashing their brains out against the stone walls. §

ART.

Stone harassing himself, with doubts whether he shall have Mrs. Stone to Manchester—also with Charles XII.

---

* "Boys to Mend," by C. D. and Morley, appeared in *Household Words*, September 11th.

† This was William Moy Thomas, who had become a contributor in 1851. He was on the staff of the *Athenaeum*. From 1868—1901 he was on the staff of the *Daily News*, for a great part of the time as dramatic critic. He died in 1910, aged 82.

‡ See letter of December 10th, 1851.

§ This paragraph is printed in "Letters," III., 141, as part of a letter of August 7th, 1853, from Boulogne.

Eminent Author.

Women in blue veils, turning out at 6 A.M. and waylaying him as he goes to the Shower Bath.

Dover Theatre.

Open.

Ever faithfully,
C. D.

Hotel des Bains, Boulogne,
Tuesday, Fifth October, 1852.

H. W.

My Dear Wills :—I don't intend to come to town as long as I remain here. I thought you understood this from our conversations at Dover. I am curious to see Horne's MS., and hope it will come out well.

I observe that Tauchnitz's bill appears to be due *today*. I enclose it. Will *you* pay it to my account at Coutts's, enquiring whether its non-presentation today affects it, and explaining how it is.

Guild.

I would certainly proceed according to Phillips's advice.

If you got ——'s account from Henry's statement or in Henry's writing, don't pay it. I will write to him myself in that case, assuming that it is an unauthorized proceeding. I think it monstrous, and doubt whether in any case we ought to pay it without protest, out of money that is not ours. Upon my word I do not think it would be an endurable item to place on record in the accounts. Conceive twelve men doing the like. "To one hundred and forty-four lace cravats, and 72 pairs of lace ruffles, £74. 8. 0. Washing, £12. 12. 0."

! ! !

Weather.

Very stormy, and a prodigious sea running.

"Bleak House."*

Just begun.

Remembrances to Mrs. Wills and you from my two ladies.

Ever faithfully,
C. D.

Hotel des Bains, Boulogne,
Thursday, Seventh October, 1852.

My Dear Wills :—I send you the proof of the No. Taboo (for the present, certainly) the Poem. I think it very bad.

See to the dashes in the article on "Epitaphs."† They are at present innumerable. "Graves and Epitaphs" would be a better name.

I have been very carefully considering the question of Horne's "Diary."‡ It is clear to me that nobody might, could, would or should understand what it means, if we were to print this portion by itself, quite ignorant of what is to follow or when it is to come. It would never do without something—at least *something*—of the "Voyage," either in the same Number or in the following one. Therefore, at any risk of Howitt's MS. making its appearance in print somewhere, hold this portion back, and insert "Penny Wisdom" (which is very interesting and good) in its stead.

---

* The first number of "Bleak House" had appeared in the previous March. The last (a double) number appeared in September, 1853.

† "Graves and Epitaphs," by Hannay, *Household Words*, October 16th.

‡ R. H. Horne had gone to Australia with William Howitt. "A Digger's Diary," by Horne, began in *Household Words*, January 29th, 1853, and continued intermittently through that year.

I shall be glad to hear whether my general objection has already presented itself to you?

Morley's (I suppose) *résumé* of the "Prairie" book is as well done as a paper of that kind can be.* Quite a model.

The "Babbleton Book Club," very weak. A kind of imbecile thing that seems to want crutches.

I never heard of such a business altogether, as you unfold in that Morton case. When I met him in Fleet Street, he told me the whole story of the Duel: I know the murderer too.

Ever yours,
C. D.

Hotel des Bains, Boulogne,
Thursday night, Seventh October, 1852.

My Dear Wills:—I think it best, in case of any miscarriage, to advise you that I returned the proof of the next No. in a packet by steamboat from here to Folkestone this afternoon.

I don't quite understand from your letter what Tauchnitz wants to know. Will you answer him, in English, and give him the explanation he requires—for me, in my absence?

"The Shot Tower of Waterloo Bridge" ought to make a good article. The Bridge itself—bridges of London in general—would be a fine subject for Sala, in another article. If the Waterloo Bridge people would give us a little information about the change in their affairs since the Railroad—and would let us lay hold of one of their *Night Toll-takers*, a very fine thing might perhaps be made of it. I wish you

---

* "Picnics in the Prairie," *Household Words*, October 9th.

would look into the subject, and see whether it will do for me, before you lay Sala on. Ever faithfully,
C. D.

HOTEL DES BAINS, BOULOGNE,
Tuesday Twelfth October, 1852.

H. W.

MY DEAR WILLS:—The No. to which you refer in your letter of yesterday's date received this morning, has not yet reached me. I will go over it when it comes.

I have thought of the Christmas No., but not very successfully, because I have been (and still am) constantly occupied with "Bleak House." I purpose returning home either on Sunday or Monday, as my work permits, and we will, immediately thereafter, dine at the office and talk it over—so that you may get all the men to their work.

The fault of Prince's* poem, besides its intrinsic meanness as a composition, is, that it goes too glibly with the comfortable idea (of which we have had a great deal too much in England since the Continental commotions) that a man is to sit down and make himself domestic and meek, no matter what is done to him. It wants a stronger appeal to rulers in general to let men do this, fairly, by governing them thoroughly well. As it stands, it is about the Tract Mark (Dairyman's daughter, &c.) of political morality. And don't think that it is necessary to write *down* to any part of our audience. I always hold that to be as great a mistake as can be made.

---

* This was, probably, John Critchley Prince (1808—1866). He was the son of a Wigan reed-maker for weavers, and worked for some time with his father. Afterwards he kept a small shop in Manchester. In 1840 he published his first volume of poems, "Hours With the Muses." Four other books came from his pen.

I wish you would mention to Thomas,* that I think the paper on "Hops" *extremely well done.*† He has quite caught the tone we want, and caught it in the best way.

In pursuing the Bridge subject, I think it would be advisable to look up the *Thames Police*. I have a misty notion of some capital papers coming out of it. Will you see to this branch of the tree, among the other branches.

Guild.

I hope Gye didn't let you have Covent Garden; for the effect of our Proscenium within that one would be so vehemently ludicrous that I think Peek would be grinned out of the field by our own carpenters.

Talking of whom, I am quite delighted with the idea of Sloman's house.

Myself.

To Chapman I will write. My impression is that I shall not subscribe to the projected Hood monument,‡ as I am not at all favourable to such posthumous honours. Ever faithfully,

C. D.

Hotel des Bains, Boulogne,
Wednesday Night, October Thirteenth, 1852.

My Dear Wills :—The No. coming in after dinner, since my letter was written and posted, I have gone over it.

I am grievously depressed by it; it is so exceedingly bad. If you have anything else to put first, don't put

---

* See Letter of August 12th, 1852, and note.
† *Household Words*, October 16th.
‡ He did not subscribe to it ; see "Letters," I., 287.

"SPORTING" AMUSEMENTS.

Sala's paper first.* (There is nothing better for a beginning in the No. as it stands, but this is very bad). It is a mistake to think of it as a first article. The article itself is in the main a mistake. Firstly, the subject requires the greatest discretion and nicety of touch. And secondly, it is all wrong and self-contradictory. Nobody can for a moment suppose that "Sporting" amusements are the sports of the PEOPLE—the whole gist of the best part of the description is to show that they are the amusements of a peculiar and limited class. The greater part of them are at a miserable discount (horse-racing excepted, which has already been sufficiently done in *H. W.*), and there is no reason for running a-muck at them at all. I have endeavoured to remove much of my objection (and I think have done so), but, both in purpose and in any general address, it is as wide of a first article as anything can well be. It would do best in the opening of the No.

About "Sunday in Paris" there is no kind of doubt. Take it out. Such a thing as that "Crucifixion," unless it were done in a masterly manner, we have no business to stagger families with. Besides, the name is a comprehensive one, and should include a quantity of fine matter. Lord bless me, what I could write under that head!

Strengthen the Number, pray, by anything good you may have. It is a very dreary business as it stands.

The proofs want a thorough revision.

In haste, going to bed,
Ever faithfully,
C. D.

---

* "The Sporting World," *Household Words*, October 23rd. It appeared as the fourth paper in the number.

I returned the wretched man's letter—evidently mad—I know nothing about him.

I want a name for Miss Martineau's paper.

"Triumphant Carriages" (or Triumphal)*.
"Dublin Stoutheartedness."
"Patience and Prejudice."

Take which you like best.

TAVISTOCK HOUSE,
Third November, 1852.

MY DEAR WILLS:—Forster wants the book "Ecclesia," in which the ballad is, sent to his chambers for him. Of course he makes out that there is a positive merit in having made the blunder, and that if it really had been the old ballad, his intention would have rather failed upon the whole. I have taken the liberty of assaulting this conclusion between the eyes, and knocking it over heads and heels.†

I send with this, the sheet of "Bleak House" paper.

Ever faithfully,
C. D.

TAVISTOCK HOUSE,
Friday, Fifth November, 1852.

MY DEAR WILLS:—Do you think it would be worth while to publish the enclosed, with an alteration here

---

* "Triumphant Carriages," *Household Words*, October 23rd.

† In *Household Words* of October 30th there was a short article by Forster ("The Reason Why") in which he had called attention to the Trelawney ballad ("And shall Trelawney die," &c.), and had quoted it *in extenso* as a genuine old ballad. As a matter of fact only three lines are old. The rest was written by the Rev. R. S. Hawker, Vicar of Morwenstow, in Cornwall, as he himself said, "after much fruitless endeavour to recover the old song, but without the slightest success." He had heard the three lines as "a choral fragment current in Cornwall" in 1824. Mr. Hawker wrote to explain this, and Forster, in a "Chip" in *Household Words* of November 20th, admitted (with some qualification) his mistake. "Ecclesia" was a volume of poems by Mr. Hawker, published in 1840.

and there, in next Wednesday week's Number—so as just to catch the Funeral?* I hate the thing myself, but it might go down with a good many. I can't quite decide. What do *you* think? Let me know, and let me have the MS. back, in the course of this morning. The sooner, the better.

Further, let me see the proof of the No. we did last night, before it goes to press. I have a misgiving that I altered a word in Morley's paper, which I intended to re-alter, but did not.

In the matter of the rappings, I think a good name for the paper would be "The Ghost of the Cock Lane Ghost."† If Morley looks to that precious business, in the Annual Register, he will find (if I understand your account) that the two spirits are greatly alike. I was thinking that

"Spirits Far Above Proof"

would be a good title. But it is a great thing in such a case to shew that the imposition is an old and exploded one.

Ever faithfully,
C. D.

[The following letter is undated, but it must be later than the preceding letter of November 5th, because in that letter "The Deeds of Wellington" is spoken of as being in MS. whereas in this letter it is mentioned as being in "slip" proof.]

MY DEAR WILLS:—You were to have sent me the rapping advertisement, and have forgotten it.

---

* The funeral of the Duke of Wellington. A long piece of verse entitled "The Deeds of Wellington" appeared in *Household Words*, November 20th. In the Office Book the author's name is entered as "Bennett (Cheapside)," no doubt W. C. Bennett.

† By Henry Morley, in the issue of November 20th.

Therefore you must go over the enclosed slip carefully, before you return it to the Printers, and fill in such blanks as I have indicated in my alterations on the margin. I will go through the No. tonight at 7, either here or at the office as you prefer—or if you will dine here at ½ past 5, better still, and we will do it after dinner. Let me know.

Faithfully ever,
C. D.

I have just got the enclosed from Lord Normanby's brother at Florence. There is not much in it, but the subject — the Bible prisoners, man and wife— attracts so much attention just now, that I think it worth a push to get it into this Number.*

Will you send the enclosed slip of "The Deeds of Wellington" to Mr. Bennett, 65, Cheapside, saying that I have not time to write to suggest any slight alterations, but will he correct and return it, and if he should observe a line halting anywhere, make it bolder if he can.

[This letter, to which Wills has prefixed the note "A curiosity from *him*. No date, no signature," is printed in "Letters," I., 299, at the beginning of the 1853 letters. I place it among the 1852 letters because there is a story by Miss Martineau, "The Deaf Playmate's Story," in the Christmas number of that year, and there is none by her in the Christmas number of 1853.]

MY DEAR WILLS :—I don't think there's enough in Thomas's story.

---

* "An Interview with the Madiai," *Household Words*, November 20th. Francesco and Rosa Madiai were imprisoned in Tuscany for possessing a Bible.

Miss Craik's * (an improvement) will do perfectly for one of our ordinary Nos. We won't put it in the Xmas No. if we can get a better. Her imitation of me is too glaring—I never saw anything so curious. She takes the very words in which Esther [Summerson] speaks, without seeming to know it.

I have not a shadow of a doubt about Miss Martineau's story. It is certain to tell. I think it very affecting—admirably done—a fine plain purpose in it—quite a singular novelty. For the last story in the Xmas No. it will be great. I couldn't wish for a better.

Mrs. Gaskell's ghost story, I have got this morning—have not yet read. It is long.

OFFICE OF *HOUSEHOLD WORDS.*
A Weekly Journal conducted by Charles Dickens.

No. 16, WELLINGTON STREET NORTH, STRAND,
Christmas Eve, 1852.

MY DEAR WILLS :—I have gone carefully through the Number—an awful one for the amount of correction required—and have made everything right. If my mind could have been materialised, and drawn along the tops of all the spikes on the outside of the Queen's Bench prison, it could not have been more agonized than by ——; which for imbecility, carelessness, slovenly composition, relatives without antecedents, universal chaos, and one absorbing whirlpool of jolter-headedness, beats anything in print and paper I have ever "gone at" in my life.

I shall come and see how you are tomorrow.

---
* "Berthalde Reimer's Voice," by Miss Georgiana M. Craik, appeared in *Household Words,* February 12th, 1853.

Meantime everything is in perfect trim in these parts, and I have sent down to Stacey to come here and top up with a final interview before I go.

Just after I had sent the Messenger off to you yesterday concerning the toll-taker Memoranda, the other idea came into my head—and, in the most obliging manner, came out of it.

Ever faithfully yours,
C. D.

Here is Mark perpetually flitting about Brydges Street and hovering in the neighbourhood—with a veil of secresy drawn down over his chin, so ludicrously transparent, that I can't help laughing while he looks at me.

TAVISTOCK HOUSE,
Wednesday, Twenty-ninth December, 1852.

MY DEAR WILLS :—It is evident that Horne (notwithstanding his outfit of tent, cart, and what not) has abandoned the Digging idea, and already begun to live upon the reserved Fund sent out to insure his capability of return. I am afraid this looks unpromising.

One of his poems very indifferent. The other (a Christmas piece) must of course stand over now.

I am concerned to see that he supposes the arrangement with Mrs. Horne never to have been discontinued. I think it would be best if you would send for her and see her on the subject; seriously representing to her that her secresy and reserve have rendered it impossible for either you or me to approach the question, or at all to divine what has been in her mind respecting it. I have not the least objection to your saying this as strongly as you like, and representing to her that you know you express my opinion. The arrangement I suppose must be resumed. She is staying with Miss Gillies at Highgate and was here the day before yesterday. If it will give you no inconvenience to see her,—don't delay. She may otherwise write to Horne with the matter in abeyance, and involve us in the Devil's own confusion—(Here I fall upon my knees, and ask your fair Secretary's pardon for my intemperate language).

I was obliged to go yesterday, to an Annual one o'clock dinner to poor people, given by Miss Coutts, which detained me later than I expected and prevented my calling on you. Today I have to get to work on the Child's History, and afterwards to go to Shepherd's Bush, and after that to preside at the dinner which you ought to assist at. The whole of the performances to conclude with a whitlow on my right forefinger, which makes it difficult for me to write, to dress myself, to brush my hair, take my bath, shake hands with anybody, or do anything.

I number all the papers I send, to prevent you falling into pits of confusion.

No. 1 is from one Caudle—to whom I have a dim idea that we gave some money for Emigration purposes. The two papers (newspapers) along with it, are, I suppose, the papers to which he refers. There is nothing to be done on that head, as I take it.

No. 2 are Murray's hints.* I see no objection to using chapter 5 as final Hints, and not using chapter 4 at all. Please to observe that these chapter numerals belong to his MSS., and have nothing to do with my present indexing for your clearer understanding.

---

* "The Roving Englishman," by Grenville Murray, was appearing in *Household Words*.

No. 3 is a letter, referring (I suppose) to the nine hundred and ninety-nine thousandth Colonial ass who wanted us to print in *H. W.* some saw-dusty Literature out of the *Port-Something Journal*. You may recollect the case. It is needless for me to see the man who writes. So I hand him over to you.

I don't think I can finish the "Child's History" in one morning, for I have got my favourite ruffian Henry the Eighth to deal with. Will you let me know, by John, your proposed Make-Up for the next No. I don't see, among my proofs, any good first article. "Child's Play" is the smallest beer I ever saw brewed from such strong materials. Don't leave out the "Dirty Old Man."* He is capital.

Ever faithfully,
C. D.

1853.

During a great part of this year Dickens was at work on "Bleak House," which was published in book-form in September. It is curious to note that, in spite of Harold Skimpole, Leigh Hunt was a contributor to *Household Words*, both this year and last (see the letters of August 5th and 7th this year). The titles of his articles were "Kilspindie," September 4th, 1852 (a poem); "The Trumpets of Doolkarnein," September 18th, 1852 (a poem); "Lounging Through Kensington," August 6th, 1853, August 20th, 1853; "Kensington," September 3rd, 1853; "Kensington Church," November 19th, 1853; and "Kensington Worthies," December 3rd, 1853.

---

* *Household Words*, January 8th, 1853, by William Allingham, the poet (1824—1889). He was a friend of Dickens and frequently contributed to *Household Words*. A volume of letters addressed him by Dickens and many others has recently been published.

Herbert Watkins, photographer.   Emery Walker Ph. sc.

Wilkie Collins.

In the spring Dickens was at 1, Junction Parade, Brighton; and in the summer he established himself at Boulogne, at the Villa des Moulineaux, his landlord being M. Beaucourt, for whom he conceived a warm regard. Here he dictated parts of the "Child's History of England," the conclusion of which appeared in *Household Words* of December 10th. It began in the number of January 25th, 1851.

In September Dickens started with Augustus Egg, A.R.A., and Wilkie Collins on a tour through Switzerland and Italy, returning to Tavistock House in December. I can find no letters written by Dickens to Wills during this tour. A long letter from Florence, dated November 21st and printed in "Letters," I., 334, is lost. From October 15th to December 24th there are no contributions by Dickens to *Household Words* except the instalments of the "Child's History of England."

This year saw the addition of Wilkie Collins to the list of contributors to *Household Words*. His story, "Gabriel's Marriage," appeared in the numbers of April 16th and 23rd. In the previous year he had taken part in the provincial theatrical tour on behalf of the "Guild," and thenceforth he became one of Dickens's best friends and, eventually, his most intimate fellow worker. He died in 1889 in his 66th year.

OFFICE OF *HOUSEHOLD WORDS*.
A Weekly Journal conducted by Charles Dickens.

No. 16, WELLINGTON STREET NORTH, STRAND,
Tuesday, Eighth February, 1853.

MY DEAR WILLS:—I think the best way will be for you to make an appointment with Collins, and talk to him on the subject of the enclosed. I don't quite understand from his letter that you explained to him that I doubt the subject of hereditary insanity—not with an eye to the feelings of the public in general, but with a consideration for those numerous families in which there is such a taint. The force of my objection lies in that range of the subject only.

On the whole I am disposed to think that it will be best to accept his offer of a new story instead. And it is desirable to explain to him that a story within a story—as this is—is complicated and difficult for our peculiar purpose.

I think there are many things, both in the inventive and descriptive way, that he could do for us if he would like to work in our direction. And I particularly wish him to understand this, and to have every possible assurance conveyed to him that I think so, and that I should particularly like to have his aid. See if he cannot strike out one or two subjects while with you, to begin upon.

Will you give Mr. Brownlow a call one day when you are near there? Seeing in the enclosed card that he was interested in a child's election for the St. Ann's Schools, I got Miss Coutts's votes—also enclosed. But I can't find the child's name in the List, and consequently can't set a No. against his name.

Ever faithfully,
C. D.

No. 16, WELLINGTON STREET NORTH, STRAND,
Thursday Night, Seventeenth February, 1853.

MY DEAR WILLS:—I have gone over the proofs and made the best of the names. I don't like Forster's paper to lead off with, but don't think Sala's better.* Also I am restless about Hobson and doubt the expediency of going back to so poor a thing—as, if I had a weak leg, or a game eye, I don't think I would call attention to it. But I leave Hobson, not to confuse the Proof. There are awful haltings in the Poem, but I have made the best of it.

Faithfully ever,
C. D.

[The following letter is printed in "Letters," III., 137 (wrongly dated 4th March, 1853), but a paragraph from a letter of 12th August, 1852, has there been substituted for the first two paragraphs.]

1, JUNCTION PARADE, BRIGHTON,
Thursday Night, Tenth March, 1853.

MY DEAR WILLS :—I have gone through this No. carefully (as you will see, on looking through my marks—I have been obliged to query twice or thrice, really not understanding what is meant) and am quite out of heart with it.

Sala, very poor. One of the noblest subjects that can be written on, with really nothing in its treatment. Quite above him.

"A Doctor of Morals," *impossible of insertion as it stands.* A mere puff for Hill, with all the difficult parts of the question blinked, and many statements utterly at variance with what I am known to have written. It is exactly because the great bulk of offences in a great number of places are committed

---

* The reference probably was to proofs of the number for March 5th, in which Forster's "Seventy-eight Years Ago" was the first article. Sala contributed "The Last Crusade," and there was a poem by "Miss Berwick" (Adelaide Procter). There is no trace of Hobson.

by professed thieves, that it will not do to have Pet Prisoning advocated,* without grave remonstrance and great care. That class of prisoner is not to be reformed. We must begin at the beginning and prevent by stringent education and supervision of wicked parents, that class of prisoner from being regularly supplied as if he were a human necessity.

Do they teach trades in workhouses, and try to fit *their* people (the worst part of them) for Society? Come with me to Tothill Fields, Bridewell, or to Shepherd's Bush, and I will show you what a workhouse girl is. Or look to my "Walk in a Workhouse" (in *H. W.*†) and to the glance at the youths I saw in one place, positively kept like wolves.

Mr. Hill thinks prisons could be made nearly self-supporting. Have you any idea of the difficulty that is found in disposing of Prison-Work? Or does *he* know that the Treadmills didn't grind the air because the State or the Magistracy objected to the competition of prison labour with free labour, but because the work *could not be got?*

I never can have any kind of prison discipline disquisition in *H. W.* that does not start with the first great principle I have laid down, and that does not protest against prisons being considered *per se.* Whatever chance is given to a man in a prison, must be given to a man in a refuge for distress.

The article in itself is very good, but it must have these points in it; otherwise I am not only compromising opinions I am known to hold, but the journal itself is blowing hot and cold and playing fast and loose, in a ridiculous way.

* "Pet Prisoners," by Dickens, *Household Words*, April 27th, 1850.
† *Household Words*, May 25th, 1850.

That heap of chips is quite out of the question. "Vegetable Miracles" had better be made a separate article, and called "Receipt of Fern Seed"—which is a phrase of Falstaff's.

The Australian article had better be called, I think, "Lost and Found at the Gold Diggings." It, too, is very poor.

As to "La Galite,"* it looks like a wretched translation from a wretched original, and I can say no more of it. But observe the horrible injudiciousness of leaving in it, at page 89, that reference to the Slave Dealer, after all the howling there has been about that infernal African who could wear his chains in peace—and be damned to him.

Starting a paper in India is very droll—to us. But it is full of references that the public don't understand, and don't in the least care for. Bourgeois, brevier, minion, and nonpareil, long primer, turn-ups, dummy advertisements and reprints, back form, imposing stone, and locking up, are all quite out of their way and a sort of slang that they have no interest in.

Let me see a revise when you have got it together, and if you can strengthen it—do. I mention all the objections that occur to me as I go on—not because you can obviate them (except in the case of the Prison paper) but because if I make a point of doing so always, you will feel and judge the more readily both for yourself and me too, at the same time, "one and indivisible," when I take an Italian flight.

* "Hermit Island," *Household Words*, March 26th. The writer was W. Hepworth Dixon, a fairly regular contributor to the paper. From 1853 to 1869 he was editor of the *Athenaeum*. He wrote "Spiritual Wives," "Her Majesty's Tower," and many other books. He died in 1879.

You.

How are the a/cs getting on ?

Me.

I have been at work all day.

Ever faithfully,
C. D.

Tavistock House,
Friday, Eighteenth March, 1853.

My Dear Wills :—When I came home last night, I found the enclosed from Brockedon on the "India Rubber" article.

It must be closely enquired into, and I should wish to have, separately, whatever Mr. Dodd may have to say on each head in which the fact is stated to be distinctly against him. Because if it should turn out—which it may not—that he has again committed and misled us, immediately after the "Gold and Silver Diets,"* it is quite clear it won't do. Nothing can be so damaging to *Household Words* as carelessness about facts. It is as hideous as dulness.

Ever yours,
C. D.

Boulogne,
Monday, Thirteenth June, 1853.

My Dear Wills :—You will be glad, I know, to hear that we had a delightful passage yesterday, and that I made a perfect phenomenon of a dinner. It is raining hard to-day, and my back feels the damp; but I am otherwise still mending.

I have signed, sealed, and delivered, a contract for a house (once occupied for two years by a man I knew in Switzerland), which is not a large one, but

* *Household Words*, March 5th, 1853.

stands in the midst of a great garden, with what the landlord calls a "forest" at the back; and is now surrounded by flowers, vegetables, and all manner of growth. A queer, odd, French place—but extremely well supplied with all table and other conveniences, and strongly recommended. The address is

> Château des Moulineaux,
> Rue Beaurepaire,
> Boulogne.

There is a coach-house, stabling for half a dozen horses, and I don't know what.

We take possession this afternoon, and are now laying in a good stock of creature-comforts. So no more at present from

> Yours ever faithfully,
> C. D.

Mrs. Dickens and her sister unite in kindest regards.

> Château des Moulineaux, Boulogne,
> *Saturday Night, Eighteenth June*, 1853.

H. W.

My Dear Wills:—I have gone over the No. and now return it. "Thomas," *very well*—but might have been a little more picturesque. Costello good enough as far as it goes, but it don't go to the Camp, and therefore is at present a *coup manqué*. If you put Forster in his place, call it "The Power-Loom."* If you have a tolerably lively process article, it would be better than "Country News." Look well to that portion yet to come of Sala's, which I have not got.

* *Household Words*, July 9th.

"Bleak House."

Thank God I have done half the No. with great ease, and hope to finish on Thursday or Friday next. O how thankful I feel to be able to have done it, and what a relief to get the No. out!

Money.

I enclose a cheque for £20.

General Movements of Inimitable.

I *don't think* (I am not sure) I shall come to London until after the completion of "Bleak House" No. 18— the No. after this now in hand—for it strikes me that I am better here at present. I have picked up in the most extraordinary manner, and I believe you would never suppose to look at me that I had had that week or half an hour of it. If there should be any occasion for our meeting in the meantime, a run over here would do you no harm, and we should be delighted to see you at any time. If you suppose this place to be in a street, you are hugely mistaken. It is in the country, though not more than ten minutes' walk from the Post Office, and is the best doll's house of many rooms in the prettiest French grounds and the most charming situation I have ever seen—the best place I have ever lived in, abroad, except at Genoa. You can scarcely imagine the beauty of the air on this richly wooded hill side. As to comforts in the house, there are all sorts of things, beginning with no end of the coldest water and running through the most beautiful flowers down to English footbaths and a Parisian liqueur-stand. Your parcel (frantic enclosures and all) arrived quite safely last night. This will leave by steamer to-morrow, Sunday, evening. There is a boat in the morning, but having no one to send to-night I can't reach it; and to-morrow being Sunday it will come to much the same thing.

I think that's all at present.

Ever, my Dear Wills,
Faithfully yours,
C. D.

Boulogne,
Monday, Twenty-seventh June, 1853.

My Dear Wills:—There was no letter from you in the parcel that came last night with the enclosed. That was all right, I suppose?

I have made various marks here. The Poem is so very poor, that it had better come out bodily until we have a very strong number. The metre is so wretchedly made out.

"Pull at the Pagoda Tree,"* very good. "Provisionally Registered,"* very good. It is rather unfortunate that we have so many foreign subjects, but it can't be helped I suppose. If we have never had Cause and Effect, I think it a better title for the Carlsruhe story. "St. Vorax's Singing Birds"* will stand over. With a chip, you won't want it.†

I am sorry that a corrected proof I once gave you of young Jerrold's "Two Gentlemen" has been mislaid. I recollect it, and my corrections, perfectly, by one stupendous absurdity that stands in the paper as it is. I wish you would tell me in what part of the town or country you know gentlemen of the present day to live under "Golden Domes." Because it is new to

---

* Wills was part author of all these articles.
† The references are to articles which appeared in *Household Words* of July 9th.

me, and I think a description of these Mansions might make a good paper.

I will send you the "History of England" in good time for the next No. and will afterwards write another paper if I can think of a subject. I will then refer to the letters you sent me yesterday, which I have not time to do this morning. Will you post the enclosed.

Ever faithfully,
C. D.

It has been blowing so hard here, that I am going down to look at the sea—with the intention of stopping the children at Folkestone by telegraphic message if feasible.

BOULOGNE,
Monday, Fourth July, 1853.

MY DEAR WILLS:—This No. will require a good deal of alteration.

In the first place, Morley must go first, beyond all question. In the second place, Morley and Sala should by no manner of means go together. In the third place the "Roving Englishman" must come out bodily; since apart from the slovenliness of the article, some of the statements are much too strong for me to commit myself to without a positive knowledge of the facts. Lastly, I think you have too much "History of England" at one time, and would do better to print one chapter in this No. and one after a week's interval.

Be very careful what you fill up with. And also, if you please, to revise the revise of the "Child's History"—taking care that it is pointed *for sense*.

How two men can have gone, one after the other, to the camp, and have written nothing about it, passes my comprehension. I have been in great doubt about the end of Sala. I wish you would suggest to him from me, when you see him, how wrong it is. Surely he cannot be insensible to the fact that military preparation in England at this time means Defence. Woman, says Sala, means Home, love, children, mother. Does he not find any protection of these things in a wise and moderate means of Defence; and is not the union between these things and those means one of the most natural, significant, and plain in the world.*

Mrs. Dickens and her sister have gone to look after Peter,† while I prepare my parcel.

Ever faithfully,
C. D.

Pray get something done in notice of the enclosed. I have forgotten it this long time.

BOULOGNE,
Sunday, Seventeenth July, 1853.

MY DEAR WILLS:—You will find a great many corrections of mine in the enclosed proof.‡

Nothing can improve the design of Miss Lynn's story ‖ (which I think very bad), but I have altered the wording of it, to avoid its looking, as it did, exactly like an indifferent translation. Unless you have promised anyone to put in that letter of Charles the First, leave it out.

---

* This paragraph is printed in "Letters," III., 140 (together with other matter wrongly dated), under date Sunday, August 7th, 1853.

† Peter Cunningham (1816—1869). For an account of him, see "Life," III., 52, 53.

‡ The proof of the number for July 30th.

‖ "Marie's Fever," *Household Words*, July 30th. Miss Lynn contributed a great deal to *Household Words*. In 1858 she married William James Linton, the wood-engraver, and afterwards became widely known, as Mrs. Lynn-Linton, for her novels and her satirical articles on certain modern tendencies, *e.g.*, her "Girl of the Period" articles in the *Saturday Review*.

See that your corrections are all attended to.

You say you have a stronger Poem. If so, and you can get it into this No. instead of the Sonnet, it will be a decided improvement. "Marie's Fever" is so twaddly that I should like to see something stronger in the place of a "Literary Lady's Maid." The No. becomes horribly weak in that place.

Will you be so kind as to hand the enclosed yourself to the little bright red round man in the inner room at Coutts's. I generally hand them the Paymaster General's Draft for Poole's quarterly pension, but, as it is payable to *me*, I cannot receive it until I come to town. Therefore I had best advance the money.

I will probably write you on one or two other small matters tomorrow.

Look at the enclosed from Hunt. I declare I don't know what to say, and have not answered it! Can you devise any means of getting out of the matter "privately and confidentially"?

The 22nd of August will suit us perfectly; but you had better come on the Saturday or Sunday previous, *in case* the passage should be queer. And we hope you will both be able to stay longer than a week.

Leech* and Mrs. Leech arrived here yesterday evening in a Devil of a gale. Everybody ill—doctors called in upon the boat (but not for them, I am glad to say)—and a most miserable scene altogether.

Ever faithfully,
C. D.

"Lounging through Kensington" is the best name, I think, for that paper.†

---

* John Leech, the *Punch* artist.
† By Leigh Hunt, *Household Words*, August 6th and 20th, 1853.

BOULOGNE,
Monday, July Twenty-fifth, 1853.

H. W.

My Dear Wills:—I received your parcel last night and return the proof * by this afternoon's boat, with a good many corrections in it. Sala's article is so badly printed that I have been obliged to put a query here and there, really not understanding what is meant.

If I *can* write an article this week, I will. But I am so full of the close of "Bleak House" that I can't, for the life of me, get at a good subject for *H. W.* as yet.

Dixon's paper admirably told, though nothing new in it.

Guild.

I think the reduction of Johnson necessary—but I would do it on not less than a month's notice.

Things in General.

I hope to begin my double No. next Monday. If I can get it done in good time, that is to say by the 18th or 19th, I shall come over with it myself. Of this I will advise you, however, in due course.

Dr. Storrar's opinion of Forster gives me great concern, though it has (as I think you know) certainly been mine for some time. I do not myself believe that Elliotson, pre-occupied with other things, has the least idea of the serious nature of his position.

* The number for August 6th.

And I am strongly inclined to think that the best course I can take is to write privately to Elliotson, and represent to him my impression of the necessity of his positively ordering Forster away. What do you think of that?

Ever faithfully,
C. D.

Haydn is the Dictionary of Dates man. This is (I think) the third time he has acted towards me in that honorable, and, in my experience, unprecedented manner.

"A Literary Lady's Maid" and "Corporation Dreams," coming together,* make me thrill and shudder with indescribable anguish.

BOULOGNE,
Wednesday, Twenty-seventh July, 1853.

MY DEAR WILLS :—There will be either three or four more—as nearly as I can judge, four more—of these slips, to complete this article.† I will send you the rest, please God, to-morrow, by the post at night.

I have also thought of another, to be called "FRAUDS UPON THE FAIRIES" ‡,—*apropos* of George Cruikshank's editing. Half playfully and half seriously, I mean to protest most strongly against alteration—for any purpose—of the beautiful little stories which are so tenderly and humanly useful to us in these times when the world is too much with us, early and late; and then to re-write "Cinderella" according to Total-abstinence, Peace Society, and

---

* In *Household Words*, July 30th.
† Probably "Gone Astray," by Dickens, *Household Words*, August 13th.
‡ This article, by Dickens, appeared in *Household Words*, October 1st.

Bloomer principles, and expressly for their propagation.

I shall want his book of "Hop o' My Thumb" (Forster noticed it in the last *Examiner*) and the most simple and popular version of "Cinderella" you can get me. I shall not be able to do it until after finishing "Bleak House," but I shall do it the more easily for having the books by me. So send them, if convenient, in your next parcel.

Acknowledge the safe receipt of this MS.

Ever faithfully,
C. D.

BOULOGNE,
First August, 1853.

MY DEAR WILLS:—I return the No.,* which is a very good one indeed. Look to the general printing and punctuation of the second article, and also of "Sick Grapes."

Enclosed is a chapter of "Child's History."

In your next parcel will you send me—

"Vergani's Italian Grammar."

"A Pocket Italian and English and English and Italian Dictionary."

"An Italian Dialogue Book."

You will get them all at De Torquet's in Tavistock Street, by the office. *Don't* send *Punch* in my parcels.

I am now going tooth and nail at "Bleak House." If I get done in time, I shall certainly come over. But it entirely depends upon my work.

I have just come back from Amiens, after a two

---

* The issue for August 27th.

days' trip. Your parcel was delivered here last night, just as I came home.

Ever faithfully,
C. D.

BOULOGNE,
Friday Evening, Fifth August, 1853.

MY DEAR WILLS:—I am too much occupied with the conclusion of " Bleak House "—just getting fairly into it—to go, with a pen, over the No. without delaying it. I therefore send the corrections of the " Child's History " chapter enclosed, and, without returning the proof in a parcel, will herein note my objections.

In the first place the No. is an awfully and solemnly heavy one—and, if you have any kind of means to that end by you, must really be lightened. I read it last night, and had a Nightmare. I doubt if anything so heavy (except stewed lead) could possibly be taken, before going to bed.

1st. "Justice to Bears." The name won't do. We have already had "Justice to the Hyæna." "BROTHER BRUIN " * would be a capital name, I think —thus introduced:

" The bear symbolises savage and primitive equality, and is therefore the aversion of the aristocracy." Such is the clue to ursine facts, according to Passional Zoology, which subject, and M. Toussenel's treatment of it, we now resume. It would appear that Mr. Sneak,† in " The Mayor of Garratt," had much reason in him when he addressed the rough personage

---

* *Household Words*, August 20th, by Dixon.

† Jerry Sneak is a character in Samuel Foote's play, "The Mayor of Garratt."

of the piece as Brother Bruin. Was he not a Bear and a Brother?

"Here again"—M. Toussenel exclaims—"is another"——

Then read the proof—you, W. H. W.—with an eye to this fact—that it wants to be made clearer all the way through, that it is M. Toussenel who is speaking, and not *H. W.* conducted by *C. D.*

Secondly, the first stage to Australia.* There is a forlorn attempt at humour about the Deputy Inspector General (page 584) that cannot be too ferociously decapitated. Pray have nothing about a detective in that connection; it looks like weakly and palely hanging on Mr. Bucket. Damn "here they are" at page 585—and dele it too. "And the onus of the idea task strangles every newly born smile that struggles for existence"—at page 584 again—strike out with a pen of iron. Look at the whole paper.

If the "Glimpse of Dublin" † be not by Allingham, strike it out. If it be, hold it over.

"Gore House" ‡ is very poor. Page 591, first column. Stop at the Graces, and dele the rest of that paragraph. It is Skimpole, you know—the whole passage. I couldn't write it more like him.

I have forgotten "Licensed to Juggle." Look to the slang talk of it, and don't let "Ya" stand for "You."

"The Stereoscope" is dreadfully literal. Some fancy must be got into the No. if John writes an article for it himself (—I mean our John: not Forster).

---

* This must, I think, refer to "A Digger's Diary," by R. H. Horne. It did not, however, appear till September 3rd.

† Presumably "The Length of the Quays," which, though written by Sala and not by Allingham, did appear on August 20th.

‡ "Gore House" was by Leigh Hunt, August 20th.

I should have thought the greater part of it written by McCulloch, edited by Rintoul.*

I am going out for a walk, after a punishing day's work.

Ever faithfully,
C. D.

P.S.—Brighten it, brighten it, brighten it!

Sunday, Seventh August, 1853.
BOULOGNE.

MY DEAR WILLS :—On the night of the day I wrote to you about there being no letter in the parcel—no, the next night—I received the letter from Barnard's office, by itself, " without note or comment."

I like the notion of the " Snow Giant " (which would be a good name) though the end is out of the question. It begins to trail off, at the smallpox part. Ask Miss Costello what it is translated from, and whether it is literally translated. If otherwise (of which there is very little hope) I think it might be well altered for the Xmas No.

Ollier's ballad will do.

I would hold " Kensington " † over,—certainly for a No. O Heaven, Hunt's not lounging, and being in earnest!

Can't possibly write autographs, until I have written " Bleak House." My work has been very hard since I have been here; and when I throw down my

---

* John Ramsay McCulloch (1789—1864) was a Scotsman, a political economist and a statistician. He wrote a great deal on taxation, the National Debt, currency and weights and measures.

Robert Stephen Rintoul (1787—1858), also a Scotsman, was a journalist and an advocate of political reform, emigration and colonisation. He founded *The Spectator*, and edited it from its first number, July 6th, 1828, till 1858, when he sold it.

† " Kensington," by Leigh Hunt, *Household Words*, September 3rd.

pen of a day, I throw down myself and can take up neither article.*

Ever faithfully,
C. D.

P.S.—My head is so pre-occupied, that I have forgotten two leading points of my note.

First. Will you send me, in a post letter, a £20 note for the enclosed.

Secondly. Will you at once make an enquiry into the Day Chancery cause, as

(1) When was it instituted?
(2) How much nearer is it now to its completion.
(3) What has been spent in costs?
(4) How many Counsel appear—about—whenever the Court is moved.†

You did ask this for me before, but I made no note of it. I should like to glance at it in the Preface. Of course I will in no degree whatever commit your informant; nor shall I even mention the cause by name. But I wish to be *within the facts.*

BOULOGNE,
Fifteenth August, 1853.
Monday.

MY DEAR WILLS:—No. 179. Want Places *not* in inverted commas as a title.‡ Pray substitute something for "Houses of Business," which is wretched

---

* This paragraph is printed in "Letters," III., 140, as the beginning of a totally different letter of the same date—which letter has no actual existence, being made up of extracts from five separate letters.

† To these queries Wills has appended the following answers in pencil:—
(1) About 1834, as near as I know.
(2) As far off as ever.
(3) At least £70,000.
(4) Formerly always 17, sometimes 30 or 40; it used to be said the whole Bar. The number has been much reduced.

‡ By Sala, *Household Words,* August 27th.

and contradictory. (I fear I am writing—it just strikes me—about a No. that is worked.)

No. 180 I will try to return tomorrow.

I see no objection whatever to Sala's pursuing that subject, as long as his matter is good.

I hope to dine at *H. W.* on *Thursday at ½ past* 6. I shall be due at London Bridge at 6—purposing to write the last little three-page chapter of "Bleak House," in town—and will come straight on in a constitutional cab. Perhaps Forster will like to dine with us.

Ever faithfully,
C. D.

Boulogne,
Fourteenth September, 1853.

H. W.

My Dear Wills:—I send you "Frauds on the Fairies" *—which I think (between ourselves) ADMIRABLE. Both merry and wise. When you send proofs, send two.

You shall have some more "Child's History" in the next parcel.

Courier.

I have been greatly diverted by your account of the Impracticable applicants. I await Kamb with interest. Mrs. Watson has written to me of another strongly recommended (by her father Lord George Quin with whom he travelled) and now at Paris; but Kamb shall have his fair chance, and if I fully like him, I will take him, supposing the other not to precede him.

---

* *Household Words,* October 1st. See *ante,* p. 110.

FAMILY

Send kindest regards.

Ever faithfully,
C. D.

BOULOGNE,
Sunday, *Eighteenth September*, 1853.

MY DEAR WILLS:—I return you the No.* with a good many corrections in pencil on it—some queries, where it is so badly printed that I cannot understand what is meant.

I have put two crosses against an expression in Ollier's poem
—"and yet it is not night"
—which you may remember in an older line, preceded by the words " The moon is up." If he be accessible, ask him to alter it.

The titles will stand

" Frauds on the Fairies."
" Tribunals of Commerce."

(here again I have queried the concluding paragraph which should be rather a suggestion, I think, than such an absolute statement)

" Bucharest."
" Starlight in the Garden."
" The Great Saddleworth Exhibition."
" Dead Reckoning at the Morgue."
" A Child's History of England."

The whole requires to be carefully gone over.

I send you another short article for the next No., chiefly *apropos* of Mr. Dunn's case.

---

* The number for October 1st.

The enclosed letter to Mr. Henry Morley came in yesterday's parcel—I suppose clearly by mistake. I send it back again.

COURIER.

Edward Kamb will bring this. He turned up yesterday, accounting for his delay by waiting for a written recommendation, and having at the last moment (as a foreigner not being an Englishman) a passport to get. I quite agree with you as to his appearance and manner, and have engaged him. It strikes me that it would be an excellent beginning if you would deliver him a neat and appropriate address, telling him what in your conscience you can find to tell of me favourably as a master, and particularly impressing upon him *readiness and punctuality* on his part as the great things to be observed. I think it would have a much better effect than anything I could say in this stage, of and from myself. And I shall be much obliged to you if you will act upon this hint forthwith.

W. H. WILLS.

No letter having arrived from the popular author of the "Larboard Fin"* by this morning's post, I rather think one must be on the way in the pocket of Gordon's son—whom, between ourselves, I don't at all want. If Kamb calls for this before Young Scotland arrives, you will understand if I do not refer to an unreceived letter. But I shall leave this open until Kamb comes first.

X— Y—

is of course an evasive humbug. Accept that story—

* A wholly imaginary nautical drama alleged (by Dickens) to have been written by Wills.

but Lord to see how he has spoilt it!!! I will re-write it, and send it you back.

Ever faithfully,
C. D.

BOULOGNE, *Tuesday Evening*,
(Just before dinner),
Twentieth September, 1853.

MY DEAR WILLS :—I have just received your letter and think Kamb appears so completely to mistake his position and functions in that ridiculous charge for expenses, that I wish you would be so kind as to send for him at once and tell him that *I shall not take him* unless it is distinctly understood between you and him that I shall hereafter reduce them, and deduct as much of this bill from his wages as I know to be right. Otherwise I know this bill to be ample ground for declaring off, and I most positively do so. I am thoroughly well acquainted with the practice and the expectations of the best Couriers, and on all grounds of common sense and justice I reject such extortion. Therefore unless you find that he perfectly understands and that he unconditionally submits, please see one of the other applicants of whom you thought favourably. His address is 4, King Street, Grosvenor Square.

I write hastily for this express purpose, and will write again to-morrow. Faithfully ever,
C. D.

BOULOGNE,
Sunday, Ninth October, 1853.

MY DEAR WILLS :—Many thanks for your kind letter, both on my own behalf, and on that of the unprotected females. They are sincerely sensible of your offer, and Mrs. Dickens begs me to say that she will not hesitate to give you all the trouble in her power!

I write before the arrival of Mark [Lemon], but leave this open in the meanwhile in case I should then have anything to add. On the second half of this sheet,* I send my line of march as far as Lausanne, whence I will write again. I shall not expect (unless in some extraordinary case) to hear from you before I get there.

When the sheets of the 3rd Volume of the "Child's History" come to you (as they will) will you put a few words into His Sowship's† life, where his writings are referred to, to the effect that he wrote, among other things, about Witches, in whom he was (as such a wrong-headed Dolt ought to have been) a strong believer. I somehow forgot to put this in to the MS. Likewise, you will find it stated that after the Gunpowder Plot some Catholics were for safety in the fens of *Lincolnshire*. It ought to be, the fens of *Ely*.

I don't remember that I have anything more to add —except that the moustaches don't look a bit better than they did. The failures desire their kindest regards. I shall come back, I hope, with no end of good things in my mind for *H. W.* Meanwhile and always, believe me,

Very heartily yours,
C. D.

[To Mrs. Wills.]

Tavistock House,
Fourteenth December, 1853.

My Dear Mrs. Wills :—I have brought you home a trifling brooch in the silver filigree-work, which has

---

* This has been torn off.
† James the First.

no value of itself, but which I hope may find some in your honest eyes, as a little sign of remembrance from your excellent husband's attached friend and fellow-workman.

Always very faithfully yours,
CHARLES DICKENS.

Mrs. Wills.

1854.

During the early part of this year Dickens gave several readings in large provincial towns for charitable purposes.

In the summer he again went to Boulogne, to a different house, the *Villa du Camp de Droite*, which he rented from the same landlord, M. Beaucourt.

"Hard Times" ran through *Household Words* from April 1st to August 12th, when it was published in book-form. Forster ("Life," III., 45) says that with "Hard Times" Dickens more than doubled the circulation of his journal.

[Wills was staying at Malvern for the benefit of his health.]

OFFICE OF *HOUSEHOLD WORDS*.
A Weekly Journal conducted by Charles Dickens.

No. 16, WELLINGTON STREET NORTH, STRAND,
Wednesday, Twelfth April, 1854.

H. W.

MY DEAR WILLS :—I have given Miss Berwick's* "Knight Errant," the benefit of the doubt, and sent

---

* "Miss Berwick" was the pseudonym of Adelaide Procter, Barry Cornwall's daughter. Her first contribution ("Old Echoes") appeared in *Household Words* of February 5th, 1853.

it to the Printers. The Spring lines I re-enclose. I would decline them, on the ground that after the Spring Sonnet we have settled Spring for this year.

Look at this letter from Mrs. Gaskell. Did *you* send it this morning—omit all mention of it by mistake—and send it in consequence of having received it with the missing paper? It has no date, but it *must* be old, I infer, because the Mr. Fairbairn matter is all arranged with her. I had a number of letters by this morning's post, and did not look at this until I had destroyed the envelope. I can't answer it without first communicating thus with you, for I can't in the least understand it.

I know all the walks for many and many miles round you, and delightful walks they are. I suppose you are already getting very stout, very red, very jovial (in a physical point of view) altogether.

Mark and I walked to Dartford from Greenwich, last Monday, and found Mrs. Horner acting " The Stranger " (with a strolling company from the Standard Theatre) in " Mr. Munns's Schoolroom." The stage was a little wider than your table here, and its surface was composed of loose boards laid on the school forms. Dogs sniffed about it during the performances, and *the* carpenter's highlows were ostentatiously taken off and displayed in the Proscenium. We stayed until a quarter to ten, when we were obliged to fly to the Railroad, but we sent the landlord of the hotel down with the following articles:

1 Bottle superior Old Port.
1 Do. Do. Gold Sherry.
1 Do. Do. best French Brandy.
1 Do. Do. 1st quality Old Tom Gin.
1 Do. Do. Prime Jamaica Rum.

1 Bottle superior small still Isla Whiskey.
1 Kettle boiling water.
Two pounds finest white lump sugar.
Our cards.
1 Lemon, and
Our compliments.

The effect we had previously made upon the Theatrical Company by being beheld in the first two chairs—there was nearly a pound in the house—was altogether electrical.

My ladies send their kindest regards, and are disappointed at your not saying that you drink two and twenty tumblers of the limpid element, every day. The children also unite in " loves," and the Plornishghenter on being asked if he would send his, replied " Yes—Man," which we understand to signify cordial acquiescence.

Forster just come back from lecturing at Sherborne. Describes said lecture as " Blaze of Triumph."

H. W. AGAIN.

Miss—I mean Mrs.—Bell's story very nice. I have sent it to the Printer, and entitled it " The Green Ring and the Gold Ring." *

This apartment looks desolate in your absence—but O Heavens how tidy!

J. W.

Mrs. Wills supposed to have gone into a convent at Somers Town.

B. AND E.

Never paid the £500! Consequently I had notice

* It appeared May 6th.

yesterday that I had overdrawn my account at Coutts'. Whereof I have given *them* notice to-day, in strong terms.

My Dear Wills,
Ever faithfully yours,
C. D.

TAVISTOCK HOUSE,
Tuesday, Eighteenth April, 1854.

H. W.

MY DEAR WILLS :—I will go over the No. when it comes, and write to you again after doing so. There is a capital paper by Sala in proof, called "Tatterboy's Rents."* I wish you would write to him from me, and tell him by all means to pursue the subject, as he intimates an idea of doing at the close of the article.

C. D.

I am in a dreary state, planning and planning the story of "Hard Times" (out of materials for I don't know how long a story), and consequently writing little. Mark and I had it in contemplation to come down to Worcester next Monday and ask you to meet us there instead of our coming to Malvern: which would have given us from five to six hours together at the Inn. But I am afraid I shall not be able to spare the day. Macready is coming to town to-day, and I have unavoidable engagements all the week which will greatly hamper me. Moreover I am greatly anxious to keep ahead. But—

W. H. W.

It appears to me that you must most decidedly stay at Malvern a full month. I don't think you can put

---

* "Tattyboy's Rents," by Sala, appeared May 13th.

the cure to any rational and fair test in a shorter time. If you decide to do that, Mark and I will overhaul our respective logs (excuse nauticality, but I have been reading a soul-stirring Drama called the "Larboard Fin,"* which *looks* to me like an undiscovered play by Shakespeare, surreptitiously modernized), and will make another appointment for next week. You are now in the Black and Blue stage. I don't apprehend that you are likely to come to a Flesh-coloured complexion in less than four weeks. You are not green yet—and *that* takes time.

W. H. W. (BROUGHT UP).

You refer in a maddening manner, to something you *don't* enclose in your letter. What do you mean by it?

T. R., HAYMARKET.

I went there to see the Easter piece last night, and I never beheld anything so dreary. The agonies of Mrs. Fitzwilliam and Buckstone were positively most distressing to see. Everything went wrong, and was bad if it had gone right. Once, before a pair of flats (clouds), Mrs. F. waved a golden patent hearthbroom about five and twenty minutes, without anything happening. Then she and Miss Featherstone and Young Farren came down to the Float, and sang and pattered *all the rest of the piece*—got it off at once—and after another long interval a carpenter was disclosed in a celestial place (but swearing awfully) and a man in black, supposed to be unseen, seized some red fire and wildly lighted it up. Buckstone meantime, perfectly idiotic and imbecile with grief, laid his head on Mrs. Fitzwilliam's bosom.

* See *ante*, p. 118 note.

J[OHN] F[ORSTER]

was there, and perpetually said, "My dear Dickens, Good God, what does this mean?" To which that eminent man replied, after the manner of Commodore Trunnion, "Hold your tongue and be damned!" For we were sitting over the stage.

B. AND E.

Have paid the £500.

ALL THE FAMILY

send kindest regards.

Ever, My Dear Wills,
Faithfully yours,
CHARLES DICKENS.

No. 16, WELLINGTON STREET NORTH,
STRAND,
Thursday, Twentieth April, 1854.

H. W.

MY DEAR WILLS:—I have gone very carefully over the whole No. and sent it down to Arry. It is a very good one, I think, and I see no occasion to alter the course of the making-up, or to change any paper. The titles are improved. I think I must have taken out almost as much as is required. If you have to take out more, take it from "Dr. Pablo"* after his marriage and the loss of his wife's fortune.

Mrs. Gaskell's missing paper has turned up at last, and is in the printer's hands.

* By Morley, *Household Words,* May 6th.

W. H. W.

It is quite clear that you must stay at Malvern a month, and come back a miracle of health. There is not the least difficulty in the way, nor have I, really, more to do than at another time, though I need not say to you that I should be more than willing to do it if I had. It appears to me from the materials on hand that we are quite safe for good numbers.

General Intelligence.

You know my man Cooper? Steady stupid sort of highly respectable creature? Seven children. Eldest boy 13 years old, "working" (I can't conceive how) at a mathematical instrument maker's "down at Westminster." On Tuesday night, the boy did not come home. Mother half distracted, and getting up at 5 in the morning to go and look for him. Father went out after breakfast to do likewise. Boy had been sent on an errand, had punctually performed the errand, and been heard of no more. Father conferring with Policeman on disappearance, up comes strange boy saying that how he has eerd tell as a boy is a lyin in the "Bonus," as was run over. Wretched father goes to the Bonus (attached to the Workhouse, I suppose), and finds his child with his head smashed to pieces! He was walking on some planks by the roadside, a plank tilted, he fell under a coal waggon as it was advancing, and was picked up as Dead as Adam. I cannot get it out of my mind—as Forster would say.

My neighbour's, Mr. Cardale's, daughter married this morning, and I was obliged to leave home at what the newspapers always call "an early hour of the morning" to avoid distraction. All the women and girls in my house, stark mad on the subject. Despotic conjugal influence exerted to keep Mrs. Dickens out of the church. Caught putting bonnet on for that purpose, and sternly commanded to renounce idiotic intentions. Bride reported by our confectioner (envious and a Roman Catholic) to have the gift of Tongues. It probably will disappear now.

Mark has just come in, and sends all manner of regards. Time of our visit is still uncertain, in consequence of "Hard Times," and great pressure of Wooden-Headedness on gifted author.

Kindest remembrances from all at home.

Ever, My Dear Wills,
Most faithfully,
C. D.

TAVISTOCK HOUSE,
Tuesday, Thirtieth May, 1854.

MY DEAR WILLS :—I think Thomas's story * very good indeed. Close, original, vigorous, and graphic. It strikes me that I see better things in it than he has done yet.

An alteration occurs to me—easily made—which I think would greatly improve it, in respect of interest and quiet pathos, and a closing sentiment of pleasure to the reader. It should be delicately expressed that the man (admirably described) who comes a-courting Miss Furbey is the old lover who has always been faithful. I think Miss Furbey might have always had a miniature of him, hanging up, or in a pet drawer and sometimes brought out, taken when he was a young man; and that when the narrator begins to observe him and his visits, she should still see in the

---

* "Miss Furbey" appeared in *Household Words*, June 17th.

grey hair and the worn face something of that portrait.

I wish you would make the suggestion in my words. Beg him not to delay the story, for I don't like to keep anything of so much merit out of print.

The young poet is not quite to any purpose at present, but I would certainly encourage him.

Ever faithfully,
C. D.

"Death's Doors" will be a better name for Morley's paper than the one I gave it yesterday.

VILLA DU CAMP DE DROITE,
Thursday, Twenty-second June, 1854.

MY DEAR WILLS:—I have nothing to say, but, having heard from you this morning, think I may as well report all well.

We have a most charming place here. I think the finest situation (Genoa excepted) I have lived in, and the best cottage house. It beats the former residence all to nothing. We have a beautiful garden with all its fruits and flowers, and a field of our own, and a road of our own away to the Columns, and everything that is airy and fresh. The great Beaucourt hovers about us like a guardian genius, and I imagine that no English person in a carriage could by any possibility find the place.

Of the wonderful inventions and contrivances with which a certain Inimitable creature has made the most of it, I will say nothing until you have an opportunity of inspecting the same. At present I will only observe that I have written exactly 72 words of "Hard Times" since I have been here.

Many thanks for the Cranstone information which is quite conclusive.

As to your account of——, though it makes me laugh, it makes me feel disposed to tear my hair off. That he should ever have been such a double-distilled ass as to marry that girl, or have anything on earth to do with that Family! The great thing to be hoped is, that she will never go back to him, and that her father and mother may fly with her—and the Devil with all of 'em—to the Antipodes.

The children arrived on Tuesday night per London boat, in every stage and aspect of sea-sickness. With them, Lally and Betty Lemon, whose parents and guardians had discreetly packed two dozen pairs of bran new stockings in their luggage. Duty on said stockings, 8 francs.

The camp is about a mile off, and huts are now building for (they say) 60,000 soldiers. I don't imagine it to be near enough to bother us.

If the weather ever should be fine, it might do you good sometimes to come over with the proofs on a Saturday when the tide served well, before you and Mrs. W. make your annual visit. Recollect, there is always a bed, and no sudden appearance will put us out.

      Kind regards,
        Ever faithfully,
          C. D.

Mr. Davey may well stand over till I return. I will tell you something *apropos* of that.

I shall be curious to hear the end of ——'s domesticity. Get him, if you can, to shew you the letter he will receive from his wife's father. O what a letter that will be!

BOULOGNE,
Thursday, Fourteenth [Thirteenth] July, 1854.

MY DEAR WILLS:—Your note received, and your parcel expected.

I am so stunned with work, that I really am not able (in sending off my own parcel hurriedly) to answer your questions—I mean, not able to consider them. I doubt if there will not be too much of "Hard Times," to admit of the conclusion all going in together. There will probably be either 14 or 15 sides of my writing. But the best thing will be for me to come over with it, the moment I have finished. *On Wednesday night at a quarter past ten,* I hope to be at London Bridge. But if I should find on Monday (though I hardly expect it) that I can come on Tuesday night instead I will let you know as much by Monday's post.

The MS. now sent, contains what I have looked forward to through many weeks.

The advertisement will simply be—

On such a day will be published complete in
One Volume, price five shillings,
HARD TIMES,
By Charles Dickens.

I will send B. and E. the two first books in your returned parcel.

Ever faithfully,
C. D.

Call the Guild again, for Monday Week.

BOULOGNE,
Saturday Night, Fourteenth [Fifteenth] July, 1854.
"HARD TIMES."

MY DEAR WILLS:—The enclosed batch of print tied up with string, to Whitefriars *at once*, if you please.

H. W.

My corrections are rather slightly made, and the No. wants carefully going over for plain pointing and setting out.

The "C. P." by R. S.* is very well done, but I cannot make up my mind to lend my blow to the great Forge-bellows of puffery at work. I so heartily desire to have nothing to do with it, that I wish you would cancel this article altogether, and substitute something else. As to the guide-books, I think they are a sufficiently flatulent botheration in themselves, without being discussed. A lurking desire is always upon me to put Mr. Laing's speech on Accidents to the public, as Chairman of the Brighton Railway, against his pretensions as a chairman of public Instructors and guardians. And I don't know but what I may come to it at some odd time. This strengthens me in my wish to avoid the bellows.†

When you want a parcel to reach me at once (if ever) I think you had better write outside, so much for Immediate Delivery. Because my friend Barnard keeps them all cooling, four or five hours. And I don't know that he can be reasonably expected under the circumstances, to do anything else.

* Probably an article on the Crystal Palace, the erection of which, at Sydenham, was completed this year.
† This paragraph is printed in "Letters," III., 140, as part of the supposed letter of August 7th, 1853.

I hope to get up to town on Tuesday night with the close of "Hard Times." Will write again on Monday night. Meanwhile, all other matters stand over without mention except—

GUILD.

The table of Sickness Fund premiums requires extension or a plain explanation appended that it presents the Minimum of Provident Investment under that head, and that so much is the Maximum. Without such addition it looks ludicrous.

Ever faithfully,
C. D.

BOULOGNE,
Monday, July Seventeenth, 1854.

MY DEAR WILLS:—I am happy to say that I have finished "Hard Times" this morning. I purpose coming over to-morrow, arriving at London Bridge at a quarter past 10 at Night. Will you tell Cooper to be there, in waiting for me.

Ever faithfully,
C. D.

BOULOGNE,
Sunday, Thirtieth July, 1854.

H. W.

MY DEAR WILLS:—I return the No. The overmatter was not in the parcel. Therefore I don't know what it is.

"Turkish Seamanship," as a separate article of one column, is ridiculous. It must be a chip.

If you have anything else of any merit, I greatly doubt the expediency of closing the No. with that "Back Ways to Fame."* I suppose it to be by Morley. But it is dreadfully heavy. It would do in another place and at another time, but I feel it to drag most wearily here.

You had better get into this No. the following advertisement—

> NEW TALE, by the author of "MARY BARTON," to be published weekly in *Household Words*.
> On Wednesday, the 30th day of August will be published, in *Household Words*, the First Portion of a New Work of Fiction, called—
> "NORTH AND SOUTH."
> *By The Author of "Mary Barton."*
> The publication of this story, &c.

(according to the first announcement of "Hard Times," at the end of No. 206).

The advertisement must always stand, afterwards, like the old "Hard Times" advertisement.

I have begged Mrs. Gaskell to send you some MS. for the printers to get up. B. and E. must do what they think necessary in the advertising way, but, if they bill the walls, they must be very careful only to have the plain, good, sensible bills used in the case of "Hard Times," that we had at the office. She objects to any title if it can be dispensed with; and altogether refuses (and no wonder) to be connected with a hideous placard all askew, invented in Whitefriars for "Hard Times," and concerning which phenomenon I wrote to Bradbury on its appearance.

Parcel for Whitefriars, enclosed. Also two letters for post.

* By Morley, *Household Words*, August 19th.

Family.

All well, and the Meteor Flag a tremendous success. Collins sends regards.

Ever faithfully,
C. D.

Boulogne,
Wednesday, Second August, 1854.

My Dear Wills:—In the next parcel will you send me both volumes of this book?

I will endeavour to come off my back (and the grass) to do an opening paper for the starting No. of "North and South." I can't positively answer for such a victory over the idleness into which I have delightfully sunk, as the achievement of this feat; but let us hope.

During a *fête* on Monday night, the Meteor Flag of England (forgotten to be struck at sunset) was—*stolen ! ! !*

—— seems to have brought his career to a noble conclusion at last. When the united bores (and the political economists) give him a piece of plate and a dinner, will you put me down for Twenty-five Pounds and a Speech.

Manage the proofs of *H. W.* so that I may not have to correct them on a Sunday. I am not going over to the Sabbatarians, but like the haystack (particularly) on a Sunday morning.

I should like John to call on M. Henri, Townshend's servant, 21, Norfolk Street, Park Lane, and ask him if, when he comes over here with his master, he can take charge of a trap, bat, and ball. If yea, then I should like John to proceed to Mr. Darke's, Lord's Cricket Ground, and purchase said trap, bat, and ball, of the best quality. Townshend* is coming here on the 15th—probably will leave town a day or two before.

Pray be in a condition to drink a glass of the 1846 champagne, when *you* come.

I think I have no more to say at present. I cannot sufficiently admire my prodigious energy in coming out of a stupor to write this letter.

Ever faithfully,
C. D.

BOULOGNE,
Monday, Seventh August, 1854.

H. W.

MY DEAR WILLS :—The No.† is very poor as it stands. I would make it up as follows. *Whatever you want to take out, you can take from Miss Lynn.* The punctuation and dashing of whose story require particular attention.

"A Little More Harmony." ‡
"Catchpennies" (without the chip heading).
"Pastimes and Plays."
"Lile Jack" (new name on the proof).
"Faithful Margaret" (Miss Lynn).
"More Splendid than a Badger."
"Back Ways to Fame."

Of the omitted articles, I have to observe : First of Sidney's, that it is such careless slip-slop as to be almost unintelligible, and quite unsuitable unless the second part be much better ; secondly of the poem,

---

* Chauncy Hare Townshend, a valued friend of Dickens. He died in 1868, and bequeathed to Dickens for selection and publication some papers on religious belief. They were published in a volume in 1869.

† The number for August 19th.

‡ By Sala.

that there is absolutely nothing whatever in it; and thirdly, of the "Roving Englishman" that it is of the same order, besides being conceited—and consequently had better be distributed at once.

Sala is very good. Don't run him too close in the money way. I can't bear the thought of making anything like a hard bargain with him.

If you have received copy from Mrs. Gaskell (as I suppose you have by this time) add the advertisement I sent you to this Number.

I am turning the Xmas No. in my mind.

And am very anxious to know whether Morley has really come into his fortune.

"Hard Times."

I was vexed to see in the *Examiner* the advertisement of the *H. W.* volume, with the parenthesis in it which I took out. I suppose it stood in all the weekly papers? Surely there was time to correct it.

Generalities.

The Meteor Flag was received with rapture and is now flying at the Masthead—to the honour and glory of England, and the confusion of the thief.

I have had a violent cold in my right ear, and am executing the present act of correspondence with my head tied up. Had poppy-heads at a boiling temperature appended to my own imaginative sconce, all day yesterday.

I have a notion of an article for *H. W.* (by myself, to be called "It is not Generally Known")* for which I want somebody to go over the file of *The Times*, and note in the Debates every night all through the

---

* *Household Words*, September 2nd.

Session, *every personal attack and personal discussion between Hon. Mems.*—who they were—on what night it happened—and what it was about. The fewest words of description will suffice for me. Now do you think you can get me such a thing done, at once? Otherwise the article would be out of date.

Ever faithfully,
C. D.

Villa du Camp de Droite, Boulogne,
Wednesday, Ninth August, 1854.

H. W.

My Dear Wills:—I would decidedly put in the advertisement of "North and South." Then I would write to Mrs. Gaskell, saying that you had heard from me you were to receive a batch of MS. for press; and that not having done so, you were uneasy (fearing it might have miscarried) and therefore wrote to say none had come to hand.

I will not maintain my opinion of the volume-advertisement against yours and Evans's united. But I should like it better, if the parenthesis were not so excessively demonstrative, and stood simply thus: (containing Hard Times).

Sorry to hear that there is not so much personality on record as I had hoped for, because it may damage the idea of the article. But *Nil Desperandum!* You may find more as you advance in your labors.

I wish you would send friend Barnard here, a set of *Household Words* in a paid parcel (on the other side is an inscription to be neatly posted into Vol. I. before sending) with a post letter beforehand from yourself, saying that I had begged you to forward the books: feeling so much obliged to him for his uniform attention and politeness. Also, that you will not fail to continue his set, as successive volumes appear.*

Your account on Bradbury authority of the Volume is capital.

I think that's all at present.

Ever faithfully,
C. D.

VILLA DU CAMP DE DROITE, BOULOGNE,
Saturday, Twelfth August, 1854.

INCLOSURES.

MY DEAR WILLS:—There is a letter for John in the parcel, also a letter for Evans, also the Barnard inscription. The rest are for the post; the American letter to be paid.

H. W.

A much better No. than the two or three last.

I enclose a list of the new names, involving one change in the order of the articles. I have bothered and worried at the Poem (which is neither English, nor verse) hoping to make something of it, but have not succeeded after all. Strike it out. If I can fuse into it an idea I have of its natural end, you shall have it in the next parcel. If you hear no more of it, give it up as unmendable.

I am not sure whether we have used the title, "A FLIGHT WITH THE BIRDS." If we have, call the paper "WINGS AND TOES."† But the name I have

---

* This paragraph is printed in "Letters," III., 141, as forming part of the supposed letter of August 7th, 1853.
† "Wings and Toes," by Hepworth Dixon, *Household Words*, August 26th

given it is a much better one if I have not used it before.

Leave three pages—or a column less—open for me in the next No. I will write an article at once, and post it to you. Of course I would do anything I could, to make your holiday the easier and longer. Therefore, count upon me for *two articles* (which will relieve you of the first article for two numbers) in the intervening time. You shall have the first one—probably on Tuesday. The second, I will buckle to as soon as Townshend shall be gone from here. He comes, that day.

Guild.

It is discouraging and vexatious, that the men should be so unreasonable—though I think the National Provident very like the-as-yet-unchanged-man in not making it easier to the members of the Council. As to Forster, if he ever makes that rheumatic remark to me, I'll choke him with a highly indigestible piece of my mind.

Holiday.

I shall be glad to hear, as soon as you know, whether you arrange to come with Mrs. Horne on the 28th. If not, I must meet her at Folkestone, for I would not on any account that she should lose a day of her short vacation after her hard work. Neither must she be allowed to pay her own charges.

I write in a hurry to get the parcel off.

Ever faithfully,
C. D.

Boulogne,
	Saturday, Nineteenth August, 1854.

H. W.

My Dear Wills:—I have gone over the No.* and now return it. Look to the punctuation of Miss Martineau and Miss Lynn.

I don't see anything in the "Children in the Wood" except a power of making nothing out of a most beautiful story. The enclosed little poem by Townshend† is far better (I have two more in hand), and will improve the No. as a substitution for the present.

It is clear that "North and South" must begin at the top of page 61—and on Mrs. Gaskell's title page (now in her possession) there is a motto from Tennyson, which I think ought to be prefixed to it. Will you write and ask her for it immediately.

It must always be resumed on the top of that page.

I am alarmed by the quantity of "North and South." It is not objectionable for a beginning, but would become so in the progress of a not compactly written and artfully devised story. It suggests to me (but I may be wrong) that the Whitefriars casting-off was incorrect. Therefore will you do what follows.

The enclosed key is the key of the round writing table in my study. In the drawer of that table, facing you as you stand looking at the table, in front of it with your back towards the windows, are two bunches of keys. One has only three cellar keys

---

* The number for September 2nd. Mrs. Gaskell's "North and South" began in it.
† "The True Voice," by Townshend, appeared September 9th.

which you have nothing to do with (unless you are thirsty); the other is a bunch of several keys. When you have found which key on that bunch will open the drawers of the writing table with the cabinet on it, by which I always sit to work and on which my envelope case always stands when I am at home, apply that key to the third drawer from the top, nearest to the fireplace, and in that drawer you will find a rough slip of notes in my writing, concerning the divisions of Mrs. Gaskell's story: and (if I do not mistake) a note from yourself, stating the Whitefriars estimate of quantity. If you cannot read my notes for your own guidance, let me have them in the next parcel; and at any rate bring them when you come.

I will go to work, please God, on my new article, next Monday.

General News.

We have had three short but strange illnesses here —two among the women servants and the third last night in Georgina, who seemed to be suddenly attacked with tic in the head, but is greatly better this morning. The rest of the story when you come.

I enclose some letters for the post.

Cooper and his charges came to hand last night.

Ever faithfully,
C. D.

Villa du Camp de Droite, Boulogne,
Sunday, Twentieth August, 1854.

H. W.

My Dear Wills:—It is perfectly plain to me that if we put in more, every week, of "North and South" than we did of "Hard Times," we shall ruin *Household Words*. Therefore it must at all hazards be kept down.

I hope the first portion is not printed "Part" I. It ought to be "Chapter." The amount you have got into 233 is quite out of the question. But this is the part from which a great deal was to be taken out. You may possibly have received the Proof from Mrs. Gaskell so altered. But in case you should not have received it, I wrote to her by this post, begging her to send you the cut down proof immediately.

Sala's "Sunday Out,"* is poor enough.

I will return the No. — probably by tomorrow's boat.

You will let me know in the course of the week, how you decide to come on Monday the 28th, so that we may be on the look-out for you.

I write hastily : having several letters to despatch.

Ever faithfully,
C. D.

BOULOGNE,
Wednesday, Twenty-third August, 1854.

H. W.

MY DEAR WILLS :—I send you my second article.† A new subject with us, and founded upon some excellent evidence you forwarded to me a little while ago, in reference to the county courts.

---

* In the issue of September 9th.
† "Legal and Equitable Jokes," printed in *Household Words*, September 23rd.

The enclosed from Mrs. Gaskell, I received this morning. Don't run beyond the present end of the second part, whatever she takes out. She can't take out too much. And bring me all of her story that is in proof, with you.

C. D.

Will you tell John to take from the bottom drawer of my wardrobe in my dressing room at home, the red shirts and the buff shirts, and to ask Mrs. Wills (on his knees) if she can find a place to pack them in, when she comes over? Further, will you bring me a little bottle of our friend Sainsbury's essence of ginger—and as large a bottle as you can stow away anywhere, of Burnett's Disinfecting Fluid?

XMAS NO.

We will, please God, settle together here.

ALL

well. I expected to have heard from you.

WEATHER

charming. With cool breezes.

EVER

Faithfully,
C. D.

Evans has again made me overdraw my account, by not paying the "Hard Times" money. I was inexpressibly vexed to receive Coutts's notice this morning, and have written to Whitefriars.

P.S. Your P.S. informs me that all the 45 Cols. are set up. If they are in your parcel, I will divide them and return them with this proof.

BOULOGNE,
Thursday, Twenty-Fourth August, 1854.
H. W.

MY DEAR WILLS :—There seems to me to be far less difficulty about Mrs. Gaskell's story than you suppose. You know what we want in a No. You can have of the 45 columns as much set up as will make about 2 Nos. and send it to me to divide. As to waiting for the Proofs, it simply cannot be done. You must tell Mrs. Gaskell, in so many words, when you *must have* the proof back, or go to Press without it. As to Forster, put him entirely out of the question and leave the settlement of any such dispute to me: saying to him merely that it was necessary to go to press, and that I persisted in going to press. (See P.S. above.)

The real difficulty is in the reckless casting-off at Whitefriars, and upon this point I must beg you to make, from me, a grave representation that it is impossible to proceed if such tricks are played with us. When I read the beginning of this story of Mrs. Gaskell's, I felt that its means of being of service or disservice to us, mainly lay in its capacity of being divided at such points of interest as it possesses. Rejecting my own estimate on that subject, I referred it to them, the Printers (of course) for a correct one. A statement was furnished to me in reply, which turns out to be entirely wrong. If I had known how it was to turn out, and that when they said in

Whitefriars "white," they meant "black," or when they said "Ten" meant "Twenty," I could not, in my senses, have accepted the story. I want to know what the Masters in Whitefriars say to this mode of doing business. It is a matter of perfect indifference to me what anybody else says. *They* enter into a certain agreement with us, upon their fidelity and exactness in discharging which, we rely. I want to know what they say to not discharging it and to shirking and shuffling it off, anyhow. And *I* say to them that I am perfectly convinced there is not another house in the trade to which I could refer a question so vital to a periodical, who would lazily mislead me altogether.

You will have received an article from me this morning. You have in hand the "Eastern Tale" you think so well of (I have not seen it yet, the parcel not having arrived), and (I suppose) other available matter. Can't you make up another No. at once; assuming "North and South" not to exceed an average portion of "Hard Times" by more than a column or two? Then, if you bring another No. with you, surely you will be easy and well beforehand.

I am unspeakably vexed by all this needless trouble and bewilderment. There is no more reason for it, than there is for a calomel pill on the top of the Cross of St. Paul's.

Ever faithfully,
C. D.

BOULOGNE,
Thursday Night, Twenty-first Septr., 1854.
H. W.

MY DEAR WILLS:—I return you the No. which is a very fair one. Some of Mrs. Gaskell's dialogue open to criticism, but I will not bring a correspondence upon you by touching it.

To "Holidays at Madame Grondet's" *—yes. I have altered it a little here and there, and return the proof.

Costello really good.

Self and Family.

Mary is quite well again, thank God, and has never had the slightest unfavourable symptom since she turned the awful corner.

I enclose a letter to be posted for Augustus.†

In your next parcel will you send me the 2nd edition of Forster's Goldsmith from the last bookcase against the wall opposite the fireplace, in my study. If I remember, it is on the second shelf from the mahogany slab outside the glass—on the second above it, I mean.

I have nearly exhausted the cigarettes I brought here. Will you use the enclosed key to open the drawer in the round table you opened before—take out the same bunch as before—find another key on it, that opens the corresponding table nearest to the drawing room—and in a drawer (I think the middle drawer on the lefthand side, nearest to the sliding book-door) you will find a cigar box with bundles of cigarettes in it. If you take out 4, tell John to put them in some little common box, go to the *Herald* Office, and ask Beard if he will bring them over; he will doubtless do so, unless he should have already

---

* This appeared on October 21st. There had been a previous article, "Madame Grondet's," on September 23rd. They were written by Miss Lee.
† His youngest brother.

left to come to us. In that case, please send them in your next parcel.

Ever, My Dear Wills, faithfully yours,
C. D.

BOULOGNE,
Monday, Twenty-Fifth September, 1854.

MY DEAR WILLS :—I really am quite shocked and ashamed on looking at the new No. to find nothing in it appropriate to the memorable time. I have written a little paper "To Working Men," * which I hope may do good, and I send it to you enclosed.

But I am so painfully impressed with a sense of our being frivolous that IF YOU HAVE NOT ALREADY GOT TO PRESS WITH No. 237, *I entreat you to unmake it and put this article first.* Forster will correct it, if you give him the copy, quite accurately I am sure; therefore it would only involve a delay of a few hours. Even if but a few 237's were printed, it would be better to cancel them—stop—and get this paper in.

No. 238 and the parcel, I will send by tomorrow morning's boat.

In haste, ever faithfully,
C. D.

BOULOGNE,
Monday Night, Twenty-Fifth September, 1854.

MY DEAR WILLS :—I have gone over the No.—which is so badly printed and so villainously read, that I have been obliged to query here and there; the sense being somewhere else.

---

* An appeal to working men to insist on better sanitary conditions. It was printed in *Household Words* of October 7th. The recent visitation of cholera had caused more than 20,000 deaths in England and Wales.

"The Ghost of Pit Pond " * is *not* the thing for a first article.

Morley has done what he could for the " Cookery," † but it is inherently conceited and stupid. I went over it before reading the " Conscript " article, and put in a clause respecting the inferior strength of the French people as compared with the English. Now, do look at those two articles, with a reference to the consistency and reliability of the Journal in which they appear! Says " Cookery," the wonderful Maltese labourers (whom I don't in the least believe in) live on coarse barley bread. Says " Cookery " further, English people neglect oatmeal. Says " Conscript," French soldiers live on barley and oats, and are therefore below the mark! The whole bestiality of the " Cookery " thing, from first to last, being—dull whole Hog.‡ Not content with showing that we might improve our commonest cookery, cheaply, and make enforced short commons at least savoury, it sets up the notorious short-comings and weaknesses of other countries as a model for us, and is more ignorant of the enormous difference made by the different requirements of different climates, than the Plornish Maroon is. Moreover, the exaggerated praise of the meatless dishes is done in a wooden-headed ignorance of the English ways of thinking, which is a recipe for raising up antagonism—the only sound recipe in the paper. I don't even find in it the common humble usefulness of the Liebig recipe for making beef tea. Ex-gra: Steep a pound of beef in a pint of cold water, for four hours. Then put the beef and water on a brisk fire for a few minutes until they begin to

* By Dudley Costello, October 7th.
† I cannot trace this article.
‡ See note to letter of August 10th, 1851.

bubble and boil. Then take them off, and let them stand until cool, when the beef is to be taken out. It will be found by that time to have deposited its utmost virtue in the water—which is the strongest and most nutritious beef tea that can possibly be made.

I think this bit of common sense might be insinuated into the article—when you soften down the points so glaringly objectionable.

There are 6 &c.'s in the compass of one column of the Chinese Francis Moore.*

The Poem is a thousand times worse than nothing and won't do.

GUILD.

I return the cheque book, with several cheques signed.

HOME.

All quite well, thank God. The Theatre took fire yesterday at about half past eleven, and is burnt down. Weather, cool, bright, and delicious. Empress arrived this afternoon.

Ever faithfully,
C. D.

BOULOGNE,
Friday, Twenty-ninth September, 1854.

MY DEAR WILLS:—I somehow lost a day, and conceived—indeed, still mistily believe—that I sent you the "Address to Working Men" on the *Monday* Night. The No. will be greatly improved by the changes you mention.

Evans will bring you this, and two letters for the

* "Francis Moore in China," October 14th, by Mylne, according to the Office Book.

post, enclosed, and one for Forster. Will you pay the enclosed £10 0. 10. at your convenience, and ask at the same time how many Terms I have to keep before being qualified to be called ? * I have no belief whatever that I shall ever keep them now; but I should like—for the gratification of an innocent curiosity—to know how many I *have* kept, after all the boredom I have suffered in that noble Institution of my country.

Mr. Gaskell's letter raises a rather difficult question. I think I would reply to him that Mrs. Gaskell is free to act in the matter—so far as we are concerned —as she thinks best; always supposing that her precautions as to time, render it *impossible* that whatever she sends out there in advance, can get back here, before its ordinary publication here. But I would add that we (I, if you like) think it very doubtful whether she would ever derive any pecuniary benefit from such an arrangement which would counterbalance the risk of such a transaction with such people.

Wonderful fine weather here. Kindest regards from all.

Reverting to *H. W.*, I observed a paragraph, either in the *Examiner* or the *Illustrated London News* the other day, to the effect that there had been "a large and influential meeting at Manchester" with a view to the prevention of Boiler explosions, and their consequent injuries to workpeople. Now, as we opened that subject, plainly and boldly, we ought to pursue it; commending the Manufacturers for any endeavour in that wise that deserves commendation, and enforcing the principle of the workpeople being always protected from accident, by

---

* Dickens entered his name as a student at the Middle Temple in 1839, but did not eat dinners till many years later. "Life," I., 160, 163.

every human precaution. By losing or delaying so apposite an occasion for pursuing a subject we have opened, we lose a chance and waste our power.

Ever faithfully,
C. D.

VILLA DU CAMP DE DROITE, BOULOGNE,
Wednesday, October Fourth, 1854.

H. W.

MY DEAR WILLS:—It is quite clear that Mr. Carleton's request cannot be complied with. I think it will be best for you to reply that you have forwarded his letter to me, as he requested; and that you write, as if I wrote, participating in the pain I should myself feel in having to convey to him the assurance that the publication is burdened with as much expense in the way of such advance, as it can possibly bear; and that, in the discharge of my first duty towards my fellow proprietors, I cannot increase the outlay.

I am very much afraid that whatever business comes within Mr. H.——'s sphere of action must be very badly done. It is important to see to this. It is not likely that other people are punctually and precisely dealt with, if I am not. Besides the absurd way in which I have received our numbers through the whole summer—getting the stamped edition, over and over again, by post, on the very day after, or on the day but one after, I have received a parcel which should have contained the unstamped No.—I have at this moment not received *the last week's No. at all* (I don't speak of to-day's—last week's) and have had two " Narratives."

There is a suggestion of bungling and messing in all this, which alarms me. There is no such thing as a man who does one part of a plain business ill, and the rest well.

I will return you Carleton's letter when I return the parcel now to come.

Guild.

I have not executed the Warrant of Attorney, because the Consul is an old fool (and a Scotch fool) and I hate to go to him. I suppose I shall be home in about a fortnight. Will that do? If you really want it sooner—why then I must encounter the Scotchman, very much against my will.

Sebastopol.

The announcement* of its being taken, at the *Review* here last Saturday, was very fine. We were very near the Emperor and Empress, and she kissed the dispatch (she is a pretty, graceful, slight little woman) in a very natural and good way. It is extraordinary to know through the evidence of one's own senses, however, that the *personal* enthusiasm and devotion of the Troops, is enormously exaggerated in the London papers. Their coldness was, to me, astonishing—so much so, as to be, under all the circumstances, almost irritating.

Egg and Muster Beard

beg to be kindly remembered.

All the Family

ditto, and all well.

Ever faithfully,
C. D.

* A premature announcement.

Boulogne,
Saturday, October Fourteenth, 1854.

H. W.

My Dear Wills :—Rather a gloomy No. Miss Martineau pretty well, but grimly bent upon the enlightenment of mankind, and quite absurdly overdoing American Education. I have taken out that passage about paper instantly rising 20 per cent. if the Newspaper Stamp were taken off, for I think it a hazardous assumption to broach so very positively.

Dodd as bad as need be. Nothing in it.

We are better without a Poem than with a Poem without an idea. Don't put in " The Best."

It appears to me that this is not only a very bad No. for Miss Lynn's paper,[*] but a very bad time. Somehow, this Balzac-imitation in poking a little knife into the social peculiarities of France seems ungraceful, ungracious, and inopportune just now. We can't afford to make mistakes which people feel to *be* mistakes almost without knowing why. " Mars à la Mode "[†] comes painfully upon the Battle Field accounts in *The Times ;* and as I don't think that an Englishman wants to dissect a Frenchman's love, at present, I would rather say nothing about France unless I had plenty to say about its gallantry and spirit. I cannot remember the subject of the paper I returned you in proof last week; marked *No. 1*—but it would be much better than Miss Lynn. I have a confidence in this " French Love " awakening a vague impression of our being ill-conditioned and inopportune. Pay for it, and let it stand over.

[*] Apparently entitled " French Love." It was not published.
[†] In the number of October 14th, by Sala.

I am sorry to hear of the Sale dropping, but I am not surprised. Mrs. Gaskell's story, so divided, is wearisome in the last degree. It would have scant attraction enough if the casting in Whitefriars had been correct; but thus wire-drawn it is a dreary business. Never mind! I am ready to come up to the scratch on my return, and to shoulder the wheel.

FAMILY.

All well. I hope to be at Tavistock House about midnight on Tuesday.

Ever faithfully,
C.D.

Possibly the note marked "Lady Bell" may suggest a subject for Morley. Her brother is Sir Charles Shaw, for many years the first surgeon at the Middlesex Hospital. She lives with him. If you want the Report alluded to, write to him for it.

TAVISTOCK HOUSE,
Friday Night, Twenty-seventh October, 1854.

MY DEAR WILLS :—I am truly sorry to hear of your poor Mother's death. What you said last night had prepared me to receive the sad news; and when I was told of a messenger being sent here to enquire for you this morning, I felt that the end was come.

Don't worry yourself about a first article for the next No. I will have one ready, please God.

Mrs. Dickens and Georgina unite with me in kindest regards to Mrs. Wills. Pray let me say that if in this sudden emergency you want any ready money, I shall consider it a breach of the confidence and friendship between us, if you seek it in any quarter where you have to pay interest for it.

Ever faithfully yours,
CHARLES DICKENS.

OFFICE OF HOUSEHOLD WORDS.
A Weekly Journal conducted by Charles Dickens.

NO. 16, WELLINGTON STREET NORTH, STRAND,
Monday, November Twentieth, 1854.

MY DEAR WILLS:—It has occurred to me that I am rather strong on Voyages and Cannibalism, and might do an interesting little paper for next No. on that part of Dr. Rae's report; taking the arguments against its probabilities. Can you get me a newspaper cutting containing his report? If not, will you have it copied for me and sent up to Tavistock House straightway.*

I don't know what Forster quite expects to ensue from "Mr. Bull's Somnambulist," † but, I think, the Downfall of the Ministry at least.

Ever faithfully,
C. D.

TAVISTOCK HOUSE,
Monday, Twenty-seventh November, 1854.

MY DEAR WILLS:—As I have had a letter from no less a person than Leigh Hunt (!) asking me to give him something soft to eat to-morrow, let us dine at the office, if convenient to you, on Wednesday—a day later than our usual day.

---

* Two articles on "The Lost Arctic Voyagers" (Sir John Franklin and his party) were written by Dickens, and appeared in <i>Household Words</i>, December 2nd and 9th.

† By Dickens, <i>Household Words</i>, November 25th.

Do you think you can manage to discover by any means where Lady Franklin is now? I should like to send her those articles, when I have revised the second one.

Ever faithfully,

C. D.

1855.

In February Dickens spent a short time in Paris with Wilkie Collins. In July he was at Folkestone, where he remained till October, and where he began to write "Little Dorrit." Thence he took his family to Paris. In December he rushed back to England (he writes to Mrs. Watson on December 23rd from Tavistock House: "Letters," I., 412) in order to give readings at Peterborough and Sheffield. The end of the year saw him back in Paris.

The "little Freehold" about which he writes to Wills on February 9th was not Gad's Hill, but a house opposite to it. The negotiations for the purchase of this house came to nothing. Later in the year, having discovered that Gad's Hill (which belonged to Miss Lynn) was for sale, he opened negotiations, and in the following year bought it.

In a letter of November 16th Dickens suggests to Wills that he should become secretary and almoner to Miss Coutts. Wills was eventually, as will have been seen, appointed to this position and filled it for many years.

OFFICE OF *HOUSEHOLD WORDS.*
A Weekly Journal conducted by Charles Dickens.

No. 16, WELLINGTON STREET NORTH, STRAND,
Friday, Ninth February, 1855.

MY DEAR WILLS :—I want to alter our arrangements tomorrow, and put you to some inconvenience.

When I was at Gravesend t'other day, I saw, at Gad's Hill—just opposite to the Hermitage where your charmer Miss Lynn used to live—a little Freehold to be sold. The spot and the very house are literally "a dream of my childhood," and I should like to look at it before I go to Paris. With that purpose I must go to Strood by the North Kent at ¼ past 10 tomorrow morning. And I want you, strongly booted, to go with me! (I have the particulars from the Agent.)

Can you?—Let me know. If you can, can you manage so that we can take the Proofs with us? If you can't, will you bring them to Tavistock House at dinner time to-morrow, ½ past 5. Forster will dine with us, but no one else.

I am uncertain of your being in town tonight, but I send John up with this. Ever faithfully,
C. D.

TAVISTOCK HOUSE,
Saturday Morning [10*th February*, 1855].

MY DEAR WILLS:—You will find a letter from me at the office when you come this morning, which I wrote on the chance of your being at home last night.

This present note, I beg to say, contains

THE LATEST INTELLIGENCE.

I have resolved (the Snow considered) not to go to Gad's Hill today, but to come to the office as we at first arranged. I will then speak to you about the little Freehold—perhaps ask you to look at it for me! Don't mention it to Charley.*

Ever faithfully,
C. D.

* His eldest son.

Hotel Meurice, Paris,
Friday, Sixteenth February, 1855.

My Dear Wills :—I received your letter yesterday evening. The posts are delayed, the roads feet deep in snow, the cold is intense, and going on to Bordeaux appears to be out of question. I have not yet seen the list of trains and boats, but purpose arranging to return about Tuesday or Wednesday. In the meantime I am living like Gil Blas and doing nothing.

I am very much obliged to you indeed, for the trouble you have kindly and promptly taken about the little Freehold. It is clear to me that its merits resolve themselves into the view and the spot. If I had more money, these considerations might—with me— over-top all others. But as it is, I consider the matter quite disposed of—finally settled in the negative— and to be thought no more about. I shall not go down and look at it, as I could add nothing to your report.

Paris is finer than ever, and I go wandering about it all day. We dine at all manner of places, and go to two or three Theatres in the evening. I suppose, as an old Farmer said of Scott, I am " makin mysel" all the time ; but I seem to be rather a free and easy sort of superior vagabond.

I live in continual terror of Poole,[*] and am strongly fortified within doors ; with a means of retreat into my bedroom always ready. Up to the present blessed moment his staggering form has not appeared.

As to yesterday's post from England I have not at the present time the slightest idea where it may be. It is under the snow somewhere, I suppose, but nobody expects it and Galignani reprints every

---

[*] See Letter of June 27th, 1850, note.

morning leaders from *The Times* of about a fortnight or three weeks old.

Collins, who is not very well, sends his " penitent regards," and says he is enjoying himself as much as a man with the weight of a broken promise on his conscience can.

Ever, My Dear Wills,
Faithfully yours,
CHARLES DICKENS.

TAVISTOCK HOUSE,
Friday, Thirteenth April, 1855.

MY DEAR WILLS :—I send you the No. with some corrections in the " Thousand and One Humbugs." * Look to the punctuation of " Soldiers' Wives." †

Do you suppose the letter I enclose to be from the Mr. Holt one has heard of? Send it me back, with a Yes or No.

I have read your MS. attentively, and return it herewith. It has interest, but it seems to me to have one great want which *I* cannot overcome. It is all working machinery, and the people are not alive. I see the wheels going and hear them going, and the people are as like life as machinery can make them— but they don't get beyond the point of the moving waxwork. It is very difficult to explain how this is, because it is a matter of intuitive perception and feeling ; but perhaps I may give two slight examples. If the scene, where the woman who dies is lying in bed, were truly done, the conversation between the heroine and the boy would belong to it—*could* do no

---

* By Dickens, *Household Words*, April 21st, 28th, and May 5th.
† "The Soldier's Wife," by Morley and Wills, *Household Words*, April 21st.

violence to it—and whatever it might be about, *would* inevitably associate itself in the reader's mind with the figure on the bed, and would lead up to the catastrophe that soon happens. If the boy on the outside of the Coach were naturally done, his illness would be a natural thing and one would receive it accordingly. Now, the conversation by the bed is an interruption to the idea of the dying woman, and the dying woman is an interruption to the conversation, *and they don't fit*. And it is plain that you, the author, make the boy ill because you want him to be ill—for, if the few closing lines of the chapter, referring to him, were taken away, the reader would have no reason whatever to suppose that anything was the matter with him. The Sir Leicester Dedlock of the story and his Mr. Tulkinghorn are open to similar objections, and the whole of the opening is much too long for what it contains.

The scene outside the Coach has a good deal of merit in it, but the same direful want. Consider if you had been outside that coach, and had been suddenly carried into the midst of a Torchlight meeting of that time, whether you would have brought away no other impression of it than you give the reader. Imagine it a remembrance of your own, and look at the passage. And exactly because that is not true, the conduct of the men who clamber up is in the last degree improbable. Whereas if the scene were truly and powerfully rendered, the improbability more or less necessary to all tales and allowable in them, would become a part of a thing so true and vivid, that the reader must accept it whether he likes it or not.

D.E.   M

There is merit too in the scene on the top of St. Paul's, and in the Engraver's house—but I still feel that Frankenstein has made the people. You are always getting into the footsteps, too, of a writer I know; and when your own shoes might otherwise leave a plain bold mark, they get so entangled with prints of his, that the reader, following on the track of both, gets confused and bothered.

I know it to be in the nature of the case that these objections to the story must inevitably become stronger as it advances, because there the difficulties grow greater. I mention them honestly; firstly, because you want me to do so; and secondly, because I usually accept so much and suppose so much, in reading Fiction, that I do not think I find more fault than another, but rather the reverse.

Faithfully ever,
C. D.

[Wills had been asked to undertake the editorship of the *Civil Service Gazette*, and had submitted the matter to Dickens.]

TAVISTOCK HOUSE,
Tenth June, 1855.

MY DEAR WILLS:—I have taken time (as I told you I would), to consider the case you put to me the other day; because, although it immediately presented itself to my mind in one plain light, I wished to be as sure as further consideration could make me, of being right.

My opinion of the matter is formed, you will presently see, entirely with a reference to *Household Words*. If I do not put your inclinations and desires in a separate place, it is because I assume your best interests to be identified with *Household Words*.

I think your impulse to take the offer made to you is altogether a mistake. I think your undertaking the conduct of any other periodical quite incompatible with your position at *Household Words*—dangerous to its individuality and responsibility—and in every way prejudicial to its interests. I have no course that I can see, but decidedly to object to such an idea.

When you proposed to me the terms of your association with *Household Words*, you expressly set forth to me necessity of your giving yourself wholly up to it. Since its establishment, you have frequently shown me that the demands made by its business on your time, have prevented your writing in it. I am perfectly sure of my own knowledge that it must always draw sufficiently on all the energies and qualities you possess for the management and conduct of any periodical work. And although I can imagine your having leisure for some literary labour apart from it, now and then, I must hold to the position that its claims are engrossing, and that it must not be put into double-harness with any other periodical editing or sub-editing.

In the case of "Hard Times," you made a speculation with the hope of a large profit. However natural it may be in you to confound the temporary sequestration of the profits on your share in *Household Words*, with the worth of the share itself, it is not so reasonable as that it can at all influence me in this case.

If, in addition to what you now do for *Household Words*, you were to help in the execution of articles that would admit of such assistance, I should think it quite fair that you should be paid extra for such work. But I am clear—to repeat it for the last time—that your entertainment of such a proposal as that made to you by Mr. Bruce is out of the question, and that I must ask you to abandon it.

I have considered the matter in every aspect, with the greatest desire to be moderate, and to make all generous allowance. I have not the least doubt that you are mistaken, and that in saying what I now do, I accept an absolute necessity which (in a mistake) you impose upon me.

Ever faithfully yours,
CHARLES DICKENS.

[Wills to Dickens. In answer to the preceding letter. From Wills's "Letter Book."]

June 11*th,* 1855.

MY DEAR DICKENS :—In deference to your wishes I have written to Mr. Bruce declining connexion with his paper altogether.

The two years during which I have engaged my whole mind and energies in the affairs of *Household Words* must have convinced you that my professional inclinations and desires are solely identified with it; but do I make a mistake in violating them—however reluctantly—by fulfilling other claims and duties, and attempting, without any abatement of my usefulness to *Household Words,* some additional means of income?

It is quite true that I did set forth at the commencement of our associations, that all my faculties would be absorbed while *Household Words* was being established; but once thoroughly organised I never for a moment doubted that, so long as my duties to it were zealously performed, I could follow another not incompatible pursuit concurrently—even when I asked the same sum, as salary, as that which I was then receiving from the *Daily News*. I ceased volunteering articles—most of which I wrote to make up the deficiencies of others—because I could not have kept up the high pressure which the first two years of my *Household Words* career imposed upon me. At the end of that time an efficient *corps* of contributors came to be formed, and it was more convenient for me to make suggestions to, and provide materials for, them—to confine myself more strictly to the duties of a sub-editor.

The *Civil Service Gazette* scheme would have made demands upon me so light that neither time nor attention would have been abstracted from my *Household Words* duties. Other projects which I have been offered I have unhesitatingly rejected because they would have absorbed too much of both. I should not have agreed to take the labouring oar in the *Household Narrative* newspaper if even that had impaired my *Household Words* strength, but would have asked for a higher berth in it.

I should never have referred to the "Hard Times" speculation, for I accept that case as it stands most cheerfully, but the fact is that my income is smaller than it has been for the last twelve years, and I cannot think that I make a very grave mistake in trying legitimately to increase it. I therefore embrace your offer of payment for helping in the execution of articles that would admit of such assistance with alacrity, for I suppose you intend to include in that expression such articles written *entirely* by me as you think worth printing.

I have said all this because I know I *may* say anything to you that is frank and honestly intended. So completely is my whole life bound up in *Household Words* and in the connexion into which it brings me with you, that I feel the giving up of any project apart from it as an escape from a grim necessity, and anything that brings me into closer association with it and with you as an increase of my best inclinations and desires.

Believe me to remain, my dear Dickens,
Ever faithfully yours,
W. H. WILLS.

TAVISTOCK HOUSE,
Tuesday, Twelfth June, 1855.

MY DEAR WILLS :—There is no fear of our misunderstanding one another.

I should be heartily glad for you to increase your income, and hope I have suggested a means by which you may do so. My letter (as I thought I expressed in it) does not apply to every conceivable kind of literary occupation, but particularizes the editing or sub-editing of a periodical not associated with *Household Words*.

Your zeal and fidelity in all respects, of course I have never doubted. How could I !

Faithfully yours ever,
C. D.

TAVISTOCK HOUSE,
Thursday, Twelfth July, 1855.

MY DEAR WILLS :—There is no doubt whatever, that the " Wife's Story " is written by a very remarkable woman.* I am quite clear that there is a strong reason to believe that a great writer is coming up in this person, whoever it is.

The story is extremely difficult of adaptation to our purpose, but I think I see a way to doing it in four parts. It would require, however, to be condensed in the beginning, and I believe the catastrophe to be altogether wrong. That part must be re-written if I accept it, and I should particularly like to see the writer on that subject.

If you have the means of communicating readily with the lady—I assume the writer to be a lady—I will see her at the office on Monday at 11, if that day and hour should suit her convenience. In the event of her living in the country, I suppose I must write; but I would prefer an interview. I think there is a surprising knowledge of one dark phase of human nature throughout this composition; and that it is expressed, generally, with uncommon passion and power.

You may quote as much of this—part or all, as you like—in writing to this author, and I particularly wish you would add that the story only came under my perusal this morning.

I enclose another MS. which will be inquired for at the office. The lady's name and address I have marked in pencil upon it. I have written to her and declined it.

Faithfully ever,
C. D.

I have seen Evans here just now, about their change

---

* Miss Emily Jolly, authoress of "Mr. Arle" and other novels. "A Wife's Story" appeared in *Household Words*, September 1st to 22nd of this year. Two letters from Dickens to Miss Jolly (July 17th and July 21st, 1855) are printed in "Letters," III., 173—175.

in the Heading. It must stand as it is until the end of the Volume, and I will tell you on Monday how I propose it shall then be.

Enclosed is a draft for 12/6 which you can place to my credit in our account.

Folkestone,
Sunday, Twenty-second July, 1855.

My Dear Wills:—I have been so very much affected by the long story without a title*—which I have read this morning—that I am scarcely fit for a business letter. It is more painfully pathetic than anything I have read for I know not how long. I am not at all of your opinion about the details. It seems to me to be so thoroughly considered, that they are all essential and in perfect keeping. I could not in my conscience recommend the writer to cut the story down in any material degree. I think it would be decidedly wrong to do so; and I see next to nothing in the MS., which is otherwise than an essential part of the sad picture.

Two difficulties then remain, which I fear are insurmountable as to *Household Words*. The first is, the length of the story. The next is, the nature of the idea on which it turns. So many unhappy people are, by no fault of their own, linked to a similar terrible possibility—or even probability—that I am afraid it might cause prodigious unhappiness, if we could address it to our large audience. I shrink from the responsibility of awakening so much slumbering fear and despair. Most unwilling therefore, I come

---

* This story was "Gilbert Massenger," by Holme Lee (Miss Harriett Parr). A letter from Dickens to her in reference to this story is printed in "Life," III., 455, note.

to the apprehension that there is no course but to return it to the authoress. I wish however that you would in the strongest language convey to her my opinion of its great merits, while you explain the difficulties I now set forth. I honestly think it a work of extraordinary power, and will gladly address a letter to her, if she should desire it, describing the impression it has made upon me. It might, perhaps, help to soften a publisher.

Miss Lynn's story* shews to considerable disadvantage, after such writing. But it is what she represented it in her draft, and it is very clever. Now, as it presents (to cursory readers) almost the reverse of the Medal whereof Miss Jolly presents the other side, I think it will be best *to pay for it at once*, and, for the present (say even for a few months), to hold it back; not telling her the exact reason, but merely saying that we are pledged first to the insertion of other stories in four parts, already accepted. Miss Jolly's is more wholesome and more powerful, because it hits the target, which Miss Lynn goes a little about, with a rifle-shot in the centre of the Bull's eye, and knocks it clean over. Therefore it should have precedence—both on its own account and ours.

But observe. I do not conceive it possible that Miss Jolly can alter her story within the time you mention. What I want done to it, is much too delicate for such swift jobbing-work. I question on the other hand, whether it may not be politic just now, to have *one monthly part without a long story*— merely for the sake of variety.

My thoughts have been upon my book† since I

---

* "Sentiment and Action," *Household Words*, November 3rd to 24th, 1855.
† "Little Dorrit," the first number of which appeared in December of this year.

came down, and I do not know that I can hit upon a subject for the opening of the new Volume. I will let you know, however, by tomorrow night's post.

When I came back from Oxford last Sunday night, I found a letter from the Mr. Meriton you speak of (dated either on that day or the Saturday night) coolly requesting to have the then enclosed MS. read and returned by the Monday evening, *when he would send for it.* I wrote a short note, declining to undertake to peruse it on such terms—and put it up at the office on the Monday Morning—and there gave it to John to take to Tavistock House in the course of the day, " where it would be called for." Pray see who is to blame for there being any more trouble about it.

I have written to Mr. Brough, whose paper *will do.* I expect my brother down today, and, if he comes, will send it and the pathetic story up to you by him.

Miss Lynn's notions of a criminal trial are of the Nightmarest description. The prisoner makes statements on oath, and is examined besides!

Ever faithfully,
C. D.

FOLKESTONE,
Wednesday, Fifth September, 1855.

MY DEAR WILLS:—I have a very strong misgiving that the " White Feather " is plagiarised from an old paper in *Blackwood*—one of the stories in the " Nights at Mess," I think. I am perfectly sure that there is a well-known paper, originally published in *Blackwood*, working out the same idea. White is coming here to a Lodging to-night, and I will consult his remembrance about it—indeed, I don't know but it was his writing—in the meantime the " White Feather " must stand over, and I have put in, in its place, Miss Lynn's "Winifred's Vow."* Which is a very pretty story indeed.

It is, however, three columns shorter; and as you have not sent me any list of the articles in hand, I cannot suggest how to fill up the deficiency. There is, however, ample time for you to communicate with Morley on the subject. They shall have my paper at Whitefriars, I hope on Saturday morning—at latest on Monday.

I hope you are enjoying your holiday.

Ever faithfully,

C. D.

FOLKESTONE,
Tuesday, Eleventh September, 1855.

MY DEAR WILLS:—I do not write because I have anything to say—for I have nothing—but merely to let you know that I have received your unanswered letters.

The "White Feather" *taboo,* on the ground of its strong resemblance, in idea, to the "Sir Frizzle Pumpkin" story. I don't think it all trenching on the "Fair Maid of Perth," but in respect of the "Frizzle" it is a plagiarism.

As the French Editorial Phalanx do not reply to your letter, but write as if they had never received it, I think it will be best not to answer this letter at all.

Mrs. Wills can answer the military woman as she thinks best—either to the effect that she knows it is of no use to ask me, or that she has asked me, and finds me to be much too busily engaged with my own

* *Household Words,* September 29th.

pursuits. Anyhow, I am not going to do what the martial woman wants.

I am just now trying to settle to No. 3 of the new book—a hideous state of mind in which I walk down stairs once in every five minutes, look out of window once in every two, and do nothing else.

Peter Cunningham has been staying at the Pavilion (and dining here) since Friday. He went up by Maidstone and Rochester yesterday, and we walked over Blue Bell Hill with him. At Paddock Wood we found that his own particular Audit Office messenger had been cut to pieces by a locomotive on Friday night.

So no more at present from
Yours always,
C. D.

FOLKESTONE,
Sixteenth September, 1855.

MY DEAR WILLS:—Scrooge is delighted to find that Bob Cratchit is enjoying his holiday in such a delightful situation; and he says (with that warmth of nature which has distinguished him ever since his conversion) "Make the most of it, Bob; make the most of it!"

(I am just getting to work on No. 3 of the new book, and am in the hideous state of mind belonging to that condition.)

Among the list of matter in hand, you will find "Peter the Great," by Peter of the Audit Office. He says there are some "new and curious facts" in it. I have not read it, but sent it straight to Arry.

What about the Paris paper?

I have not a word of news. I am steeped in my

story, and rise and fall by turns into enthusiasm and depression.

Ever faithfully,
C. D.

FOLKESTONE,
  Tuesday Night, September Eighteenth, 1855.

"THE ERARDS."

MY DEAR WILLS:—I don't know that I have the least knowledge of Mr. Robertson, though he addresses me as "Dear Dickens." I send you his letter. Will you answer it to the effect that the article* is accepted (it is a very good one for us). I send it to Arry to be printed, by this post. It should go into the next No. made up, as it is *apropos* of the Queen's late visit to Paris and will get out of date. Will you take care that Hogarth has it to look over, in order that there may be nothing in it against his positive knowledge.

"THE RIVAL QUEENS."

I am sorry to say, Taboo. I will enclose it to Holdsworth, with instructions to retain it for your directions.

"THE OLD CATHEDRAL CITY."

I will try to read to-morrow.

"OUT OF TOWN."†

(an article of mine for next week's No.). I sent Breach of the Pavilion a proof it, and he is in the Seventh Heaven of Delight and wants 500 copies

---

* "Pierre Erard," *Household Words*, October 6th, 1855. In the Office Book it is ascribed to "Robinson." See, however, the letter of November 10th, this year.

† *Household Words*, September 29th. In the article Folkestone is called "Pavilionstone."

of the No. Will you instruct Holdsworth to send them down on the Tuesday night by the mail train, so that Breach may have them on the Wednesday morning; and will you forward him a note from yourself to Breach, to go in the parcel, to the effect that you have the pleasure of forwarding them at my request and begging his acceptance of them. (He was so extraordinarily kind to me when I was ill, that I am glad of the opportunity of being able to make the little present.)

YOU

I suppose are fat and rosy.

I

am in the variable state consequent on the beginning of a new story.

YOU AND I

I suppose will foregather before long.

Ever faithfully,
C. D.

FOLKESTONE,
Sunday, Twenty-third September, 1855.

H. W. 289.

MY DEAR WILLS:—" Sportsmanship in Earnest "* for the first article most decidedly.

I wish you would ask Sala so to remodel that paper on the Kensington Gardens Band,† as not to argue the question with so ridiculous an antagonist as the *Sentinel*, and not to refer to the verses. What their writer wants is notoriety, and why should we give it

---

* By Dixon, *Household Words*, October 6th, 1855.
† "Sunday Music," *Household Words*, October 13th, 1855.

to the blockhead? Sala's description is very pretty —perhaps he may see something else, to amplify it a little. But what I wish to do, is, not to argue the question and elevate these *Sentinels* and their preposterous sentry-boxes. I wish you would explain to him what I mean, and tell him that I want to rest the subject upon its common sense and common humanity, without reference to any braying jackass with a head —and nothing in it.

You have something to substitute, no doubt?

Nor would I just now put in " From Kraiova through Orsova " *—though it may be paid for. If for no other reason, because there is a reference to Mazzini in it. I have a great regard for him, but this is not exactly the time to call him " a keen player " with his " Manifesto to the Neapolitans " in our hands.

Where is " Peter the Great " ? Where is " Erard " ?

I should like to see the re-modelled No.

I

cannot very well come up to town before Saturday, as I am very hard at work, and rather slowly. But I will arrange to come on Saturday, and on Saturday week. Will that do for you, Bob ?

I send you No. 2—not corrected. When you have read it, let Forster have it.

And I think that's all I have to say this morning. Except

CHARLEY.†

On Wednesday I got a letter from Mr. Bates saying

---

* " From Kraiova to London," *Household Words*, October 20th, by E. C. Grenville Murray.

† Dickens's eldest son.

that when he recommended Charley's going to the Brokers, he could not foresee that so good an opening would arise in Baring's as had suddenly presented itself. That the Brokers gave Charley the highest character for ability and zeal, and that he would be glad to take him into Baring's (instantly if I pleased), beginning at £50 a year. I immediately sent off to Charley, and he goes to Baring's tomorrow. I expect the Brokers to have been a device and trial altogether—to get a telescopic view of a youth with the double suspicion on him arising out of his being an author's son and an Eton boy.

Ever faithfully,
C. D.

FOLKESTONE,
Tuesday, Twenty-fifth September, 1855.

MY DEAR WILLS:—I write hastily, after a day's work.

"Half a Life Time Ago" * will be well divided, I think, as you propose. I have marked a place at page 235 where the effect would be obviously served by making a new chapter. Is such a thing to be done with that lady? If so, do it.

I don't like three such short articles in one No. as "London Stones," "The Caitiff Postman," and "The Erards." Can't you remedy this? It looks so patchy.

I think you ought to set your want of participation in No. 288 right by reading "Out of Town" in every one of Breach's 500 copies.

It would be particularly well-timed if we could hit

---

* By Mrs. Gaskell, *Household Words*, October 6th to 20th, 1855.

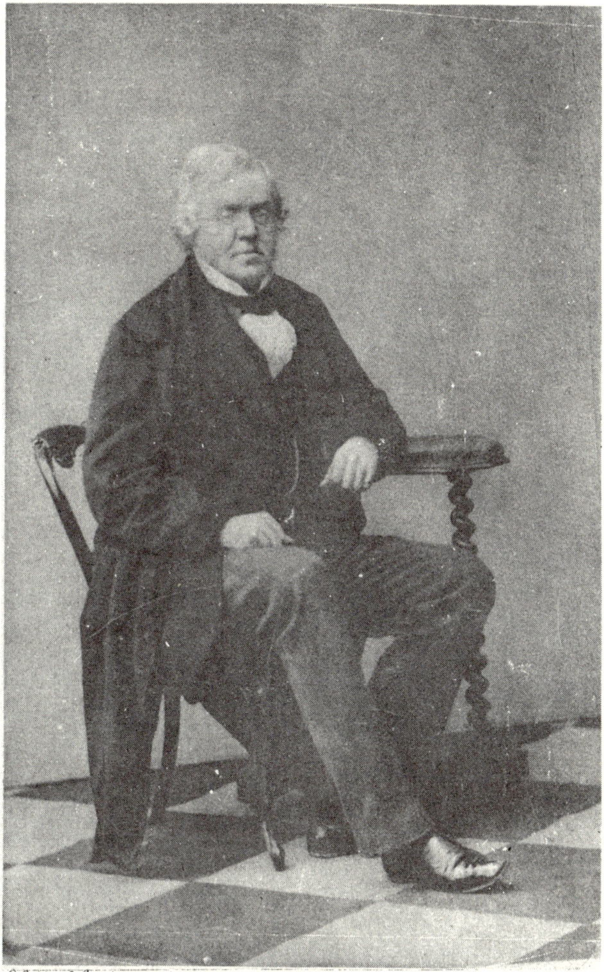

L. Caldesi & Co., photographers — Emery Walker Ph. sc.

W M Thackeray

the Charter House again, hard. Can anything be done out of private information, young Hale's pamphlet, and a communication in reference to Thackeray's distorted praise of it (which I remonstrated with him about), in the *Examiner* two Sundays ago? I should particularly, of course with all respect for and praise of Thackeray, [like] to knock that destructive bit of sentiment in connexion with the poor brothers slap over as with a rifle-shot.*

    Yours always faithfully
     (and at present addle-headedly),
           C. D.

  49, AVENUE DES CHAMPS ELYSÉES, PARIS,
   Friday, October Nineteenth, 1855.

MY DEAR WILLS:—After going through unheard-of bedevilments (of which you shall have further particulars as soon as I come right side upwards—which may happen in a day or two) we are at last established here—in a series of closets, but a great many of them—with all Paris perpetually passing under the windows. Letters may have been wandering after me to that house in the Rue de Balzac, which is to be the subject of more law suits between the man who let it to me and the man who wouldn't let me have possession, than any other house that ever was built. But I have had no letters at all, and have been—ha ha!—a maniac, since last Monday.

Will you give my address to B. and E. without loss of time, and tell them that although I have communicated at full explanatory length with Browne, I have heard *nothing of or from him.* Will you add

* See "The Charter-House Charity," by Morley, *Household Words*, December 1st, 1855.

that I am uneasy and wish they would communicate with Mr. Young, his partner, at once. Also that I beg them to be so good as send Browne my present address.

I will try my hand at that paper for *H. W.* tomorrow, if I can get a yard of flooring to sit upon. But we have really been in that state of topsy-turvy-hood, that even that has been an unattainable luxury—and may yet be for eight and forty hours or so, for anything I see to the contrary.

Ever faithfully,
C. D.

49, AVENUE DES CHAMPS ELYSÉES, PARIS,
Sunday Night, Twenty-first October, 1855.

MY DEAR WILLS:—Coming home from a walk this afternoon, I found your letter of yesterday awaiting me. I send this reply by my brother Alfred who is here, and who returns home tomorrow. You should get it at the office, early on Tuesday.

I will go to work tomorrow, and will send you, please God, an article by Tuesday's post which you will get on Wednesday forenoon. Look carefully to the Proof, as I shall not have time to receive it for correction. When you arrange about sending your parcels, will you ascertain and communicate to me the prices of Telegraph messages? It will save me trouble, having no foreign servant (though French is in that respect a Trump), and may be useful on an emergency.

I have two floors here—entresol and first—in a Doll's house, but really pretty within, and the view without, astounding—as you will say when you come. The House is on the Exposition side, about half a quarter of a mile above Franconi's, of course on the other side of the way, and close to the Jardin d'Hiver. Each room has but one window in it, but we have no fewer than six rooms (besides the back ones) looking on the Champs Elysées, with the wonderful life perpetually flowing up and down. We have no spare-room, but excellent stowage for the whole family, including a capital dressing room for me, and a really slap-up Kitchen near the stars! Damage for the whole, 700 francs a month.

But Sir—but—when Georgina, the servants, and I, were here for the first night (Catherine and the rest being at Boulogne,) I heard Georgy restless—turned out—asked "What's the matter?"—"Oh it's dreadfully dirty. I can't sleep for the smell of my room." Imagine all my stage-managerial energies multiplied, at daybreak by 1,000. Imagine the porter, the porter's wife, the porter's wife's sister, a feeble upholsterer of enormous age from round the corner, and all his workmen (4 boys) summoned. Imagine the partners in the proprietorship of the apartment—old lady, and martial little man with François Premier beard—also summoned. Imagine your inimitable chief briefly explaining that Dirt is not in his way, and that he is driven to madness, and that he devotes himself to no coat and a dirty lace until the apartment is thoroughly purified. Imagine co-proprietors at first astounded—then urging that " it's not the custom "—then wavering—then affected—then confiding their utmost private sorrows to the Inimitable—offering new carpets (accepted), embraces (not accepted), and really responding like French Bricks. Sallow, unbrushed, unshorn, awful, stalks the Inimitable through the apartment until last night. Then all the improvements were concluded, and I do really believe the place to be now worth 800 or 900 francs per month. You must picture it as the smallest place you ever saw, but as exquisitely cheerful and vivacious—clean as anything human can be—and with a moving panorama always outside, which is Paris in itself.

If this should cross a letter and projected No. from you tomorrow night, I shall of course understand *that this announcement of my coming article governs everything else,* and that you will arrange accordingly. I mention this now, as I may have no time to write with the MS.

You mention a letter from Miss Coutts as to Mrs. Brown's * illness, which you say is " enclosed to Mrs. C. D."

It is not enclosed —and I am mad to know where she writes from that I may write to her. Pray set this right, for her uneasiness will be greatly intensified, if she hears no word from me.

I thought we were to give £1,700 for the house at Gad's Hill. Are we bound to £1,800 ? Considering the improvements to be made, it is a little too much, isn't it ? I have a strong impression that at the utmost we were only to divide the difference, and not to pass £1,750. You will set me right if I am wrong. But I don't think I am.

I write very hastily, with a Piano playing and Alfred looking for this.

Ever, my Dear Wills,
Faithfully,
C. D.

* Mrs. Brown was for many years Miss Coutts's companion and intimate friend.

49, Avenue des Champs Elysées,
Wednesday, Twenty-fourth October, 1855.

My Dear Wills:—I infer from your letter just now received (the Foreign Post is not delivered in this part of Paris until between 1 and 2), that you had not then got my letter posted by Alfred. This morning you will have received my article, promised therein. And this, I hope, will have set you up.

No news whatever, of the missing Miss Coutts letter.

In the Gad's Hill matter, I too would like to try the effect of "not budging." *So do not go beyond the* £1,700. Considering what I should have to expend on the one hand, and the low price of stock on the other, I do not feel disposed to go beyond that mark. They won't let a purchaser escape, for the sake of £100, I think. And Austin was strongly of opinion, when I saw him last, that £1,700 was enough.

You cannot be in any doubt about this place, if you will only recall it as the great main road from the Place de la Concorde to the Barrière de l'Etoile. Immediately above the Jardin d'Hiver, is this house.

You cannot think how pleasant it is to me to find myself generally known and liked here. If I go into a shop to buy anything and give my card, the officiating priest or priestess brightens up, and says, " Ah ! C'est l'écrivain célèbre ! Monsieur porte une nomme très distingué. Mais ! Je suis honoré et interessé de voir Monsieur Dick-in. Je lis un des livres de Monsieur tous les jours." (In the *Moniteur*). And a man who brought some little vases home last night, said, " On connaît bien, en France, que Monsieur Dickin prend sa position sur la dignité de la Littérature. Ah ! C'est grande chose ! Et ses caractères (this was to Georgina while he unpacked), " sont si spirituellement tournés ! Cette Madame Tojair (Todgers) Ah ! Qu'elle est drôle, et precisément comme une dame que je connais à Calais ! "

Ever faithfully,
C. D.

Great haste to save post.

49, Avenue des Champs Elysées,
Sunday, Twenty-eighth October, 1855.

My Dear Wills :—Don't be uneasy about the letters. All has come right. Miss Coutts is here and poor Mrs. Brown* with her. The instant I received the two notes, I wrote to her at Montpellier. She crossed that letter on her way here. Enquiring at the Hotel Bristol, I found they were coming directly, and I immediately guessed what had happened. The body has been embalmed, and has been sent home to Stratton Street. She will be able, it being in that condition, to bury it under her own Church—which is a comforting idea to her, and which she thinks Mrs. Brown will like. I shall have to come over to the Funeral, but I hope it will be so long delayed as to bring me near to our Audit day.

All right as to No. 293, also as to getting a Number ahead—which stormy weather may make desirable; though it but rarely happens that the Mail Boat doesn't cross.

I will in future acknowledge the receipt of your letters, and you will do the like by me. We shall then be sure that we miss nothing.

You may imagine that I have been put out by this

* See letter of October 21st, 1855, note.

unexpected event. In Miss Coutts's peculiar circumstances—so isolated in the midst of her goodness and wealth—it has been a great blow to her. And I have that respect and admiration for her, that I cannot bear to see her distressed. They are both as quiet and well as it is possible to hope, however.

Faithfully always, C. D.

PARIS, 49, AVENUE DES CHAMPS ELYSÉES,
Saturday, Tenth November, 1855.

MY DEAR WILLS :—I had a rather heavy passage, but was not even squeamish. Arrived here in very good time, and with great success.

Will you tell Mark [Lemon] with my love, that I found them playing that piece in Boulogne, and that I observed it to be becoming very well known, not only among the French, but among our countrymen going to and fro. Consequently, if he do anything with it, it should be done at once.

There has called on me in my absence, a Mr. John Robertson,* 15, Rue de Monceau, Faubourg St. Roule. I believe this to be the writer of the "Erard" paper. Will you address a letter to him, explaining that in a multiplicity of communications his letter was unfortunately mislaid, but that you have heard from me that I think that is his address. And that you beg the favour of knowing whether you are right, in order that you may remit him the amount due to him for his contribution.

Don't forget the early almanac for Miss Coutts.

I am impatient to know how the Gin Punch succeeded with you. It is the most wonderful beverage in the world, and I think ought to be laid

* See *ante*, p. 173.

on at high pressure by the Board of Health. After sleeping only two hours on the H. W. sofa, I arose yesterday morning like a dewy flower.

Mentioning which object, I am reminded by contrast that your friend Wheatstone was on board yesterday; and that at Boulogne with his boredom developed, and his visage creased by abject sea-sickness, he was the most terrific phantom—the shrunken spectre of the Ancient Mariner.

Ever faithfully,
C. D.

P.S. 1. I think I gave you, sometime ago, some Xmas Verses of Townshend's.* If you will send them me in type when you send other things, I will try to put them into shape for the ordinary No.

P.S. 2. About the 1st or 2nd of next month, it will be well to write to the hotel at Peterboro',† ordering our accommodation; as Mrs. Watson‡ and (I believe) her two boys, will be with us. I have written to her about it, and will prime you with our requirements in good time.

PARIS, 49, AVENUE DES CHAMPS ELYSÉES,
Thursday, Fifteenth November, 1855.

MY DEAR WILLS:—I return the No.—a most alarmingly shy one, and really requiring something better to bring it up at last than that "Much Ado About Nothing." Pray overhaul your stock, and see if you can't find something better than *that* at any rate.

"Charter House Charity,"|| most decidedly first. I

---

* Probably "Work for Heaven," by Townshend, in *Household Words* of November 24th. For Townshend, see letter of August 12th, 1854, note.
† Dickens was engaged to give a reading there.
‡ The Hon. Mrs. R. Watson, of Rockingham Castle.
|| See *ante*, p. 177.

would make that the name, and have so altered it in the No. Look to my corrections, and particularly in "Literal Claims," where the Italics (of which, take care that not one is left), and the marks of elision where the vowels are omitted, are as irritating and vulgar as the offences complained of. I suppose it to be Dixon. It is as weak as the Paris flies are in this post.

I hope, by Monday's post, to send you my part of the Xmas No.*

My people are all gone to see the distribution of prizes at the Exposition (I recusant); in reference to which demonstration I have been driving Landseer out of his senses by telling him, that, no matter what the Queen and Lords tell him, if they give him money (as it is said they will), he is bound in self-respect and in respect for his art and his country to send it politely to the Prefect tomorrow for the Poor of Paris.

Ever faithfully,
C. D.

49, Avenue des Champs Elysées,
Friday, November Sixteenth, 1855.

My Dear Wills :—A very short note—I am driven into the smallest corner for time.

You will probably receive a note from Miss Coutts, asking you to call upon her. She wants to have, for the present, a confidential Secretary, to write her letters, and see that the money she gives away is well bestowed. For the two things, Saunders has occurred to me; for the last thing only, Johnson. Since then, for both and on all grounds, You. And if she tells

---

* "The Holly Tree," to which Dickens contributed three parts—" Myself," " The Boots," and " The Bill."

you that she has communicated with me on the subject, and that I replied I would write to you and tell you my views and the people I had thought of, then I counsel you (if you see no personal objection) to propose yourself. The duties would not be inconvenient at all—the connexion would be extremely valuable and pleasant to you—the money would not be unacceptable—and the post is fit for any gentleman, in association with such a lady. Don't be amazed by the suddenness of this note. I have an idea that it may possibly be useful to you. Will write again on Sunday.

Ever faithfully,
C. D.

49, AVENUE DES CHAMPS ELYSÉES, PARIS,
Sunday, Eighteenth November, 1855.

MY DEAR WILLS :—I have just received your letter of yesterday.

XMAS NO.

I send you my paper complete. The title of the next one, after we arrange the order, will follow on at the end of it. There will be a page and a half or two pages, to carry out the idea and close the Number. These you shall have in the course of the week.

You are mistaken in supposing White to be here. They are not coming until next Friday. Perhaps you may as well address a line to him at once, at Bonchurch.

SHEFFIELD.

I think it highly desirable, under the circumstances, to avoid going there—which will be a great relief to me, and will enable me to get back in better time. Will you write a careful note, to the effect that I highly esteem the plain-dealing of the communication, and that as the particular usefulness I had proposed to myself does not appear to be attainable, I shall consider the redemption of the promise Mr. What's-his-name obtained from me, postponed for a time.

The Home.

I **would** take Mr. Jephson's case, if you see no reason to the contrary.

The Literary Fund

may be paid, if you please.

The Tailors' Society

I cannot of course render the required service to, now. Similar answer to all such applications.

Gad's Hill

bothers me, because Austin was so **strongly** of opinion that £1,800 would be too **much**. I should think he has by this time returned from Scotland. Will you write to him a note, and let him know how the case stands. *If* he thinks it advisable, let us finally offer £1,750. If he does not—let it go, since they won't take our money. I think myself that, all things considered, £1,700 is quite enough. Let my opinion be as one Vote among three. *Observe. They are building on that spot—have begun since you saw it.*

Miss Coutts.

I am anxious to hear if it be brought to bear. It may not be within her plans, but I have strongly recommended it to her.

H. W.

Will you tell Holdsworth to post me 2 copies of the missing No.—the No. for November third.

Forster's Bulletins

about things in general, you know pretty well by this time. He certainly doesn't find [found] this one on any report of mine, for I have held no communication whatever with him on the subject of the great G. P. Night.

Ever faithfully,
C. D.

49, Avenue des Champs Elysées, Paris,
Saturday Night, November Twenty-fourth, 1855.

My Dear Wills:—I begin my letter to you to-night, under the impression that one from you is on its way to me. The post has been so irregular lately, that I *may* not get it before I shall be obliged to send this off. If I do, I shall of course reply to it on this sheet.

I have received for the Xmas No.—with very blank feelings—besides your paper and "The Inn Pensioner," "A Question of Mistaken Identity," "The Landlady" and "The Actor," all running, by an extraordinary fatality, on criminal actions and criminal trials.

"The Actor" is altogether out of the question. By Miss Lynn, I suppose. By whomsoever—unmitigated Rot.

"The Question of Identity," I can make do, by cancelling at least a page. (I suppose to be Sidney's.)

Do., "The Landlady," by cancelling about half a column.

I trust in our good stars that we shall get better matter than this, or by Heaven we shall come poorly off! The way they *don't* fit into that elaborately described plan, so simple in itself, amazes me.

I return the No. The Poem must really be polished before it can appear: it is so painfully defective and broken. Make the best change you can—taking it out.

Another Poem received, "Amy's Return," is so full of strange conceits and strange metre, that I am very doubtful of it. Don't put it in, until I mention it again. I take it to be by Ollier. Tennyson is ruining all these writers.

My corrected Proof of my own Papers (which I *do* think suitable to the purpose), I return in one letter; the Proof of the new No. in another letter.

Myself.

Will you tell John to get me a new Shower Bath cap made at the Ironmonger's—like the old one? Any old hat of mine in the Schoolroom cupboard, will give him the size. It will then be ready for me at home, when I come to town. My former one reposes in the Pavilion at Folkestone.

Peterboro'.

Mrs. Watson warns me that the best Inn is small, and that we had best order our accommodations at once. She also tells me the name of it, but Mrs. Dickens has cleverly lost her letter, and for the soul of me I can't remember. Will you write her one line (Hon. Mrs. Watson, Rockingham Castle, Northamptonshire), and ask her? Then, what we shall want at the hotel will be

A Bedroom for each of us—You and me.

The largest sitting-room—for all of us.

A bedroom—for Mrs. Watson.

Some sort of sitting-room attached, if possible, for do.

A double bedded room for her 2 boys.

Dinner at 4—certainly for 5—probably for 7 or 8.

But of this we may perhaps apprise them 2 days before.

Sunday, Twenty-fifth.

I want to give Scheffer the Painter, a complete set of *H. W.* Will you direct one—in the Double Volumes as far as they go—to be sent to me in a Parcel.

I have received your letter of yesterday, and shall expect you on Wednesday night. Come straight here. We will have a bed ready, near at hand. We shall have the Olliffes and young Bulwer at dinner that day, but you can go straight into my dressing-room, and preen your feathers. I fully expected your announcement of your intended arrival: feeling that we could never get thro' the No. without it.

The Almanack

ought to have done more. It is a pity (I observe now) that my name is nowhere upon it.

Ceilings

all right. Everything in the apartment right now.

Miss Coutts

I have heard no more from.

Myself.

Not working very well at "Little Dorrit," since I went back to her from the Xmas No.

Ever faithfully,
C. D.

More Proofs have arrived by this last Post.

Paris,
Sunday, Thirtieth December, 1855.

H. W.

My Dear Wills :—No. 203 [303] is not yet arrived, but I think the Post has not come in. I will go over it on Tuesday (shall be busy tomorrow, finishing "Little Dorrit," No. 4), and will write a paper for the following No. and will also think of your enquiry concerning subjects.

Delighted to hear of the Xmas No.

If an article comes to the office from Charles Whitehead,* will you immediately read it, and— unless it be out of the question : which I hope it won't be—immediately get it cast off, and immediately pay for it : with a turn of the scale in his favour ? He is going to New Zealand.

To this man (envelope enclosed) who wrote about a case of Distress that he don't know what to do with, will you write that you forwarded his letter to me at present in Paris, and that I begged you to say, with great regret, that after giving the subject my best consideration, I could think of no Institution applicable to such a peculiar case, and could not—from this distance, and without personal observation of the unfortunate young lady—advise him what to do.

The Turkey

seems to have been a stunner.

The Ham

Ditto.

---

* " Nemesis," by Whitehead, appeared in *Household Words*, April 19th, 26th, 1856.

WHITE*

is in one of his fits of depression, and talks of going home the moment his time is up.

DICK†

is in one of *his* fits of depression—rather uncommon with him. Thinks he has overworked himself.

Many happy years,
Ever faithfully,
C. D.

1856.

Dickens remained in Paris until the middle of May, Wilkie Collins being also there during part of the time. Dickens, however, made several visits to London. In the summer he was again at Boulogne at the Villa des Moulineaux. The purchase of Gad's Hill was concluded on March 14th, but he did not move into it until the following June.

He was working hard at "Little Dorrit" throughout this year.

The mention of Miss Martineau in the letters of January 3rd and 6th deserves something more than a passing word. During the year 1855 a striking series of five articles had appeared in *Household Words*.‡ They were all written by Henry Morley, as I learn from the Office Book, and they dealt trenchantly and vigorously with the question of accidents to life and

---

* The Rev. James White, of Bonchurch, historian and writer of tragedies. "With Dickens," says Forster ("Life," II., 395), "White was supremely popular for his eager good fellowship."
† One of his names for himself.
‡ Their titles and the dates of their appearance were :—"Fencing with Humanity," April 14th; "Death's Cyphering Book," May 12th; "Deadly Shafts," June 23rd; "More Grist to the Mill," July 28th; and "Two Shillings per Horse-Power," September 8th.

limb in factories, and the combination of manufacturers in the North of England " in what they are pleasant enough "—so runs the second article—" to call a National Association for resistance to the law which requires accidents to be prevented by the fencing of their dangerous machinery." Hereupon Miss Martineau took up her pen—for the manufacturers. She wrote an essay for the *Westminster Review*, which, however, declined it on account of its manner of treatment. It was then issued as a pamphlet by the aforesaid National Association of Manufacturers.

In this pamphlet Miss Martineau accused *Household Words* of " unscrupulous statements, insolence, arrogance, and cant." She abused " Mr. Dickens or his contributor," whom she called " his partner in the disgrace," and she charged Dickens personally with " conceit, insolence, and wilful one-sidedness." She said, " I like courtesy as well as anybody can do ; but when vicious legislation and social oppression are upheld by men in high places, the vindication of principle and exposure of the mischief must come before the consideration of private feeling." Vicious legislation meant the provisions of the Factory Law ; its enforcement was social oppression ! She bade Dickens, " if he must give the first place to his idealism and his sensibilities," to " confine himself to fiction ; and if he will put himself forward as a social reformer, let him do the only honest thing—study both sides of the question he takes up. . . . The issue," she added, " to which the question is now brought is that of the supersession of either the textile manufacturers or the existing factory law. The two cannot longer coexist."

To this pamphlet Morley replied in an article entitled " Our Wicked Mis-Statements," which was printed in *Household Words* of January 19th, 1856. In language which is all the more forcible on account of its studious moderation and courtesy, he takes up

Miss Martineau's challenge, and demolishes her figures, her statements of fact, and her arguments. It is to the proof of this article that Dickens refers in his letter of January 6th. It is not difficult, in reading the article itself, to perceive that he himself added some touches to it.

In the letter of January 10th Dickens says that "Mr. Paine might do this," *i.e.*, an article on the old coaching houses. The reference must have been to James Payn, the novelist, who was at this time a fairly regular contributor to *Household Words*. His first article, "Gentleman Cadet"—it is entered in the Office Book, by the way, as being by "J. Payne and Morley"—had appeared in the issue of April 9th, 1853. He speaks of it in his book, "Some Literary Recollections":—"My first prose article," he says, "found acceptance in *Household Words*. It was the forerunner of scores and scores contributed to the same periodical, but no other gave me a tithe of the pleasure this one did. . . . I don't know how many attempts I had made to obtain that *status* [of being an author, not a mere private person] before I succeeded; the perseverance of Bruce's spider as compared with mine was mere impatience. If I could have foreseen how long it would be before I was fated to be successful again, my happiness would have been not a little dashed;* but as it was I was in the seventh heaven. Up to this day, when I look back upon the letter I received, announcing the acceptance of 'Gentleman Cadet' (a short sketch of life at the Academy), it awakens emotions. The writer was W. H. Wills, who assisted Dickens in his editorship, a man of kindly nature and (of this I was especially convinced just then) of excellent judgment. He was devoted to his chief, conscientious to his contributors, and an excellent fellow, as I had afterwards good reason to

* Payn's next contribution appeared on November 5th of the same year.

know; but it was a disappointment to me that I had not heard from 'the Master' himself. Even that, however, I almost forgot when I received the *honorarium* (three guineas)* for my little paper. It seemed to me that fame and fortune had both opened wide their gates to me at once." Payn then goes on to describe how he invested this money in the purchase of a genuine Berkshire pig as a gift for his tutor in Devonshire, where, he declares, "there are no pigs worthy of the name, only a kind of dog with a pigskin on it." Returning after the next vacation he took the pig with him in a large hamper by train to Devonshire. It was a hot day in August, and when Payn got out of the train at Bristol for some liquid refreshment, it struck him that the pig must be thirsty. A porter fetched a pan of water and together they got the hamper and opened it. "There was a cry of panic, rage and fear— a squeal is no word for it—a broken pan, a prostrate porter, and a mad pig *gone!* . . . The next moment the creature was in the market—the 'open market,' as it is called, but altogether out of my reach. He had joined a great band of pigs (though the owner denied it), and identification was out of the question. Such was the fate of the pecuniary proceeds of my first article."

Payn, who was a most prolific and successful novelist, became editor of *Chambers's Journal*, and afterwards editor of *The Cornhill*, and "reader" to Messrs. Smith, Elder & Co. He died in 1898. There is a charming biographical account of him, by Sir Leslie Stephen, prefixed as an introduction to "The Backwater of Life," a book of Payn's essays, published in 1900.

The references in the letters of February 12th and 14th to Forster's share require some explanation. The original agreement for the establishment of *Household Words* (March 28th, 1850) was made, as I

---

* The actual sum paid, as I find from the Office Book, was half-a-guinea more.

have already mentioned, between Dickens, William Bradbury, Frederick Mullett Evans, Forster, and Wills. Dickens was to take a half share of the profits, Bradbury and Evans together one-quarter, Forster an eighth, and Wills an eighth, it being stipulated "that in consideration of the share hereby reserved to him the said John Forster shall from time to time contribute literary articles to the said publication without any additional remuneration for the same." Later on there appears to have been a further agreement, for I find amongst Wills's papers an unsigned copy of a memorandum of agreement purporting to be made on February 22nd, 1854. Herein it is recited that Forster has communicated to his co-proprietors his inability henceforth to contribute literary articles to *Household Words;* and it is agreed, notwithstanding, that he shall retain his eighth share on condition that he shall, on February 22nd, 1856, pay to his co-proprietors the sum of £1,100. Failing this payment, Forster's share is to revert to the other proprietors. Whether this agreement was executed in those very terms I cannot say. It will be noted that in the letter of February 12th Dickens assumes to control the disposal of Forster's share, and it is possible that he may have made some subsequent and subsidiary arrangement with Bradbury and Evans. Be that as it may, it appears that half the share was conferred upon Wills, whose pecuniary interest in the profits of *Household Words* was thus raised from one-eighth to three-sixteenths, while Dickens retained the other sixteenth for himself.

As bearing upon this matter, I add here a copy of a loose fragment, in Dickens's handwriting, which I found amongst Wills's papers. There is no date to it:—

RESOLVED,—

That the one-eighth share in the property of *Household Words* relinquished on the 23rd day of February in the present year by Mr. John Forster, has become the property of Mr. Charles

Dickens, and is hereby declared to belong to him during his life.

That one-half of that one-eighth share, is, on the proposal of Mr. Charles Dickens, now by him conferred upon and made over to Mr. William Henry Wills (in addition to the share Mr. W. H. Wills already holds), to remain his property so long as he shall continue to be Sub-Editor of *Household Words*, or so long as he and Mr. Charles Dickens shall both live.

That in the event of the death of Mr. W. H. Wills, or of his ceasing to be Sub-Editor of *Household Words*, this said one-half of the one-eighth share now allotted to him by Mr. Charles Dickens, shall revert to Mr. Charles Dickens; who will then exercise his own discretion as to retaining it, or bestowing it, or any part of it upon any future Sub-Editor; as he may think most advantageous to the interests of *Household Words*, and the efficiency of his own connexion with it.

That in the event of the death of Mr. Charles Dickens, the whole one-eighth share referred to in the first paragraph of this Memorandum shall become the property of his successors in his half proprietorship of *Household Words* under the deed of partnership, and of the other surviving partners, jointly; in trust honorably to employ it, according to their discretion, in rewarding future Editors, or Sub-Editors, or both, with an interest, beyond and over and above a salary in the character and success of *Household Words*.

Paris,
First January, 1856.

My Dear Wills:—Many Happy New Years! And so, as Tiny Tim observed, &c.—

I return the Proofs. As you observe in your note, they will want to be looked over, very carefully.

"The Flag of England"—Taboo.

"Across the Street"—highly desirable to be postponed for the present. It is too manifestly a remnant from the Xmas No. and would now come too near that story of Thomas's.

Lead off the No. with "The Guards and the Line."*

---

* "Nob and Snob," *Household Words*, January 12th, 1856; ascribed to Measom in the Office Book. This was Malcolm Ronald Laing Measom (born in 1824), formerly a soldier—he served in the Afghan and Gwalior campaigns.

With the new name I have given it (see to the proof, the punctuation, and slovenly composition here and there), it is the best thing we can do. It has a distinct and appropriate purpose.

Howitt, all right. But take his German poetry out altogether, or make him render it in English also.

"Zoological Auction,"* also licensed and returned herewith.

Ever faithfully,
C. D.

I will write again in a day or two.

49, CHAMPS ELYSÉES,
Thursday, Third January, 1856.
(After Post time.)

H. W.

MY DEAR WILLS :—I am sufficiently irritable—though, as you know, the most amiable of men!—to desire to avoid reading Miss Martineau's outpouring of conceit, unless I should feel myself positively obliged to do so. I have therefore put the precious packet by, without opening it. I will come to a decision upon Morley's notice of it, when I see the Proof of his article. But my present impression is, that I would rather (if only for the mortification it will cause her), not notice it at all. The Proof has not yet arrived.

BONBONS.

Mrs. Dickens has already sent to her sister at Tavistock House, instructions there anent. It is to go back there.

* By Frank Buckland, *Household Words*, January 12th, 1856.

POOLE'S*
quarter I have paid him. Enclosed is his proof of life. After you shall have sent me the receipt to sign, and after I shall have signed it, please pay the usual Paymaster General order, to my account at Coutts's.

Friday Afternoon.

The Proof has arrived. I will read it and write to you about it, when I have done my article. Expect it on Monday morning. From 3 to 4 pages.

I send by this post a paper of White's. I have not read it, but I know the design and it is a good subject.

He wants an order on Lafitte's for all we owe him, including "Old Blois" *and* this paper—an order to pay Revd. James White † so many pounds sterling. This will be as advantageous to him as gold—and if you will make a parcel of those books and so send them to him, he will Ever Pray, &c.

Ever faithfully,
C. D.

[The original of this letter is wrongly dated 1855.]

49, CHAMPS ELYSÉES,
Sunday, January Sixth, 1856.

MY DEAR WILLS:—I have read Morley's article, and gone very carefully over that part of it which refers to Miss Martineau. Supposing the facts to be closely examined and verified, I think it should be printed, and should go into the opening of the next No. as I have arranged it in the enclosed proof. I do not quite distinctly see how it is proved that the

---

* See letter of June 27th, 1850, note.
† See letter of December 30th, 1855, note.

renunciation of the idea of paying the penalties dates from that seventh of August beyond all doubt. I should like it made clearer.

Miss Martineau, in this, is precisely what I always knew her to be, and have always impressed her upon you as being. I was so convinced that it was impossible that she *could* be anything else, having seen and heard her, that I am not in the least triumphant at her justifying my opinion. I do suppose that there never was such a wrong-headed woman born—such a vain one—or such a Humbug.

If you think any little thing I have put in, too hard, consult Forster. If you both think so, take it out. Not otherwise.

I should like Morley to do a Strike article,* and to work into it the greater part of what is here. But I cannot represent myself as holding the opinion that all strikes among this unhappy class of society who find it so difficult to get a peaceful hearing, are always necessarily wrong; because I don't think so. To open a discussion of the question by saying that the men are "*of course* entirely and painfully in the wrong," surely would be monstrous in any one. Shew them to be in the wrong here, but in the name of the Eternal Heavens shew only, upon the merits of this question. Nor can I possibly adopt the representation that these men are wrong because, by throwing themselves out of work, they throw other people, possibly without their consent. If such a principle had anything in it, there would have been no civil war; no raising by Hampden of a troop of Horse, to the detriment of Buckinghamshire Agriculture; no self

---

* See "The Manchester Strike," by Morley, *Household Words*, February 2nd, 1856.

sacrifice in the political world. And O Good God when Morley treats of the suffering of wife and children, can he suppose that these mistaken men don't feel it in the depths of their hearts, and don't honestly and honorably—most devoutly and faithfully —believe—that for those very children when they shall have children, they are bearing all these miseries now!

I hear from Mrs. Fillonneau that her husband was obliged to leave town suddenly, before he could get your parcel. Consequently he has not brought it, and White's sovereigns—unless you have got them back again—are either lying out of circulation somewhere, or are being spent by somebody else.

I will write again on Tuesday. My article to begin the Vol. enclosed.

Ever faithfully,
C. D.

49, Champs Elysées,
Thursday, January Tenth, 1856.

Miss Coutts.

My Dear Wills:—I am happy to find from the enclosed letter (which you are to read, after reading this), that I exercised a wise discretion in saying nothing to you of a conversation I had with Miss Coutts on the day after my arrival in town last time. She then told me that she was under particular articles of agreement with her Partners in the Bank, never to associate herself with anyone, in any kind of engagement or business, who was connected with any House or Enterprize; and that she had doubted, since her interview with you, whether your position in respect to *Household Words* might not be construed in the Strand as coming within the line drawn. Observing my invariable custom of taking the perfectly independent course in any such matter, and of justifying no jealousy or suspicion, and of having nothing in common with anybody's intrigues or approaches towards her, I told her that if she had that doubt it was enough—that it was enough for me—that it would be enough for you—and that there was an end of it. She then begged me to explain it to you. But I thought I saw so distinctly that her mind was *not* made up and that there was a strong probability of her coming to an opposite conclusion, that I resolved to make no explanation to you for some little time. All this I now disclose to you in the strictest confidence —my confidence with her, being involved therein. You will see from her letter that she now contemplates the kind of relation I pointed out to you as desirable. I have told her in reply that I expect to be in town again about the 10th of February, and that I shall then be very happy to pursue, and I hope settle, the subject with her.

ME.

When you write next, will you enclose some stamps for cheques?

Is there any news of Gad's Hill Place?

Will you send John to Mr. Morgan, our family apothecary (John knows his house near Russell Square), with a note asking him to call upon you at the office at a certain time? When he comes, will you tell him that you have it in charge from me to beg him to charge his attendance, medicines, &c., for Mrs. Hogarth in her illness to my account, and just to say nothing at all about the matter to her, or her family, or any one else.

X. Y.

came here at 12 o'clock on Tuesday, by appointment, at his solicitation. It was the second appointment. On the first occasion he was 20 minutes behind his time (but I really believe by an accident), and of course I had gone out. He sat here *two hours*, telling me about his reputable friends at Erith, and so forth. I had no suspicion that he was postponing a request for money and couldn't make up his mind to make it, until he at last stammered out a petition for £5. I gave it him. Please place that sum to his debit and my credit. He told me he had sent two articles to you.

I derived the idea that he was living very queerly here, and not doing himself much good. He knew nothing, I observed, about the pieces at the Theatres, and suggested a strong flavour of the wine shop and the billiard table. In *Galignani*, I see a quotation from the *Leader*, which unless my memory deceives me (which I don't think it does), is a part of that article he wrote about the Young Man and his Uncle, and called, I think, " Parisian Nights Entertainments." You didn't give it back to him, did you? If you did, it was a mistake. I meant it to stand over, until Collins should come here.

H. W.

Forster does not think those two little poems are otherwise than original. That is to say, he cannot find them anywhere, though he has my general impression about them. Therefore get them back from him and insert them.

My head is necessarily so full of my own subjects, that I have not thought of that point to any advantage, though I have thought of it at various times. The "Police Enquiry" was never done, though I spoke to you about it when you were here. Accounts of the constitution of foreign armies, especially as to their officering, and as to the officer's professional business being his professional pride and study and not a bore, are highly desirable. An article on the prices of fares on Foreign Railways, on the cost of making them, on the public accommodation and the nature of the carriages, &c.—contrasting their law with our law, and their management with our management—would be highly desirable. I suppose Dixon could do it directly. Would it be possible to strike out a new man, to write popularly about the monstrous absurdity of our laws, and to compare them with the Code Napoleon? Or has Morley knowledge enough in that direction, or could he get it? It is curious to observe here that Lord Campbell's Acts for making compensation to bodily-injured people, are mere shreds of the Code Napoleon. That business of the Duke of Northumberland and his tenantry. Couldn't Sydney do something about it? It would be worth sending anybody to that recusant Farmer who leads the opposition. Similarly, the Duke of Argyll, whom the papers drove out of his mind by agreeing to consider him a Phenomenon, simply because he wasn't a born ass. Is there no Scotch source from whence we can get some information about that Island where he had the notice stuck upon the Church Door that "no tenant under £30 a year, was to be allowed to use spirits, at any marriage, christening, funeral, or other Gathering." It would be a capital illustration of the monstrous nonsense of a Maine Law. Life Assurance. Are proposals ever refused—if so, often—because of their suspicious character as engendering notions that the assured life may possibly be taken? I know of Policies being refused to be paid, on the ground that the person was murdered—and could insert an anecdote or two. Poisoning. Can't Morley do something about the Sale of Poisons—I suppose Miss Martineau's doctrine of never never never interfering with trade, is not a Gospel from Heaven in this case.

For a light article, suppose Thomas went round, for a walk, to a number of the old coaching houses, and were to tell us what they are about now, and how they look. Those great stables down in Lad Lane whence the horses belonging to the "Swan with two Necks," used to come up an inclined plane. What are they doing? the "Golden Cross," the "Belle Sauvage," the Houses in Goswell Street, the "Peacock" at Islington, what are they all about? How do they bear the little ricketty omnibuses and so forth? What on earth were the coaches made into? What comes into the Yard of the General Post Office now, at 5 o'clock in the morning? What's up the yard of the "Angel," St. Clement's? *I* don't know. What's in the two "Saracen's Heads"? Any of the old brains at all?

Mr. Paine* might do this, if Thomas † couldn't. But Thomas would do it best.

Your letter of yesterday has just arrived as I close this. Morley always wants a little screwing up and tightening. It is his habit to write in a loose way.

* See introduction for this year.
† See letter of August 12th, 1852, note.

Certainly *not* the Burns at that price for White,* I undertake to say. The Xmas Bills in the parcel, if you please.

Ever faithfully,
C. D.

49, Champs Elysées, Paris,
Monday, Fourteenth January, 1856.

H. W.

My Dear Wills :—I enclose the Proof of "The Friend of the Lions."† Will you have the corrections made at once, and then enclose a revise, by post, to Sir Edwin Landseer, 1, St. John's Wood Road. I have told him that you will send it to him, and that he need not answer. He is not a ready writer.

I think I have a good idea for a series of Paris papers into which I can infuse a good deal of myself, if Collins comes here (as I think he will) for some time.

If X. Y. really has not sent those papers, it is a very, very bad business. But he described one of them to me; and I shall still hope that they may turn out to have been on the road while we have been communicating about them.

Poole.

I enclose the document duly signed. It is to go to my account at Coutts's, you observe; and *no* remittance is to be made to Paris.

---

* See letter of December 30th, 1855, note.
† "The Friend of the Lions," by Dickens, *Household Words*, February 2nd, 1856.

Begging Letters.

I return three (see P.S.); retaining Miss Walpole's, late of the St. James's Theatre. She has been a begging-letter writer, within my knowledge, these fifteen years.

Mrs. Ramo Samee is a case that there is no doubt about. John has been there once, and can do the needful again. Something like a couple of guineas, I should think, would be the sum most useful to her. But if there were any hope (I fear there is not) of doing her any real good with more, I should not object to more.

The other two letters I really cannot form a judgment upon. But I a little distrust " E. Martell " who advertised in the *Chronicle*. Do you think them worth enquiring into?

I bear such a long, long train, that I am never rich, and never was, and never shall be. But (———— excepted), I always want to make some approach towards doing my duty, and I could give away £20 in all just now to alleviate *real distress*—should be as happy to do that, as I should be the reverse in lazily purchasing false comfort for myself under the specious name of charity.

Miss Coutts.

When you next see her, will you mention, if you remember it, that there was a sum she was to have paid to my account at the bank, which I had laid out for her (I forget whether it was forty pounds or sixty, but I gave her the Memorandum), which was not entered in my book when I last saw it. I have forgotten to mention it in writing to her; but I know she will prefer its being recalled to her recollection, in case there should have been any mistake.

I think that's all at present.

Ever faithfully,
C. D.

P.S.—To save postage, I return no letter, but describe them.

1. Mrs. Ramo Samee lives at John knows where.
2. Mrs. or Miss E. Martell lives at 18, John Street, Holland Street, Blackfriars.
3. Mrs. Mortlock—poor woman, unable to pay her rent—husband ran away from her four years ago, and left her with two small children—lives at 8, Molyneux Street, Bryanstone Square. Says she never wrote a begging letter before.

49, CHAMPS ELYSÉES, PARIS,
Saturday Night, Nineteenth January, 1856.

MY DEAR WILLS:—

You have forgotten that I asked you to send, in the next letter you should write me, some stamps for cheques. I am demented for want of them.

H. W.

The No. did not arrive today. Will come, I suppose, tomorrow.

Albert Smith has sent me a proof of his pamphlet about hotels. I, in my turn, have sent it to Sala, and suggested to him that he may write an article on the subject. I have *begged him* to send it to me, here; thinking that may expedite him.

I

report that White's parcel arrived safely.

Also that if B. and E. want to buy the collection of criticisms, for themselves, they are heartily welcome. As to me, I don't want it.

MARK

with his usual depth of diplomacy has made no mention to me of the Boots at the Adelphi. Though I had a letter from him two days ago, with a deal about the Adelphi in it.

MUD

at Paris, is 3 feet and $\frac{7}{8}$ deep.

Sunday, 20th.

The No. having arrived this morning, I have gone over it, and here it is. It wants careful correction (as usual) for pointing, avoidance of confusion in meaning, and making clear. I never saw such confused writers as we seem to vaccinate.

The Cricket Club paper is desperately poor; but I have no Taboo to interpose.

BUCKSTONE.

Does he ask whether I can recommend them to a chairman, or what they are to do for a chairman? Have I anything to answer on that head?

Ever faithfully,
C. D.

49, CHAMPS ELYSÉES,
Monday, Twenty-eighth January, 1856.

H. W.

MY DEAR WILLS:—This is a very shy No. and White's is a very bad first paper. I suppose there is nothing else?

D.E.

My corrections (which are pretty numerous) are made in pencil, but I hope you will find them legible. "The Rector Abroad," most relentlessly and ruthlessly Taboo.

In your Programme of the No. something called "The Russian Budget" is in that place. Anyway, the "Rector" is out of the question.

GAD'S HILL.

I must come to town sooner than I intended, because February is the short month, and I want to get back to my work. I think I shall come on Monday or Tuesday in next week. Will you tell Ouvry* therefore that I shall be glad to complete the purchase *at the end of next week*, if he will make the arrangements accordingly.

MISS COUTTS

I will write to, as soon as I can positively fix any day.

NO MORE

at present.

From yours ever faithfully,
C. D.

H. W. OFFICE,
Friday, Eighth February, 1856.

MY DEAR WILLS:—I think you may like to know the result of my talk with Miss Coutts, without waiting until tomorrow.

She asked me if I had thought of any precise acknowledgement for the services you rendered her, as she felt it very difficult to suggest an amount herself— much greater than she would have felt if she had been

---

* Frederic Ouvry, Dickens's solicitor and friend.

able to place everything in your hands. I said that whatever I might have thought, it seemed right that she should form her own opinion on the subject and suggest her own proposition. She then said, as there would be some little expenses incurred now and then in going about, and as she wished her offer to include everything, what did I think of £200 a year? I replied that I thought it was handsome, and that I would communicate it to you.*

I hope you approve? You will have a friend for life, who is worth having.

Ever faithfully,
C. D.

[To Mrs. Wills.]

H. W. Office,
Friday, Eighth February, 1856.

My Dear Mrs. Wills :—Pray acccept my hearty thanks (and a halfpenny,† or we shall quarrel) for your welcome remembrance of me yesterday. It gave me the greatest pleasure, and the pretty knife shall be my constant companion.

Always, My Dear Mrs. Wills,
Very faithfully yours,
Charles Dickens.

49, Avenue des Champs Elysées, Paris,
Tuesday, Twelfth February, 1856.

My Dear Wills :—I arrived here in the most brilliant and pleasant manner, to dinner yesterday.

---

* In Wills's "Letter Book" there is a copy of a letter from him to Miss Coutts accepting this arrangement.

† The coin, which bears date 1806, is attached by white silk ribbon to the back sheet of the original of this letter.

H. W.

It seems to me that when you meet to return Forster's bills and note the end of that transaction, the future disposal of that share had better be arranged. What I propose to do with it, is, to divide it between you and me, equally, so long as we both live and you are the Sub-Editor of the Journal. That in the event of your death or your ceasing to be Sub-Editor, the whole of it shall revert to me, in trust to bestow it or part of it upon any other Sub-Editor as I may think best and most to the advantage of the property. And that in the event of my death, the whole of it shall revert to the other proprietors, in trust to be similarly employed at their discretion.

My Birthday.

Stanfield called at the office on Saturday as I was dressing to go out to dinner, and had not the least idea that I was in town. The note of invitation he received did not mention that I was coming, and had no signature to it. He addressed his answer to you at random, and called on Saturday to ask you if he had done right.

Faithfully ever,
C. D.

49, Champs Elysées,
Friday, February Fifteenth, 1856.

My Dear Wills :—I enclose you the promised article for *H. W.*

I have just received your letter, and am truly pleased to know that you are gratified by what I have done respecting the share. I hoped you would be; and in this, and in all other little ways in which I can ever testify my affection for you and my sense of the value of your friendship and support, I merely gratify myself by doing what you more than merit.

In haste,
Ever faithfully,
C. D.

49, Champs Elysées,
   Sunday Night, Seventeenth February, 1856.

My Dear Wills:—On the principle that one XX number is better than two X ones always, I could so re-arrange this No. as to begin with "Why," and get Collins (who, so far, is *admirable*) into the opening. I have taken some things out of Sala, where he is wrong. He has not been in Italy, I feel sure.

The Poem, very good. But it is a remarkable thing, especially when that contrast is to be presented between the flourishing and the wasted Babylon, that the thriving city has not a single living figure in it! It is a very curious example of the incomplete way in which some writers seem to see their pictures.

"Looking Out of Window," is so ridiculously printed in the huddling up of the sentences, that I really cannot understand it. There appears to be a good idea in it, but I have become hopelessly confused by it and have given it up in despair.

The same remark applies to "Far East," which, in one place especially, I can't at all understand. Pray look to the Proof and the Copy.

Reverting to my article, "Why," I am not sure but that in a former article called "A Few Conventionalities," I noticed the theatrical way of opening a letter. Will you refer back? And if I did notice it, take that passage out.*

* The various articles above referred to appeared in *Household Words*,

I wish you would write, for 311, a temperate but strong article about the cost of administering the Literary Fund.* It will be the No. before the Annual Meeting. I would recite the object and intention of the Institution, recite the monstrous expenditure, and plainly call upon the Subscribers to look into the thing at the next Annual Meeting on such a day. If you are too busy to do it get Morley to do it; but let us have it in that No. I will go carefully over it.

Ever faithfully,
C. D.

To Mr. Snow, say it was a mistake of Mr. Carlyle's. We have made no investment in the *Mitre* Office, and I know nothing about it.

49, CHAMPS ELYSÉES, PARIS,
Seventeenth February, 1856, *Sunday.*
H. W.

MY DEAR WILLS ;—I will go over the proof tonight, and write you what I think we had best do in respect of Collins's story tomorrow. At the same time I will return my Proof.

Pray take care that they always strike out that infernal dash which I myself have taken out five hundred times, between the heading "In so many Chapters," and the numbering of the chapter. I am vexed to see it in the last No. after all.

March 1st. "Why," was by Dickens. Wilkie Collins's "A Rogue's Life" began in this number and was concluded in the number of March 29th. Sala's article was "The Great Hotel Question." The poem was "A Vision of Old Babylon," by Ollier. "Looking Out of Window" and "Far East" were by Morley.

* This was written by Morley, and appeared in the number of March 8th.

C. D.

My agreement with the French booksellers for the complete translation, binds me to let them have a copy of everything I have written. Will you have, in the course of a week, a complete collection made of my papers in *H. W.*? (It would be no bad thing, while our people are about it, to have it made in duplicate, so that we may keep one at the office and regularly keep it up to the time); and when it is finished will you label it " From Mr. Charles Dickens's contributions to *Household Words*," and send it to B. and E., to go into a parcel they are making for the said French booksellers? You will of course except all composite articles and all such *pièces de circonstance* as the opening address and the reference to the almanack.

And will you ascertain from Augustus what wine of mine has come to hand? There is some very precious champagne wandering about, somewhere.

Ever faithfully,
C. D.

49, CHAMPS ELYSÉES, PARIS,
Sunday, March Second, 1856.

MY DEAR WILLS :—I have been so occupied with " Little Dorrit" that I could not return you the revise of No. 311, in time for it to be of any use. I am sorry to see the Cold Water cure classed in Morley's article among the humbugs of the time. Firstly, because I believe that in reason there is a good deal in it. Secondly, because you were at one of the great Malvern Doctors' and my wife was at another's. Perhaps this may have occurred to you and you may have taken it out.

The Gad's Hill purchase seems to me to be a sort of amateur Chancery suit which will never be settled.

Will you tell John that Walter* is coming home on Tuesday, and that I shall be glad if he will meet him at the London Bridge station on Tuesday night at 10.

If Johnson has not acquitted himself of that selection-job, the parcel (tell Bradbury and Evans) must come at once without it. The French booksellers are impatient for it, and worry me like sharp dogs. Pray tell B. and E. to get it dispatched at once.   Ever faithfully,
                                    C. D.

P.S.—Your letter received, since I wrote the foregoing.

You remember my telling you some time ago that I greatly mistrusted ——'s affairs.

To the Gentleman who wants to play "The Lighthouse" please say that I am in Paris—that I have referred his request to Mr. Collins the Author of the piece—and that Mr. Collins, with every disposition to oblige him, would desire to keep the MS. in his desk where it now lies.

49, Champs Elysées, Paris,
Thursday, March Sixth, 1856.
C. G. T.

My Dear Wills:—I am deeply grieved that such a Fire† should have come off in my absence. Am inconsolable.

---

* His second son, Walter Landor Dickens.

† An allusion to the great fire at Covent Garden Theatre on March 5th, 1856. There had been a *Bal Masqué* all night; it was not quite ended when the fire broke out in the carpenter's shop, between ceiling and roof, just before 5 a.m., as the band was being bidden to strike up "God Save the Queen." Two hundred revellers were still there: a stampede—where no guest behaved well—was curbed by the police.

I

think I shall come to town in the night of Sunday; being so abominably used up as to the Calais Railway, that I feel desirous to be relieved from the contemplation of that enterprise by daylight. After brightening myself up in my usual beaming manner I will come down to the office; and—as I shall be dining out every day that week—if we dine together in peace at the Office *that* day (meaning Monday) it will perhaps be the usefullest thing we can do. Come and dine with me at Gravesend on the following Sunday. Forster and Charley are coming down to take a respectful look at the outside of the Giant Property.

Mark,

I understand, is helping the country to that noble representative, Mr. Herbert Ingram. In case he should return before I come, will you tell him of the change in my arrangements (he supposes me to be due at London Bridge on Monday Night, which was my original intention), and that I am his, at *Household Words* at 8 on Monday Evening.

John

perhaps will come to the Station to receive me, at about 8 on Monday Morning. I purpose being there, unless it should blow Great Guns.

Gad's Hill

I suppose stands where it did?

"Little Dorrit"

has completed her sixth; and that wonderful man the writer thereof is in that state of weary excitement which is a part of him at such periods.

Will you tear off, put in an envelope, address to my bootmakers, Hall & Co., Quadrant, Regent Street, and send at once by John (he knows the place), t'other side.

Ever faithfully,
C. D.

49, Champs Elysées,
First April, 1856.

My Dear Wills:—You will have seen by a letter from me received this morning, that we are all right.

I think, in such a case as that of Collins's, the right thing is to give £50.* I think it right, abstractedly, in the case of a careful and good writer on whom we can depend for Xmas Nos. and the like. But further, I know of offers for stories going about —to Collins himself for instance—which make it additionally desirable that we should not shave close in such a case. I therefore tell him that you have paid in £50.

In great haste (at work),
Ever faithfully,
C. D.

49, Champs Elysées, Paris,
Sunday, Sixth April, 1856.

My Dear Wills:—

Fifty Pounds in all its aspects
all right.
Sala.

I enclose my reply. Need not repeat its terms, as you will open and read it for your own guidance. I

---

* This was the sum paid for "A Rogue's Life."

wonder whether you anticipate its contents. I shall be curious to know.

"THE SIGN."

I think not. I am doubtful, but I *think* not.

CHRISTMAS.

Collins and I have a mighty original notion (mine in the beginning) for another Play* at Tavistock House. I purpose opening on Twelfth night, the theatrical season of that great establishment. But now a tremendous question. Is

MRS. WILLS!

game to do a Scotch Housekeeper, in a supposed country-house with Mary, Katey, Georgina, &c. If she can screw her courage up to saying Yes, that country house opens the piece in a singular way, and that Scotch housekeeper's part shall flow from the present pen. If she says No (but she won't),† no Scotch Housekeeper can be. The Tavistock House Season of 4 nights pauses for a reply. Scotch song (new and original) of Scotch Housekeeper, would pervade the piece.

YOU

had better pause for breath.

Ever faithfully,
C. D.

POOLE.

I have paid him his money. Here is the Proof of life. If you will get the receipt for

* "The Frozen Deep."
† She didn't.

me to sign, the money can go to my account at Coutts's.

BOULOGNE,
Thursday, Seventh August, 1856.

MY DEAR WILLS :—I do not feel disposed to record those two Chancery cases; firstly, because I would rather have no part in engendering in the mind of any human creature a hopeful confidence in that den of iniquity.

And Secondly, because it seems to me that the real philosophy of the facts is altogether missed in the narrative. The wrong which *chanced* to be set right in these two cases was done, as all such wrong is, mainly because these wicked Courts of Equity, with all their means of evasion and postponement, give scoundrels confidence in cheating. If justice were cheap, sure, and speedy, few such things would be. It is because it has become (through the vile dealing of those Courts and the vermin they have called into existence) a positive precept of experience that a man had better endure a great wrong than go, or suffer himself to be taken, into Chancery with the dream of setting it right—it is because of this, that such nefarious speculations are made.

Therefore I see nothing at all to the credit of Chancery in these cases, but everything to its discredit. And as to " owing " it to Chancery to bear testimony to its having rendered justice in two such plain matters, I have no debt of the kind upon my conscience.

In haste,
Ever faithfully,
C. D.

TAVISTOCK HOUSE,
Tuesday, Sixteenth September, 1856.

MY DEAR WILLS:—I have been thinking a good deal about Collins, and it strikes me that the best thing we can just now do for *H. W.* is to add him on to Morley, and offer him Five Guineas a week. He is very suggestive, and exceedingly quick to take my notions. Being industrious and reliable besides, I don't think we should be at an additional expense of £20 in the year by the transaction.

I observe that to a man in his position who is fighting to get on, the getting his name before the public is important. Some little compensation for its not being constantly announced is needed, and that I fancy might be afforded by *a certain engagement*. If you are of my mind, I wish you would go up to him this morning, and tell him this is what we have to propose to him today, and that I wish him, if he can, to consider beforehand. You could explain the nature of such an engagement to him, in half a dozen words, far more easily than we could all open it together. And he would then come prepared.

Of course he should have permission to collect his writings, and would be handsomely and generously considered in all respects. I think it would do him, in the long run, a world of good; and I am certain that by meeting together—dining three instead of two—and sometimes calling in Morley to boot—we should knock out much new fire.

What it is desirable to put before him, is the regular association with the work, and the means he already has of considering whether it would be pleasant and useful to him to work with me, and whether any mere trading engagement would be likely to render him as good service.*

Ever faithfully,
C. D.

Tavistock House,
Thursday, Eighteenth September, 1856.

My Dear Wills :—Don't conclude anything unfavourable with Collins, without previous reference of the subject, and the matter of your consultation, to me. And again put before him clearly, when he comes to you, that I do not interpose myself in this stage of the business, solely because I think it right that he should consider and decide without any personal influence on my part.

I think him wrong in his objection, and have not the slightest doubt that such a confusion of authorship (which I don't believe to obtain in half a dozen minds out of half a dozen hundred) would be a far greater service than dis-service to him. This I clearly see. But, as far as a long story is concerned, I see not the least objection to our advertising, at once, before it begins, that it is by him. I *do* see an objection to departing from our custom of not putting names to the papers in *H. W.* itself; but to our advertising the authorship of a long story, as a Rider to all our advertisements, I see none whatever.

Now, as to a long story itself, I doubt its value to

---

* I think some arrangement of this kind was made between Dickens and Wilkie Collins, for I observe that from October 4th of this year onward no entry of any payment is made in the Office Book opposite his contributions. This would, I presume, signify that he was paid a regular salary as a member of the *Household Words* staff.

us. And I feel perfectly convinced that it is not one quarter so useful to us as detached papers, or short stories in four parts. But I am quite content to try the experiment.* The story should not, however, go beyond six months, and the engagement should be for twelve.

Faithfully ever,
C. D.

Tavistock House,
  Sunday Morning, Twenty-eighth September, 1856.

My Dear Wills :—I suddenly remember this morning, that in Mr. Carter's article, "Health and Education," I left a line which must come out. It is, in effect, that the want of Healthy Training leaves girls in a fit state to be the subjects of Mesmerism. I would not on any consideration hurt Elliotson's feelings (as I should deeply) by leaving that depreciatory kind of reference in any page of *H. W.* He has suffered quite enough, without a stab from a friend. So pray, whatever the inconvenience may be in what Bradbury calls "The Friars," take that passage out. By some extraordinary accident, after observing it I forgot to do it.

Ever faithfully,
C. D.

Tavistock House,
  Wednesday, October Fifteenth, 1856.

My Dear Wills :—Will you and Mrs. Wills come to the reading of the Play,† next Monday Evening at

---

* Wilkie Collins's "The Dead Secret" ran in *Household Words* from January 3rd to June 13th, 1857.
† "The Frozen Deep."

a quarter before 8. Stanfield has not returned yet; but there is so much to do with it that I think it best not to wait for him, so far as the Dram : Pers : is concerned.

Ever faithfully,
C. D.

OFFICE OF *HOUSEHOLD WORDS*,
A Weekly Journal conducted by Charles Dickens.
No. 16, WELLINGTON STREET NORTH, STRAND,
Thursday Evg., 13th *Novr.*, 1856.

MY DEAR WILLS :—Yes, to the " Christmas Carol." —No, to the " Song of the Stars."

I am glad you like "The Wreck,"* though you have not seen all of it, I think. I find the "Narrative" too strong (speaking as a reader of it, not as its writer) to be broken by the stories. I have therefore devised with Collins for getting the stories in between his " Narrative " and mine, and breaking neither.

I never wrote anything more easily, or I think with greater interest and stronger belief.

The almanack I returned to the Printer tonight. I chose the longer quotation, because the quotation without the Sun seems to want its source of Life.

Ever faithfully,
C. D.

TAVISTOCK HOUSE,
Nineteenth November, 1856.

MY DEAR WILLS :—On the lists being added up, I find that we can still (as I hope), book some more

---

* The Christmas number this year was " The Wreck of the *Golden Mary*," in which Dickens wrote " The Wreck," while Collins wrote " John Steadman's Account " and " The Deliverance."

names. I have therefore put down Mr. Payn. And if you have any names to suggest, now is the time.

Of course if you have any at any time, wherein you may be interested or not, you will let me know what they are. But this is the time at which such lines have the best chance of falling into pleasant places.

Ever faithfully,
C. D.

TAVISTOCK HOUSE,
Twenty-fourth December, 1856.

MY DEAR WILLS :—Will you represent to Mr. Sala the necessity and vital importance—quite as much to himself as to *Household Words*—of his being punctual and faithful in the performance of the work he has undertaken.

Pray take care that he distinctly understands beyond all possibility of misconception, that he can have money from you while he is at work, as he wants it; and that when we come, on the completion of "Due North," to close our accounts I shall arrange all things with him for his advantage, in exactly the same spirit as if he had not given me occasion to decide that *Household Words* must not do him the injury of accepting any further service at his hands.*

Faithfully always,
CHARLES DICKENS.

1857.

In January of this year several performances of Wilkie Collins's play, "The Frozen Deep," were given at Tavistock House, where a special stage had been

---

* See *ante*, p. 46. Sala's "A Journey Due North" ran through *Household Words* from October 4th, 1856, to March 14th, 1857.

constructed. Dickens, who took the part of Richard Wardour, was the stage-manager; the audiences were crowded and enthusiastic, and everything went off with brilliant success. "The Frozen Deep," I may add, was produced at the Olympic Theatre in 1866, but it failed to draw the public, and had only a short run.

On June 1st Dickens took up his residence at Gad's Hill Place. In that month Douglas Jerrold, his intimate friend, died, and Dickens at once set about organising a series of entertainments for the benefit of Jerrold's family. These included performances of "The Frozen Deep" in London and Manchester; readings of the "Christmas Carol" in both these towns; performances of two of Jerrold's plays by professional actors, and a lecture by Thackeray. Dickens ("Life," III., 145) had expressed a "confident hope that we shall get close upon two thousand pounds," and Forster declares that "the result did not fall short of his expectations."

For the business management of these various entertainments Dickens had secured Arthur Smith, brother of Albert Smith. "I have got hold," he writes ("Life," III., 145), "of Arthur Smith as the best man of business I know, and go to work with him tomorrow." Arthur Smith's services in this capacity were invaluable, and when Dickens in the following year gave his public readings Smith again became his business assistant, and so remained until his death in October, 1861. Dickens had a great regard and liking for him.

On September 7th (see letter of September 6th, *post*) Dickens and Wilkie Collins set off together on a tour in the North of England, the object being to gather notes for a series of articles to appear in *Household Words*, under the title "The Lazy Tour of Two Idle

Apprentices" (*Household Words,* October 3rd, 10th, 17th, 24th, and 31st). On September 9th they climbed Carrick Fell, and lost their way in coming down. To make matters worse Collins fell and sprained his ankle, and could hardly manage to move. They got down eventually, after running great risks. (See a letter from Dickens to Forster, "Life," III., 147).

TAVISTOCK HOUSE,
    Saturday, Third January, 1857.

MY DEAR WILLS :—I am sorry that I cannot do what Mr. —— asks. But the substitution of an uninvited visitor for an invited one* is really put out of the question by the large reserved list of friends whom we have been unable to ask for want of room. No longer ago than Thursday, I could not do exactly the same thing for my old and intimate friend Maclise. His place falling in (through his being unable to move his leg, which is injured), I could not accept his proposed substitute, but gave it to the first on our old neglected list. And I must beg to exercise the same privilege in respect of Mrs. ——'s.

                  Ever faithfully,
                      CHARLES DICKENS.

TAVISTOCK HOUSE,
    Sunday, Fourth January, 1857.

MY DEAR WILLS :—I have of course no other reply to your note than that I *cheerfully* acquiesce. I wish however, in thorough good humour, that you did not argue the principle with me, because it does not

---

* At the performance of "The Frozen Deep," at Tavistock House. The next letter refers to the same matter.

reasonably admit of any discussion out of myself.
The less I know of the people concerned, the more
unreasonable such a substitution is in my mind, and the
greater the liberty *is* of so misusing an act of attention.
(This remark applies solely, I need not add, to Mr. ———.)
It is worth remembering that among nearly four
hundred people no such thing has been thought of—
except by Maclise, who expressly said in his note that
he still did not consider it a kind of thing to be done.

I should like to see you sometime tomorrow morning
about the seats; which will require a little management when you have got the Theatre nearly full, and
will need to be perfectly understood beforehand. I
am going to Newgate Market with Mrs. Dickens after
breakfast to shew her where to buy fowls; but I shall
be back directly. Shall we appoint 12 o'clock?

I shall then have one or two things to give you for
H. W. also, and a question to ask you about Frederick.*

Will you impress upon Mrs. Wills† from me, this
last never-to-be-departed-from rule. Imagine it
written in Golden characters.

WHEN THEY APPLAUD, INVARIABLY STOP, UNTIL THE
APPLAUSE IS OVER.

Ever faithfully,
C. D.

Yes to the Poems—too golden-haired, and marble,
and all that; but meritorious I think.

TAVISTOCK HOUSE,
Wednesday, Seventh January, 1857.

MY DEAR WILLS:—All right. Half past one tomorrow!

---

* His second brother.
† Mrs. Wills was acting the part of Nurse Esther in "The Frozen Deep."

I am in perfect order. Calm—perfectly happy with the success—about to make more Gin Punch. Draught of that article enormous.

Macready has just been here, perfectly raging because Forster took him away, and positively shouldered him out of the Green Room Supper, on which he had set his heart.

You write Diabolically plain this morning. I can't do *that*.

Ever faithfully,
C. D.

[To Mrs. Wills.]
Tavistock House,
Eighth February, 1857.

My Dear Mrs. Wills :—Pray accept my cordial thanks for your elegant little present. It has a treble value to me. Firstly as a mark of your remembrance. Secondly, as replacing a loss that I have much regretted. Thirdly, as a gift from Nurse Esther, and an association with the pleasant times in which I made that worthy woman's acquaintance, and conveyed to her previously benighted mind the complete assurance that I am not a Dragon, but a villified Lamb. (Note. An L too many in the last word but one.)

Believe me always,
Very faithfully yours,
Charles Dickens.

Tavistock House,
Monday Night, Ninth February, 1857.

My Dear Wills :—Will you be so kind as to make an expedition to the India House for me? I get so mobbed if I go to a place of that sort myself, that I ask the favor. I did not know of the necessity when you were here to-day.

Walter Landor Dickens,* being now of an age to go up to be examined for a Direct appointment as a Cadet, to which he is nominated (the Director nominating him, being, as I remember Mr. Lock), the business merely is to ask for his necessary papers. I suppose the Secretary's office to be the right one; but the name Walter sends me this morning as the name of the gentleman to be asked for is Mr. Hollyer.

It is a mere matter of form. Walter is going up in about a fortnight. He is now with Messrs. Brackenbury and Wynne at Wimbledon (if that be anything to the purpose). The papers are wanted, I believe, directly—or at all events should be applied for directly.

Ever faithfully,
C. D.

Tavistock House,
Sunday, Second August, 1857.

My Dear Wills :—

I write hurriedly, on my way back to Gad's Hill.

You I suppose are somewhere in Cheshire or Staffordshire, as you didn't turn up yesterday.

"Frozen Deep."

Get the Circular out, directly. Nights of acting,

---

* Dickens's second son. He went to India in July of this year as a cadet in the East India Company's service, was then transferred to the 42nd Highlanders, and died in India on December 31st, 1863.

Friday, 21st and Saturday, 22nd.* Company to go down on the afternoon of Thursday, 20th. Rehearsal of 3rd Act to be called in town beforehand, on account of Actresses instead of Amateur ladies. Also in the Free Trade Hall on the Friday morning at 11.

H. W.

Can you come down to Gad's Hill with the next proofs? If yes, when? I purpose not coming up (unless obliged) before Friday.

Ever faithfully,
C. D.

GAD'S HILL PLACE,
Thursday, Thirteenth August, 1857.

MY DEAR WILLS :—I send this up to town to be posted by our Doctor—come down to see Mrs. Dickens —still very poorly.

I have altered the names thus:

"A Journey in Search of Nothing."
"The Self-made Potter."
"Burning, and Burying."
"The Leaf."
"Sepoy Symbols of Mutiny."
"Eleanor Clare's Journal."
"On Her Majesty's Service." †

—But I have a misgiving that we have used the last title before. If we have not, retain it. If we have, call the article either

"PUBLIC BUSINESS."

or

"HOW THE WRITER WAS DISPATCH-BOXED." ‡

---

* At the Free Trade Hall, Manchester.
† These articles formed the contents of the issue of September 5th.
‡ This was the title chosen.

Perhaps the latter is the better title of the two. "On Her Majesty's Service" is the best title of the three, if we have not anticipated it.

I will try to knock out a subject or two. In the event of my Sleepy Head engendering anything, the great suggestion shall come to you by Post.

Ever faithfully,
C. D.

GAD'S HILL PLACE,
Sunday, Sixth September, 1857.

MY DEAR WILLS:—

MRS. WILLS

I hope is better. I have filled them with sympathy here, by my vivid descriptions of your descriptions. They all send loves and messages. Don't forget to let me know how she goes on when you write.

H. W.

I find in my official drawer, the card of the Writer of some foreign paper I left for you on your table. In case his address should not be attached to the paper, I send the card to you.

JERROLD REMEMBRANCE.

In the left hand drawer of my table at the office, is a roll of the usual Theatrical MS.—"The Spendthrift," by poor Jerrold. Will you have it put up in a parcel for Buckstone with the enclosed note, and left at the Haymarket Theatre?

"THE IDLE APPRENTICES" *

go straight to Carlisle, by 9 A.M. North Western Train on Monday Morning. After casting about a good

---

* Wilkie Collins and Dickens. See Introduction to this year.

deal, the Cumberland Fells look promising to them. I will write you one line from Carlisle on Tuesday, giving you any new address we may fix on. Until you have a new address from me, write (if you have occasion to write) to me at the Post Office there—that is to say, at Carlisle.

I think I am becoming rather inventive again.

Ever faithfully,
C. D.

CARLISLE,
Monday Night, Seventh September, 1857.

MY DEAR WILLS :—Conglomeration prevailing in the Maps—and our minds—to an alarming extent, I have the faintest idea of our trip. But I think I am perfectly right in this direction :—You writing to me from London not later than Wednesday night, address me at the Post Office, Maryport, Cumberland. After that, address me at the Post Office, Doncaster. I think we shall leave the Maryport (that is to say, the coast) regions, about Friday or so. We shall not arrive at Doncaster until Sunday night. It is quite uncertain what we may be about in the interval. Once at Doncaster, the address is always Doncaster until you hear to the contrary.

Of course you will expect copy (as we agreed) on Saturday morning.

You will be charmed to hear that two bedrooms and a sitting room are not to be got at Doncaster for the race week at less than the moderate charge of

TWELVE GUINEAS!

But we have a grotesque idea of describing the

town under those circumstances, which I hope may be worth (if anything can be worth) that money.

Will you let Evans know the directions I give you, as he will probably wish to write to me while we are out.

Collins's kind regard.

Ever faithfully,
CHARLES DICKENS.

ANGEL HOTEL, DONCASTER,
Thursday, Seventeenth September, 1857.

MY DEAR WILLS :—The day post has brought me your note, and I write you by return a few words in reply.

The other halves of the notes I believe are all safe. One in Arthur Smith's hands; one in mine. I cannot remember the correspondent's name, or anything about him, except that he dated from Exchange Buildings, Liverpool.

All of my part—three pages and a half—of the second portion of the "Lazy Tour" is already here, and in corrected type. Collins is sticking a little with his story, but I hope will come through it tomorrow. He is much obliged by your enquiries and sympathy, and sends his kind regard. He can't walk out, but can limp about the room, and has had two Doncaster rides in a carriage. Is to be treated to another tomorrow if he has done.

Happy to hear so good an account of Mrs. Wills.

Ever faithfully,
C. D.

ANGEL, DONCASTER,
Sunday, Twentieth September, 1857.

MY DEAR WILLS:—I am going into the country this morning; and I answer your letter briefly, before starting.

I see no other objection to the Manchester article[*] than that it is commonplace.

"The Bristol Prayer Monger"[†] I have never had sent me, and therefore can do nothing to. But the name suggests care and caution.

You will see that the second part of the "Lazy Tour" is very long. The third will be much shorter—not more than half this quantity, if so much.

My next address will be Gad's Hill. I *think* I shall leave here on Tuesday, but I cannot positively say. Collins and I part company tomorrow. (He can walk now—walked a mile yesterday, with a stick.) I did intend to return home tomorrow, but have no idea now of doing that. Whatever I do, I shall of course come up to the scratch with the third part. Indeed I have half done it.

I am very sorry to hear of Mrs. Wills, to whom my kind regard again. But you know how constantly it happens that the first effect of the sea is to exaggerate and stimulate an illness.

Ever faithfully,
CHARLES DICKENS.

Collins sends kind regard.

---

[*] Presumably "The Manchester School of Art," by Wills, *Household Words*, October 10th.
[†] I cannot trace this article.

OFFICE OF *HOUSEHOLD WORDS.*
A Weekly Journal conducted by Charles Dickens.
No. 16, WELLINGTON STREET NORTH,
STRAND,
Saturday, Twenty-Sixth September, 1857.

MY DEAR WILLS:—I write you a line with such slight official intelligence as I have.

Part 3 of "The Lazy Tour" I have corrected, and introduced Collins's copy (received this morning) in to [it]. I have instructed B. and E. to send him down proof to Scarborough to-night and have instructed *him* to send back proof to B. and E. tomorrow night. There are some descriptions of mine in it (particularly one, of a Railway Station), that I think very good indeed.

Part 4, I am at work on.

Oxenford* has sent a paper "Touching the Lord Hamlet,"† giving a very good account of the old Saxo Grammaticus history. I have sent it to the Printer, with instructions to send proof to him.

I have, at Gad's Hill, a pretty little paper ‡ of a good deal of merit, by one Mr. Hollingshead, who addressed me as having tried his hand in *The Train*.§ This, too, I will send to the Printer's. (I ought to have brought it from Gad's Hill this morning, but forgot it.) I am inclined to hope that the writer may be very serviceable to us.

---

* John Oxenford (1812—1877) wrote many articles for *Household Words.* He was the dramatic critic of *The Times* from 1850 for more than a quarter of a century.

† *Household Words,* October 17th.

‡ "Poor Tom," *Household Words,* October 17th. The author was John Hollingshead, who became a regular contributor to the periodical. Later on he become celebrated as lessee of the Gaiety Theatre, where—to use his own words—he kept the sacred lamp of burlesque burning.

§ In January, 1856, G. A. Sala and Edmund Yates established a monthly magazine called *The Train,* which did not survive long.

Collins I have made the new proposal to, as we agreed.*

Evans has been with me this morning, to ask me, Would I have a Posting-Bill of "The Lazy Tour"? I replied, most decidedly Yes. I think it will give us a good push into the public mind, at a very dull time—will probably do us good at Christmas.

I spent while I was away, £75. 1 shall make a very handsome deduction indeed, if I take off £15 for any personal peculiarities in the order of march. That I will do, however, and therefore *H. W.* has to pay £10 to my account at Coutts's.

Which reminds me:—Will you make a memorandum that whenever you settle accounts with Miss Coutts, I have to receive £5 for her subscription to the Reverend Mr. Ford, which I have paid.

Trusting that Mrs. Wills continues to improve,
Ever faithfully,
C. D.

GAD'S HILL PLACE,
Friday, Second October, 1857.

MY DEAR WILLS:—I have yours of yesterday, this morning.

Know, that I yesterday sent to B. and E. the greater part of "The Lazy Tour," Part IV.; and that by this post I send the rest—having stuck to it and finished it this morning. A very odd story, with a wild, picturesque fancy in it.

I write to John, to tell him not to come, *if* he has only to come for copy.

Monday, so far as I know at this moment, will suit me very well. In case I should have occasion to go to town that day (possible, but not probable), I will write to you again in the meantime.

* See next letter.

I don't remember whether I have told you that I have made the arrangement with Collins—that he is extremely sensible of the extra Fifty, and was rather unwilling to take it—and that I have no doubt of his being devoted to *H. W.*, and doing great service.

Ever faithfully,
C. D.

1858.

In May of this year Dickens and his wife separated. Out of this private matter there arose between him and his publishers, Messrs. Bradbury and Evans, certain differences of opinion. These led to negotiations (which are referred to in some of the letters towards the end of the year) and resulted ultimately in Dickens's decision to wind up *Household Words* and to start *All the Year Round* in its place.

Hitherto Dickens had given readings either for a charity or for some other public purpose. This year he decided to read for his own profit. With the assistance of Mr. Arthur Smith as his business manager he planned and carried out a tour through England, Scotland and Ireland, which began on August 2nd and ended on November 13th. I append a copy of the printed list setting out the places at which he was to read and the dates of his visits.

Charles Allston Collins, who is referred to in the letter of August 9th, was the younger brother of Wilkie Collins, and was born in 1828. In early life he devoted himself to painting and became attached to the Pre-Raphaelite Brotherhood. He then turned to literature, became a contributor to *Household Words* and *All the Year Round*, and published essays, novels, and books of description, amongst which may be mentioned "A New Sentimental Journey" and "A Cruise upon Wheels." In 1860 he married Dickens's younger daughter, Kate. He died in 1873.

MR. CHARLES DICKENS'S TOUR,
During the Autumn of 1858.

CLIFTON	Monday,	Aug.	2...8 o'clock	Bath Hotel.
EXETER	Tuesday,	,,	3...8 ,,	London Hotel.
PLYMOUTH	Wednesday,	,,	4...8 ,,	} Elliot's Royal Hotel.
,, ...	Thursday,	,,	5...3&8 ,,	
CLIFTON	Friday,	,,	6...8 ,,	Bath Hotel.
WORCESTER	Tuesday,	,,	10...8 ,,	Mr. Stratford's Music Warehouse, The Cross, Worcester
WOLVERHAMPTON	Wednesday,	,,	11...8 ,,	Swan Hotel.
SHREWSBURY ...	Thursday,	,,	12...8 ,,	Mr. Leake, Bookseller.
CHESTER	Friday,	,,	13...8 ,	Royal Hotel.
LIVERPOOL	Wednesday,	,,	18...8 ,,	
,, ...	Thursday,	,,	19...8 ,,	} Radley's Adelphi Hotel.
,, ...	Friday.	,,	20...8 ,,	
,, ...	Saturday,	,,	21...3 ,,	
DUBLIN	Monday,	,,	23...8 ,,	
,, ...	Tuesday,	,,	24...8 ,,	} Morrison's Hotel.
,, ...	Wednesday,	,,	25...3&8 ,,	
,, ...	Thursday,	,,	26...8 ,,	
BELFAST	Friday,	,,	27...8 ,,	} Imperial Hotel.
,, ...	Saturday,	,,	28..3&8 ,,	
CORK	Monday,	,,	30...8 ,,	} Imperial Hotel.
,, ...	Tuesday,	,,	31...1½&8 ,,	
LIMERICK	Wednesday,	Sept. 1...8	,,	} Cruise's Hotel.
,, ...	Thursday,	,,	2...8 ,,	
HUDDERSFIELD ...	Wednesday,	,,	8...8 ,,	George Hotel.
WAKEFIELD	Thursday,	,,	9...8 ,,	Stafford Arms.
YORK	Friday,	,,	10...8 ,,	Mr. Henry Banks, Music Warehouse, Stonegate.
HARROGATE	Saturday,	,,	11...3&8 ,,	Mr. W. Dawson, Cheltenham Pump Room.
SCARBOROUGH ...	Monday,	,,	13...3&8 ,,	Assembly Rooms.
HULL	Tuesday,	,,	14...8 ,,	Mr. R. Bowser, Music Hall.
LEEDS	Wednesday	,,	15...8 ,,	Scarboro' Arms Hotel.
HALIFAX	Thursday	,,	16...8 ,,	White Swan Hotel.
SHEFFIELD	Friday	,,	17...8 ,,	King's Head Hotel.
MANCHESTER	Saturday,	,,	18...8 ,,	Royal Hotel.
DARLINGTON	Tuesday,	,,	21...8 ,,	Mr. Robert Swale, Bookseller.
DURHAM	Wednesday,	,,	22...8 ,,	Mr. Procter, Bookseller, Market Place.
SUNDERLAND	Thursday,	,,	23...8 ,,	Bridge House Hotel.
NEWCASTLE	Friday,	,,	24...8 ,,	} Mr. T. Horn, Music Warehouse, Grey-street.
,, ...	Saturday,	,,	25...3&8 ,,	
EDINBURGH	Monday,	,,	27...8 ,,	
,, ...	Tuesday,	,,	28...8 ,,	} Waterloo Hotel.
,, ...	Wednesday,	,,	29...3&8 ,,	
,, ...	Thursday,	,,	30...8 ,,	
DUNDEE	Friday,	Oct.	1...8 ,,	} Mr. Chalmers, Bookseller.
,, ...	Saturday,	,,	2..8 ,,	
ABERDEEN	Monday,	,,	4...3&8 ,,	Mr. John Marr, Music Saloon.
PERTH	Tuesday,	,,	5...8 ,,	Mr. Drummond, Bookseller.
GLASGOW	Wednesday,	,,	6...8 ,,	
,, ...	Thursday,	,,	7...8 ,,	} Mr. John Muir Wood, Music Warehouse
,, ...	Friday,	,,	8...8 ,,	
,, ...	Saturday	,,	9...3 ,,	
BRADFORD	Thursday,	,,	14...8 ,,	Mr. C. Ollivier, St. George's Hall.
LIVERPOOL	Friday,	,,	15...3&8 ,,	Radley's Adelphi Hotel.
MANCHESTER	Saturday,	,,	16...8 ,,	Royal Hotel.
BIRMINGHAM	Monday,	,,	18...8 ,,	
,, ...	Tuesday,	,,	19...8 ,,	} Hen and Chickens Hotel.
,, ...	Wednesday,	,,	20...8 ,,	
NOTTINGHAM	Thursday,	,,	21...8 ,,	Mr. T. Forman, Guardian Office.
DERBY	Friday,	,,	22...8 ,,	Royal Hotel.
MANCHESTER	Saturday,	,,	23...8 ,,	Royal Hotel, Manchester.
YORK	Monday,	,,	25...8 ,,	Royal Station Hotel.
HULL	Tuesday,	,,	26...8 ,,	} Royal Station Hotel.
,, ...	Wednesday,	,,	27...3 ,,	
LEEDS	Thursday,	,,	28...8 ,,	White Horse Hotel.
SHEFFIELD	Friday,	,,	29...8 ,,	King's Head Hotel.
LEAMINGTON	Tuesday,	Nov.	2...3&8 ,,	Assembly Rooms, Leamington.
WOLVERHAMPTON	Wednesday,	,,	3...8 ,,	Swan Hotel.
LEICESTER	Thursday,	,,	4...8 ,,	Bell Hotel.
OXFORD	Friday,	,,	5...8 ,,	} Star Hotel, Oxford.
,, ...	Saturday,	,,	6...3 ,,	
SOUTHAMPTON	Tuesday,	,,	9...8 ,,	} Mr. Sharland, Bookseller, High Street.
,, ...	Wednesday,	,,	10...3 ,,	
PORTSMOUTH	Thursday,	,,	11...3&8 ,,	Mr. Atkins, Music Warehouse, Portsea.
BRIGHTON	Friday,	,,	12...8 ,,	} Bedford Hotel.
,, ...	Saturday	,,	13...3&8 ,,	

TAVISTOCK HOUSE,
Monday Night,
Twenty-second February, 1858.

MY DEAR WILLS :—Letter No. 1, enclosed, is the Stereoscope people's favour that I spoke to you of this morning. Will you kindly write them an obliging reply, to the effect we mentioned?

Letter No. 2 is the usual thing. I know no more about it.

Collins wishes to read his new play to me, next Thursday. I mean to propose to him that you be of the party, and I have no doubt the idea will give him much pleasure. If all things else should be "in a concatenation accordingly," what do you say to our dining at Gad's Hill (under John convoy), reading there after dinner, sleeping there, and coming up next morning? I have broached this notion to our respected contributor.

I will be in Wellington Street on Wednesday in good time, and we can arrange details then.

Ever faithfully,
C. D.

TAVISTOCK HOUSE, TAVISTOCK SQUARE,
LONDON, W.C.,
Saturday, Third April, 1858.

MY DEAR WILLS :—I have been so hustled by a crowd of cares since I came home, that I have not written to you—the rather because, until I received yours from Edinburgh, I had nothing to say.

Yours arrived very opportunely. On the previous

night, I had been going through Arthur Smith's suggested list of readings, and had demurred to his idea of returning to several large places. His reason for this, was exactly yours. I felt bound to send him your unconscious confirmation of his opinion, immediately. And he was extremely glad to receive it.

It is an unspeakable satisfaction to me, to have left such an impression in Edinburgh. I felt that night, that it was a very great success; but your account of it, even exceeds my hopes.

Arthur Smith told me on my return, that he had written to you in Edinburgh. I suppose you received his letters? I believe he had nothing important to say, in consequence of the Glasgow man, the brother of the Edinburgh music seller, having communicated with him direct.

The Queen wants to hear the "Carol." I have represented my dutiful hope that she will form one of an audience, as I consider an audience necessary.*

I have not a scrap of news. The usual papers come tumbling into the office in the usual way, and John cleans the windows all day in a kind of melancholy stagnation of mind. Holdsworth smiles on me with a limp and sickly benevolence.

All the chance men who have been got in to help the gardener at Gad's Hill ply the pump, have run away, one after another (I am serious) and been heard of no more in that country. The last man became so desperate as to work seven hours, and fly without his money. The machinery must be altered, and I must establish a revolving pony.

* A difficulty arose about this matter, and it was eventually found impossible to gratify the Queen's wish. See "Life," III., 466.

All the rest of my world turns as it did, and that's not saying much for it.

With kind regards to Mrs. Wills and all about you,

Ever faithfully,
C. D.

GAD'S HILL PLACE,
 HIGHAM BY ROCHESTER, KENT,
Monday, Ninth August, 1858.

H. W.

MY DEAR WILLS :—I was at the office on Saturday at Noon, but did not expect to find you there.

Send me a Proof of the next No. you make up. I must put a new name to Charles Collins's story.*

I hope Mrs. Gaskell will not stop, for more than a week at all events.†

I am very glad to heard from Wilkie that he is at work again.

I

have done exceedingly well, I think, so far. It is out of season at Clifton, and half the houses are shut up. The Yacht Squadron too, was gone from Plymouth to Cherbourg, and there were races at Plymouth, and public balls. Nevertheless we took nearly £400 last week. Exeter was tremendous. You never saw such a reception, and we might have stayed there a week. The first night at Plymouth (very wet) not good. The next morning (great talk about it spreading in the town) admirable. That night (greater talk

---

* "Her Face," *Household Words,* August 28th.

† Mrs. Gaskell's "My Lady Ludlow" was appearing in *Household Words*.

about it spreading in the town) enormous. Similarly at Clifton. There was a very great increase of Numbers on the second night, and the local Magnate said "Now they know what it is, Mr. Dickens might stay a month and always have a cram." Contrary to my impression of those Western people, I have never seen a finer or more subtly apprehensive audience than at Exeter. Nor did I ever know the minutest touches in "Little Dombey," go better in London than at Plymouth. As to the "Boots" at Plymouth, the people gave themselves up altogether (Generals, Mayors, and Shillings, equally) to a perfect transport of enjoyment of him and the two children.

Arthur shall have the packet tomorrow morning (when we start for Worcester), that I received from you this morning.

I have no printed lists of my tour here, but will send Miss Coutts one straight.

I think that's all at present,
Ever faithfully,
C. D.

ADELPHI HOTEL, LIVERPOOL,
Saturday, Twenty-first August, 1858.

MY DEAR WILLS:—I send this to Sheffield at a flying venture.

The Liverpool audience has been altogether different from our Theatrical experience of it. Quite as good as St. Martin's Hall. A great call, every night. Every point taken. The nicest and finest bits in "Little Dombey," hitting like chain shot. Last night, we had the greatest house, both in numbers and money, we have ever had: London included. There were 2,300 and 200 guineas. The turn-away from the shilling part was very large. On each of the two previous nights we had 100 guineas, and (if the day should keep moderately fine) we expect a very good afternoon to-day at 3.

The crossing to Ireland to-night is not likely to be very agreeable, for it has been exceedingly squally these last two days.

I observe in *H. W.* that that " Running the Gauntlet "* (an article with good stuff in it) has been very badly looked over. " That " is constantly put for " who," which is a great vulgarity. Such an expression too as " vowed him revenge " is extremely bad.

Wilkie's paper, very funny.† Just what we want.

With kind regard to Mrs. Wills, and all kinds of remembrances from Arthur,

Ever faithfully,
C. D.

P.S. As new places are constantly proposing themselves to be brought into the Tour, I have arranged with Arthur that it shall now be wound up, so that I may be able to get to work in London, *on the 15th of November*, with a view to the Xmas No.‡ I will talk over my idea with Wilkie, and ascertain if he feels up to it. If he should not, when I expound it to him,—then perhaps it might be best to have a round of Stories. But *nous verrons.*

---

* " The Last Victim of the Gauntlet," by Von Goetznitz, *Household Words*, August 21st.
† " The Unknown Public," *Household Words*, August 21st.
‡ " A House to Let," containing one contribution by Dickens, two by Collins, and one by Dickens and Collins jointly.

ROYAL HOTEL, LIMERICK,
Thursday, Second September, 1858.

MY DEAR WILLS :—I purpose being at the office *next Tuesday afternoon*, before starting again. I hope to be at Tavistock House at noon on Saturday, and to start for Gad's Hill on Sunday forenoon.

Belfast and Cork, as great successes as Dublin. Fancy, at Cork (by no means a large place) more than 1,000 stalls being engaged for the three readings. I made last week clear profit, £340; and have made in the month of August, a profit of one Thousand Guineas! This, after paying our expenses back to London, and halfway to Huddersfield. Pretty well, I think?

This is the oddest place—of which nobody in any other part of Ireland seems to know anything. Nobody could answer a single question we asked about it. There is no large room, and I read in the Theatre—a charming Theatre. The best I ever saw, to see and hear in. Arthur says that when he opened the doors last night, there was a rush of—three Ducks! We expect a Pig to-night. We had only £40; but they seemed to think *that*, amazing! If the two nights bring £100, it will be as much as we expected. I am bound to say that they are an admirable audience. As hearty and demonstrative as it is possible to be. It is a very odd place in its lower-order aspects, and I am very glad we came—though we could have made heaps of money by going to Dublin instead.

Arthur sends you his kindest regard. He has been nearly torn to pieces in the shilling rushes, and has been so flattened against the walls that he is only now beginning to " come round " again.

My kindest remembrance to Mrs. Wills.

Ever cordially,
C. D.

STATION HOTEL, NEWCASTLE,
Friday afternoon,
Twenty-fourth September, 1858.

MY DEAR WILLS:—I return the cheque, duly signed.

I have just now walked over here from Sunderland (1 o'clock) and have barely had time to look at the room. It is new since we acted here—large—and capable of holding a good deal of money. I hope it will have a good deal to hold, tonight and tomorrow. The Let is a very good one, and we expect a large Take in payment at the doors.

You will be amazed to hear that we reaped very little profit at Sunderland last night! I read in a very beautiful new Theatre, and it *looked* a fine house. But it was not fine enough to pay well. Half a million of money, *belonging to Sunderland alone*, was lost in the last Bank-Smash there; and the town has never held up its head since, they say.

I suppose the people who were there, had either not lost any money, or had found it again. I never beheld such a rapturous audience. And they—and the stage together: which I never can resist—made me do such a vast number of new things in the " Carol," that Arthur and our men stood in amazement at the Wing, and roared and stamped as if it were an entirely new book, topping all the others.

You must come to some good place and hear the
"Carol." I think you will hardly know it again.

Little Darlington — in a mouldy old Assembly
Room without a Lamp abutting on the street, so that
I passed it a dozen times and looked for it, when I
went down to read—covered itself with glory. All
sorts of people came in from outlying places, and the
town was drunk with the "Carol" far into the night.
At Durham we had a capital audience too—led by
Dean and Chapter, and humbly followed up by Mayor
and local Bores—but the Hall not large enough, and
the City not large enough, for such a purpose as your
friend's.

So, we are working our way further North. I
walked from Durham to Sunderland, and made a little
fanciful photograph in my mind of Pit Country, which
will come well into *H. W.* one day. I couldn't help
looking upon my mind as I was doing it, as a sort of
capitally prepared and highly sensitive plate. And
I said, without the least conceit (as Watkins might
have said of a plate of his) "it really is a pleasure
to work with you, you receive the impression so
nicely."

I mark this note "Immediate," because I forgot to
mention that I particularly wish you to look well to
Wilkie's article about the Wigan schoolmaster, and
not to leave anything in it that may be sweeping, and
unnecessarily offensive to the middle class.* He has
always a tendency to overdo that—and such a subject
gives him a fresh temptation. Don't be afraid of the
Truth, in the least; but don't be unjust.

* "Highly Proper," *Household Words*, October 2nd, 1858. The article protested against the conduct of a schoolmaster who had refused to keep Mr. Alfred Wigan's son at his school on the ground that Mr. Wigan was an actor.

Arthur sends kindest regards. Give my love to Mrs. Wills. I hope my wholesome influence lasts? Ever faithfully,
CHARLES DICKENS.

TAVISTOCK HOUSE,
TAVISTOCK SQUARE, LONDON, W.C.,
That is to say:
DUNDEE,
Saturday, Second October, 1858.

MY DEAR WILLS:—Pray, pray, *pray*, don't have Poems unless they are good. We are immeasurably better without them: "Beyond," is really Beyond anything I ever saw, in utter badness.

You instructed Payn and White, that no storyTeller must have been a Lodger in the House.* I don't understand that, at all. A Lodger may give variety to the thing, and cannot possibly (that I see) weaken the carrying out of the Idea.

To Wilkie's queries I reply:

1. I *think* I had best write the framework in the first person—unless I should think of any new and odd way of doing it. I will certainly avoid the plain third person in which the stories will be narrated.

2. I am not clear about following up the old Materials, and making them doomed and destructive. I think it would end the thing with unseasonable grimness. If I could build them into a good school, or infirmary, or child's hospital, or something of that sort, it might be a more pleasant end, and a working round of the thing to something brighter.

---

* An allusion to the Christmas number, "A House to Let." Neither Payn nor White, however, contributed to it.

3. If I were Wilkie, unless I got an idea which would not admit of it, I would certainly make the story of some people who kept the house, *the* story. Indeed, I supposed that to have been understood.

There was certainly in Edinburgh, a coldness beforehand, about the Readings. I mention it, to let you know that I consider the triumph there, by far the greatest I have made. The city was taken by storm, and carried. "The Chimes" shook it; "Little Dombey" blew it up. On the two last nights, the crowd was immense, and the turn-away enormous. Everywhere, nothing was heard but praises—nowhere more than at Blackwood's shop, where there certainly was no predisposition to praise. It was a brilliant victory, and could have been represented in no mere money whatever.

My profit there was £200. My profit at Newcastle £170 (the room in the latter place, very large). My profit in September is £900. No doubt in reason this sum will have passed £1,000 before I begin the next Thousand in Glasgow.

"The Carol" will be read one night at Birmingham, and at Nottingham. Those are the places nearest to your hand I think.

My love to Mrs. Wills, in which the girls unite. They were delighted with Edinburgh, and saw it, and all about it, on beautiful days. Payn went with us to Hawthornden, and we laughed all day. Conceive his telling me that Miss Martineau once told him and a certain Lake Doctor, face to face, that the reason why *The Times* succeeded with their Foreign correspondence was because—they kept a clairvoyante to do it!!! "You may observe," says she, "that the *Daily News* is rapidly improving in that particular. Why? Because they have lately engaged a clairvoyante, too!"

With which large button of arrogant conceit from the head and front of a strait waistcoat, I beg to subscribe myself,

  Ever Anti Politico-Economically,
    Anti De Morganically,
      and the like,
        C. D.

[James Payn was at this time in Edinburgh as editor of *Chambers's Journal*. He describes this, his first, meeting with Dickens in "Some Literary Recollections":—

"He was full of fun and brightness, and in five minutes I felt as much at my ease with him as though I had known him as long as I had known his books. It was not one of the days on which Hawthornden was open to the public, and we had much difficulty in obtaining admittance at the lodge; and when we got to the house we were detained there again, and there was a difficulty about seeing the glen. I went within doors and expostulated; but for a long time without success: the inmates, I am sorry to say, did not seem to be acquainted with Dickens's name—a circumstance which, though it would only have made him laugh the more, I did not venture to disclose. The fancy picture which he drew of my detention in that feudal abode, and of the mediæval tortures which had probably been inflicted upon me, made ample amends, however, for what I had suffered on behalf of the party. In the end we saw all that was to be seen: and never shall I forget the face of the hereditary guide and gatekeeper when Dickens tipped him in his usual lavish manner. This retainer had not thought much of him before—indeed, had obviously never heard of him—but his salute at parting could not have been more deferential had the author of 'Pickwick' been the Lord of the Isles. The humours of the day must have made some impression upon Dickens himself, for in a letter two years afterwards he reminds me of the imprisonment I had suffered for his sake in the gloomy cells of Hawthornden. Late that night I supped with him—after his reading—at his hotel, alone; after which I discarded for ever the picture which I had made in my mind of him, and substituted for it a still pleasanter one, taken from life."]

HEN AND CHICKENS HOTEL, BIRMINGHAM,
Monday Night, Eighteenth October, 1858.

MY DEAR WILLS:—I forgot three things in my hurried note of to-day from London.

1. After the "Smallport Monte Christo"* (which is very whimsical and good), I think the "Great Dunkerque Failure"† may go in. It should be in the next No. you make up. (Let me see the Proof of any other printed paper by him. A very little erasure here and there, makes a considerable difference in his case.)

2. When you come to advertise in *H. W.* my readings for November, put, and keep as long as the advertisement stands, this line after Brighton, 13th Nov., *in small caps.—in a line by itself—*

WHICH WILL TERMINATE THE SERIES OF READINGS.

3. The "Carol" is not read here. It is read at Nottingham on Thursday, and at Manchester on Saturday.

A very, very, wet night.

Ever faithfully,
C. D.

ROYAL HOTEL, DERBY,
Friday, Twenty-Second October, 1858.

MY DEAR WILLS:—If you look at the passage in Macready's letter, which refers to Mrs. Meredith,

---
* By Charles Collins, *Household Words*, October 16th.
† Also by Charles Collins, *Household Words*, October 30th.

you will see what I mean when I ask you if you will write to him, and enquire whether he will receive the money for the paper, or what is to be done with it; telling him at the same time how much the sum is.

Was she paid for her former paper or papers? That passage in her note looks to me as if she never had been paid.

Immense at Nottingham last night. Immense final night at Birmingham. Let, very good here.

I have a bad cold all over me.

Ever faithfully,
C. D.

WOLVERHAMPTON,
Wednesday, Third November, 1858.
H. W.

MY DEAR WILLS:—You remember that at one of our Audit Meetings—I think, the last—I suggested to Mr. Evans that we ought to have the vouchers for the payments made, and charged as being made, by their Firm, on account of *H. W.* It arose out of our speaking of paying for the paper in ready money.

Mr. Evans replied to that, that we, the other proprietors in *H. W.* were not responsible for the paper. He said so, with confidence; and I did not urge the point, though I had great doubts of his being legally right.

I have now ascertained that we *are* legally responsible. Will you therefore let Mr. Evans know that at the Audit of next week, we wish to have produced to us, the Vouchers for their payments on account of *Household Words.* There can be no Audit, I am assured, without such Vouchers, except in the mere name.

Pray do not fail to see to this.

Ever faithfully,
Charles Dickens.

Swan, Wolverhampton,
Wednesday Third November, 1858.

My Dear Wills:—I enclose you the note that I think best calculated to be shewn or sent by you to B. and E. on the voucher question.

In reference to my own copyrights, you seem to have omitted by accident, the most important question of all. It is, *whether I, being the largest proprietor in the books, can change the printer and publisher of them if I choose?* On this, the whole question of the extent of our power and the manner of its exercise, depends. There is no sub-agreement whatever, as to printing and publishing.

Now, will you again see Ouvry* on this vital question—which absolutely governs our proceeding as to *Household Words*—and communicate his opinion on that point, to Forster, along with his opinion on the other points? I cannot consult with Forster to any purpose, until we know exactly how we stand on this head.

As to Wilkie's paper—I see no necessity whatever, for altering Fauntleroy's name. But I wouldn't use it in the Title. I would call it a "A Paradoxical Experience" †—or "A Curiosity of Life"—or something like that.

I purpose being at the office, at 1 on Friday.

Little Leamington came out amazingly yesterday.

* See *ante*, p. 210, note.
† *Household Words,* November 13th.

We took £130, and turned away many hundreds of people. We have 200 stalls let here for to-night; which, considering the size of the town, is unusually large.

And I think that's all I have to say, at present.

Ever faithfully,

C. D.

Royal Hotel, Southampton,
Wednesday, Tenth November, 1858.

My Dear Wills:—The Audit Meeting appears to have gone off, pretty much as I expected it would. I felt sure of their producing the documents—I meant to have written, Vouchers.

In the Forster matter I do not agree with you. For this reason. It is clear to my mind that no discussion *can* take place between me and Bradbury and Evans. My being there would shut up any approach to it,—simply because I have steadily refused to enter on any approach to it, however distant, and have left Evans's advances disregarded. Now, with Forster they are under no such restraint, and even in the event of no discussion taking place with him at the meeting (which is the most probable aspect of Monday), they still have him legitimately in the business, and can at any time go to him or write to him. They could not do so with me, because they have already found it to be unavailing.

As to his management of the interview, I have not a doubt of his arranging it as I shall entreat him to do, and I can write to him from Brighton, expressly laying down the course that I want him to take. That course shall be, accommodation if it be possible. It is not possible with me, in a matter in which I have so deep a personal feeling. It never can come about, unless they have a third person before them, without seeking such person.

For these reasons, I would get the Power of Attorney—a Power to Forster to act for me, in matters relating to *H. W.* I must execute it. Could you not come down to Brighton with it? We shall be there by mid-day on Friday. I would write my letter to Forster then and there, and you should see it, and see that it is to your satisfaction. I feel convinced that he would not depart from a course agreed upon. You know how emphatically he feels that the first thing above all others, is, not to injure the property.

In order to avoid unnecessary conglomeration of our accounts, let me give you a check for your part of the Audit Day balance. It is enclosed.

Don't go to press with Wilkie's paper about Sidney Herbert, Guizot, The Heir of Redclyffe, and Dr. Dulcamara,* without my seeing it.

Ever faithfully,
C. D.

OFFICE OF *HOUSEHOLD WORDS*.
A Weekly Journal conducted by Charles Dickens.
No. 16, WELLINGTON STREET NORTH,
STRAND, W.C.,
Saturday, Twentieth Novr., 1858.

MY DEAR WILLS:—As I find you are not coming here to-day, I post this to let you know that we have returned to Tavistock House.

---

* "Dr. Dulcamara, M.P.," by Dickens and Wilkie Collins, *Household Words*, December 18th, 1858. The article was directed against some opinions on literature expressed by Sidney Herbert in an address at the Warminster Athenæum, in which he had quoted with approval M. Guizot's praise of "The Heir of Redclyffe."

Also, that Wilkie and I have arranged to pass the whole day here, on *Monday Week, the* 29*th*, to connect the various portions of the Xmas No. and get it finally together. If you arrange to have them ready at the Printers, for such cuts and such short bits of copy as we shall send them from time to time in the course of that day, we can finally correct it before we leave here that night, and you can send your last revise for Press next day.

This will enable you, now to settle on what day the Xmas No. shall be published, and to announce the said day in our No. sent to Press next week.

Ever faithfully,
C. D.

No. 16, WELLINGTON STREET NORTH,
STRAND, W.C.
Thursday, Twenty-fifth Novr., 1858.

MY DEAR WILLS :—I want to prepare you for an H. W. disappointment, in case it should come off. My introduced paper for the Xmas No. involves such an odd idea—which appears to me so humorous, and so available at greater length—that I am debating whether or no I shall cancel the paper (it has gone to the Printers today) and make it the Pivot round which my next book shall revolve.

Ever faithfully,
C. D.

TAVISTOCK HOUSE, TAVISTOCK SQUARE,
LONDON, W.C.,
Monday, Twentieth December, 1858.

MY DEAR WILLS :—You will see from the enclosed, that we are quite right.

Will you go round to Ouvry's, and ask them to write the notice they recommend, for me to sign. *If they approve*, I should wish it to be served on B. and E. from their office, and it certainly had best be served at once—today. A duplicate of it should be served upon you. I am finishing my little paper for the New Year, and will wait at home until you bring or send me the legally copied notices for my signature.

Ever faithfully,
C. D.

IV

ALL THE YEAR ROUND

THE AGREEMENT FOR *ALL THE YEAR ROUND*.

1859.

The last number of *Household Words* was published on Saturday, May 28th, and the first number of *All the Year Round* on Saturday, April 30th. The two periodicals thus overlapped one another by five numbers. The office of *Household Words* had been at 16, Wellington Street; the office of *All the Year Round* was at No. 11 in the same street. The price of the new periodical was the same as that of the old—2*d*. As a consequence of the differences, previously referred to, between Dickens and Messrs. Bradbury and Evans, a bill in Chancery had been filed, and by order of the Court "the right to use the name of the periodical *Household Words*, together with the printed stock and stereotyped plates of the same," was put up to auction in one lot on Monday, May 16th. Dickens himself was the purchaser. Accordingly the words "with which is incorporated *Household Words*" were added to the title of *All the Year Round*" in the fifth number (May 28th). The formal legal agreement (of which I have a copy) "for the carrying on of a Periodical called *All the Year Round*" was not executed until August 2nd. It is made between Dickens and Wills, and the following are its chief provisions :—

(1) Dickens and Wills are to be the proprietors.
(2) Both in regard to profits and losses Dickens is to be interested as to $\frac{3}{4}$ and Wills as to $\frac{1}{4}$.
(3) Dickens is to be Editor at a yearly salary of £504.
(4) Wills is to be General Manager with control (subject to powers reserved to Dickens) of the Commercial Department.
(5) Wills is to be Sub-Editor at a yearly salary of £420.
(6) If Wills retires from the Sub-Editorship Dickens is to have a $\frac{7}{8}$ share, Wills retaining $\frac{1}{8}$.
(7) The name *All the Year Round* and the goodwill attached to the publication to be the exclusive property of Dickens.

"A Tale of Two Cities" ran in *All the Year Round* from April 30th to November 26th. It also appeared concurrently in monthly parts from June to December. In October Dickens went on another reading tour in England.

Edmund Yates (1831—1894), who is referred to in the letter of April 11th, was a contributor both to the old and the new periodicals. For many years he had a place in the Post Office, but left in 1872. In 1858 Dickens had taken the part of Yates in a dispute with Thackeray, which led to Yates's expulsion from the Garrick Club, and Dickens and Thackeray consequently became temporarily estranged. Yates wrote several novels, and in 1874 founded *The World*, which he continued to edit until he died.

I have no Office Book for *All the Year Round* such as I have used for the references in the letters to *Household Words*. It will, therefore, be impossible for me to identify the authors of articles in the former publication, except in the case of Dickens himself. His contributions to *All the Year Round* were, I believe, identified from the office "set" of the journal by the late Mr. F. J. Kitton. Where that set may now be I do not know. Dickens's contributions to both journals were included by Mr. B. W. Matz in Vols 35 and 36 of "The National Edition of the Works of Charles Dickens" (Chapman & Hall, 1908).

GAD'S HILL PLACE,
 HIGHAM BY ROCHESTER, KENT,
  Saturday, Eighth January, 1859.

MY DEAR WILLS :—This is the first of some papers by "The Clergyman's Wife" I told you of.* Get it printed for the next No. we make up.

* Mrs. Blacker. She contributed two papers under the title of "The

I have rather a strong hope that she may turn out a very useful contributor. I have read several of her papers, and have generally advised her how to make them better. She will have another to follow this with. She has an excellent knowledge of a poor country parish, some very pretty womanly humour, some very good womanly observation, and a decided faculty for writing.

Ever faithfully,
C. D.

[This letter is written on the back of the letter from John Forster which follows. Dickens had an idea of letting Tavistock House on a long lease, and from this Forster and Wills dissuaded him.]

Friday Evening,
Fourteenth January, 1859.

MY DEAR WILLS:—I will no longer doubt that you are right, and I thank you heartily for the affectionate earnestness with which you have represented me to myself, as wrong. Will you, as early as practicable tomorrow morning, communicate to the agent, That I find my daughters so averse to the long term that I must withdraw from that proposal, even if the other party should make it. But that I beg him to complete the Inventory (if it be not already done), and to take the house upon his books, as being to Let from and after next June inclusive, for any term not less than 6 months, or more than 12.

Ever faithfully,
C. D.

Clergyman's Wife" to *Household Words*, January 22nd and 29th. Another paper from her pen was "The Highest Testimonials," in *Household Words*, March 5th.

[From John Forster to Dickens.]

19, WHITEHALL PLACE,
14th January, 1859.

MY DEAR DICKENS :—Lizzie* must judge for herself, and I will not utter a word to influence her. But at once I must say for *my*self that I entertain no doubt whatever that such a step would *most decidedly be very damaging indeed*. With you I say, it is not matter of reasoning so much as of feeling : and I would not have you at this moment do such a thing for 8,000, far less 800 pounds. Do not laugh at this. I feel it very strongly.

Nay, I cannot tell you how I would grieve if you did not give the girls some society at Tavistock House before you think of letting it at all. Only this morning at breakfast I was talking to Lizzie about it, and I must ask her to tell you exactly what I said.

You read in a very masterly way last night, indeed. I was immensely moved altogether by your execution of both pieces of reading.

Always affectionately,
JOHN FORSTER.

TAVISTOCK HOUSE, TAVISTOCK SQUARE,
LONDON, W.C.,
Monday, Eleventh April, 1859.

MY DEAR WILLS :—Wilkie has done a few very good paragraphs for the " Register." † You will have them from him to-day.

---

* Mrs. John Forster.
† The " Occasional Register," a series of crisp paragraphs on matters of current interest, was a feature of the early numbers of *All the Year Round*.

It occurs to me that for that purpose Edmund Yates is likely to be very useful. He reads all the newspapers and periodicals, and is smart. I have told him that you will write to him on the subject. But perhaps the best way will be if you will make an appointment with him—say for today or tomorrow—then shew him the proof and explain the little idea, and see if he can get some paragraphs ready for No. 2. (He will be at the Post Office all today.)

Wilkie has a notion that if he could see what matter we have at the Printers, he might find out for himself what kind of articles would be most useful for No. 2. He will join us at the office at about 2 tomorrow. Will you have your slips there?

If I should find to-day that the St. Alban's business yields any good notion, I will come down to the office early tomorrow morning, and write another short paper for No. I.—to strengthen it. But this is, of course, contingent on there being anything in what I am going to see.

I send with this, for Whiting's, two more weekly parts of the "Tale of Two Cities."

I have just heard from an excellent practical man, that nothing could be better done than our posting in the great towns. At Birmingham particularly it is described as quite wonderful.

Ever faithfully,
C. D.

Gad's Hill Place,
   Higham by Rochester, Kent,
      Thursday, Twenty-eighth April, 1859.

My Dear Wills :—Very glad to get your letter this morning, and to receive the latest possible report of our goings on.

The result of the Whitefriars circulars will be, in the main—as we pretty well know—to heap over them, a vast accumulation of expensive miscellaneous matter.

But, there can be no harm in your writing to as many people as come into your mind, from time to time, some such letter as this,

> "DEAR SIR:—I beg, on behalf of Mr. Charles Dickens, to inform you that if it should be compatible with your engagements to write for this Journal, it would afford him the greatest pleasure to secure your valuable co-operation.
>
> Now, or at any other time, I shall be happy to pursue this subject and to enter into details with you, if you will allow me."

I would send this, *at once*, to both the Trollopes, and to George Eliot, care of Blackwood—with a private seal on the latter letter. I would also address it to Ruffini,* with a note to Mrs. Carlyle, asking her if she can direct the envelope. I would also write to Mrs. Gaskell, referring back to that story she mentioned.

Ever faithfully,
C. D.

GAD's HILL PLACE,
  HIGHAM BY ROCHESTER, KENT,
    Thursday Night, Twenty-Eighth April, 1859.

MY DEAR WILLS:—I write this, for John to bring up in the morning.

---

* Giovanni Ruffini, an Italian refugee and an English novelist: author of 'Dr. Antonio, &c." A slight account of him and a longer one of his brother, Agostino, appears in the late Professor Masson's "Memories of Two Cities," recently published.

It grieves me to hear that you are still so unwell. Pray tell me by next post how you are. I am quite remorseful that you should have had to go down to the Rolls Court.

Hullah's* daughter (an artist, who is here), tells me that certain female students have addressed the Royal Academy, entreating them to find a place for *their* education. I think it a capital move, for which I can do something popular and telling, in the "Register." Adelaide Procter is active in the business, and has a copy of their letter. Will you write to her for that, and anything else she may have about it: telling her that I strongly approve, and want to help them myself.

Do get better,
     And believe me ever,
        Yours,
         C. D.

    Gad's Hill Place,
     Higham by Rochester, Kent,
      Saturday, Thirtieth April, 1859.

My Dear Wills :—I hope and trust you are better today. I cannot tell you how distressed I am to think of your being ill at this time, with its anxieties necessarily upon you.

Referring to the Liverpool newspaper and its Piracy, I find it expressly stated in the Piracy that the act is not to be repeated. I think, therefore, that I should *not* communicate with Ouvry. What I recommend is

---

* John Pyke Hullah (1813—1884), musical composer and teacher of singing. He had, in 1836, composed the music of "The Village Coquettes" to the libretto of Dickens.

your writing to Mr. Whitly, telling him you have received this from me :—

"I received this morning, the Liverpool paper you sent me, and, at first, felt with you the imperative necessity of stopping that injustice. But on looking to Mr. Whitly's introduction of the reprint, I observe that he expressly states that he does not mean to repeat the offence. Under these circumstances I think it would be ungenerous—though I most strongly object to his proceeding—to put him to any expense. And if you will tell him so from me, good-humouredly, I hope the matter may be considered as ended."

Very sorry to hear of Chapman and Hall's confusion. I shall be at Tavistock House again on Monday afternoon.

Ever faithfully,
C. D.

OFFICE OF *ALL THE YEAR ROUND*.
A Weekly Journal conducted by Charles Dickens.
No. 11, Wellington Street North,
Strand, London, W.C.,
Tuesday Evening, Third May, 1859.

My Dear Wills :—All right.

I have corrected Yates's article carefully, and it really is very good. Morley's so so. Also corrected.

Thornbury's* is only this moment come in, and (not having yet read it), I cannot yet say whether it is good or no. I thought Mrs. Blacker's article so very

---

* George Walter Thornbury (1828—1876), novelist, writer of books of travel, &c. He was a frequent contributor to *Household Words*.

good—the Nurse's story so exceedingly well done—that I considered it best to send it to the Printer's at once. I shall not have it for another hour. I will then decide between it and Thornbury's; selecting for this No. the better of the two. I have prepared Whitings for the uncertainty between them.

I send a few letters—thinking I may confuse you, if I answer them myself. Perhaps we had best see the Russian papers referred to in one of them.

I shall see you again tomorrow.

Be quite comfortable. All as right as possible.

Love to Mrs. Wills.

Ever faithfully,
C. D.

Gad's Hill Place,
Higham by Rochester, Kent,
Thursday, First July, 1859.

My Dear Wills:—Very funny indeed, about the amiable Mr. Joyce. What fools they are! As if a mole couldn't see that their only chance was in a careful separation of themselves from the faintest approach or assimilation to *All the Year Round*!*

I am very much relieved by finding that you had Parts enough yesterday. Shall I still write that note to Chapman and Hall? Or issue solemnly friendly summons to council at the office next Tuesday?

Whitings have made a mistake this morning, for which I dare say I am myself mainly responsible, through having used the word "Proofs," instead of "revises."

They have sent me my own soiled and cut-about

---

* An allusion, no doubt, to *Once a Week*, the periodical started by Messrs. Bradbury and Evans after their breach with Dickens.

Proofs of Chapters X., XI., XII., and XIII. What I wanted, was, *fair revises of those chapters.* Will you send round for them, and then post them.

I don't think I am any better to-day. I am rather disposed to feel it in my general health, and am languid and short of starch. Original complaint, much where it was.

Ever faithfully,
C. D.

P. S. I once asked you, or thought of asking you (I cannot recollect which), if you would let the house agent know that I would now let Tavistock House, for not less than 4 months or more than 12? Also that the Stanfield room has been done since he saw it? Also that the house is generally dismantled for the preservation of the furniture, but that he himself knows what its normal state is.

Have you ever done so? If not, will you give him a call when near?

CRIPPLE'S ARMS,
GAD'S HILL PLACE,
HIGHAM BY ROCHESTER, KENT,
Friday, Eighth July, 1859.

MY DEAR WILLS:—A line—to say that I got your letter this morning, and that Wilkie and I have been much delighted by your account of Meredith's[*] Poem. It is too hot to do much, but I am at work, and see the story[†] in a wonderful glass.

Ever faithfully,
C. D.

---

[*] George Meredith had been an occasional contributor to *Household Words*.
[†] "A Tale of Two Cities."

Gad's Hill Place,
 Higham by Rochester, Kent,
  Saturday, Twenty-third July, 1859.

My Dear Wills:—First, as to the agreement. I have had a letter from Ouvry, in which he said that Hobhouse did not see the possibility of making you Sub-Editor in any other way. I told him that as he knew what was meant, he had best explain his difficulties to you—which he seems not to have done.

If the other points about your share and salary, are really as you take them to be, they are wrong, of course. But as to the Title, I must be quite positive and immoveable, and place myself at once beyond the possibility of mistake with you. My design is, and always has been (I have purchased the experience on which I formed it, rather dear) that if I choose to abolish the thing it is abolished, and that the Title is *Mine.* Nothing would induce me to depart from this.

In the matter of petitioning the Court, I quite understood what you had done, but was alarmed by Ouvry's having given them to understand that we had any idea of doing such a thing.

As to Evans—I have some reason to believe that what he reports in reference to Harper's is quite true. I do not think it at all discouraging or surprising, but I believe it to be true.

                              Ever faithfully,
                                         C. D.

Gad's Hill Place,
 Higham by Rochester, Kent,
  Sunday Evening, Sixteenth October, 1859.

My Dear Wills:—I found the enclosed letter marked A with a lot of printed documents, and six pints of eau de Cologne, and two small boxes of eau de Cologne, at Tavistock House last night. Will you return the article, saying that it is not admissible, and that the eau de Cologne awaits his directions.

In reference next to the enclosed marked B.

I have a letter from Poole reminding me that I have not remitted his quarter's pension, and that he is aground for the means of going on. Will you kindly—*at once*—hand the order to Coutts's for its remittance to him by Monday night's post.

My Readings List is on the other side.

The missing letter to you, I posted at the Ipswich chief Post Office, last Tuesday morning about 11.

Will you have the enclosed for Lever posted and prepaid.

Will you remind Whitings that I have not yet seen a Proof of my own No. 6.

Ever faithfully,
C. D.

[In Dickens's handwriting on the back-sheet of the preceding letter.]

Date.	Place.	Address.
Monday, 17th Oct.	Cambridge	Post Office.
Tuesday, 18th ,,	Cambridge	Post Office.
Wednesday, 19th ,,	Peterborough	Railway Hotel.
Thursday, 20th ,,	Bradford	George Hotel.
Friday, 21st ,,	Nottingham	George Hotel.
Saturday, 22nd ,,	Nottingham	George Hotel.
Sunday, 23rd ,,	London	Office.
Monday, 24th ,,	Oxford	Star Hotel.
Tuesday, 25th ,,	Oxford	Star Hotel.
Wednesday, 26th ,,	Birmingham	Hen and Chickens.
Thursday, 27th ,,	Cheltenham	Messrs. Hale & Son, Piano Forte Warehouse.

HEN AND CHICKENS, BIRMINGHAM,
Wednesday, Twenty-sixth October, 1859.

MY DEAR WILLS :—The wonderful thing in your letter is, that you don't say whether Evans has paid any money! I take it for granted that he has paid none, but you don't say so. The rest of the prospects and projects all right.

Great doings at Oxford. Princes of Wales, and what not. Last night there, was as bad a night as ever you saw, but the people really came up nobly. It has rained here ever since last Wednesday—is raining now—is all mud and water—and I do not think it possible that we can have a good room tonight.

I shall come up from Cheltenham in the night tomorrow, and shall be at the office about 1 or 2. Of course you won't come out, or think of coming out, unless and until you are quite well.

Ever faithfully,
C. D.

OFFICE OF *ALL THE YEAR ROUND.*
A Weekly Journal conducted by Charles Dickens.

No. 11, WELLINGTON STREET NORTH,
STRAND, LONDON, W.C.,
Friday, Twenty-eighth October, 1859.

MY DEAR WILLS :—I have read the letter to Evans (which is as plain as a pike staff), and have duly given it out to Johnson to be posted with the account.

We felt the bad weather at Birmingham, though the people did really, under the circumstances, "tumble up" extremely well. At Cheltenham yesterday we had a splendid day and a great go. My share after Arthur's percentage and all the large expenses, was some £70 for the day's work. We came up by the Mail at night—got to town at 5—and even *I* feel a little tired (though really not much) today.

Oxford came out brilliantly. Princes of Wales and the like attended.

I go down to Gad's Hill early tomorrow morning, as it is Katie's birthday. I am not quite sure whether I may or may not propose to defer our making-up till Wednesday. It depends on how long the Forsters stay with us. I will write you again from Gad's Hill, as soon as I know.

Your cold could scarcely be expected to be better, under such trying circumstances of weather. Write me a line tomorrow night to Gad's Hill, and tell me how you are.

I didn't tell Arthur the Printing joke, because I thought it better to keep the name quite close,

      Ever faithfully,
        C. D.

  Gad's Hill Place,
    Higham by Rochester, Kent,
      Sunday, Thirtieth October, 1859.

My Dear Wills :—I say Decidedly *No* to the Stephenson paper—solely on the ground, as to Sidney, that I consider it will be behind the time and after the Fair—as between you and me, on the additional ground that the thing has already been done in *Once a Week* (wretchedly) and quoted in *The Times*—further, that I really do honestly think enough has been said and sung on the subject. *Pay well for the article nevertheless.* Certainly don't use it.

I am glad to hear such good accounts of the cough. I will come up on Wednesday by the Train that arrives at London Bridge at 10 minutes past 10. If I don't find you at the office, or coming to the office, I will come on to your house. It makes not the least difference to me where we make up the No.

All here, including the Forsters and Wilkie, send kindest regard to Mrs. Wills and you.

Ever faithfully,
C. D.

OFFICE OF *ALL THE YEAR ROUND.*
A *Weekly Journal conducted by Charles Dickens.*

No. 11, WELLINGTON STREET NORTH,
STRAND, LONDON, W.C.,
Saturday, Nineteenth November, 1859.

MY DEAR WILLS :—I don't see my way through this letter of Lewis's at all.

I shall be back here at 3 today to meet Alfred. Don't wait for me if you have anything else to do. If you have nothing else to do—why, then I shall find you.

On what strange, sad, errand do you think I am going now? To Highgate, to choose a Grave for— poor Stone,* who died yesterday!

Ever faithfully,
C. D.

---

* Frank Stone, A.R.A., an intimate friend of Dickens, and father of Mr. Marcus Stone, R.A. The son succeeded "Phiz" as Dickens's illustrator. He drew the design for the cover of "Our Mutual Friend."

1860.

Dickens began "The Uncommercial Traveller" in *All the Year Round* of April 21st. These papers continued to appear until 1869.

"Great Expectations" began in *All the Year Round* of December 1st.

In September Dickens finally disposed of Tavistock House to a Mr. Davis, a Jewish gentleman (see letter of September 4th).

On November 1st Dickens and Wilkie Collins started for a tour in Cornwall and Devon, one of their objects being a visit to Clovelly, where the scene of the Christmas story, "A Message from the Sea," was to be laid.

Tavistock House, Tavistock Square,
London, W.C.,
Wednesday, Twenty-eighth March, 1860.

My Dear Wills:—There is not a hope of my doing the "Uncommercial," in time for Saturday's American Mail. When I got home last night, I found a note from the lady with whom my mother lives, who is terrified by the responsibility of her charge and utterly relinquishes it. Consequently I must at once devote myself to the difficult task of finding good hands for my mother, and getting her into them without alarming her, and how this is to be done, and done at once, I am at a great loss to settle.

The "Uncommercial" being announced, I am very unwilling to postpone it as to England. Can we make up the No. without it, for America, and afterwards re-make it up, with it, for this country? I will come to the office in the course of this afternoon.

Ever faithfully,
C. D.

OFFICE OF *ALL THE YEAR ROUND.*
A Weekly Journal conducted by Charles Dickens.
No. 11, WELLINGTON STREET NORTH,
STRAND, LONDON, W.C.,
Monday, Twenty-third April, 1860.

MY DEAR WILLS:—This is only a word, to say that I have received your letter here today and that all is well in the official regions.

When I came to make up the No. I found it impossible to get in the "Eye Witness,"* and was forced to substitute " Friends on all Fours." † I wish you would write the distinguished E. W. a line, explaining that it was driven out at last by impossibility of fitting, and that it is in the following No. I make a rule of never speaking to him on Editorial topics.

I have had a very admirable letter from Mrs. Linton —which shall be yours when you come back.

The newspaper extracts for the current No. I duly made out. I have also read "Warious Gammon" addressed to myself, in the way of contributions, and have returned the same.

It is cold and wretched here, and hails every five minutes. But I always believe Paris to be one of the coldest—and hottest—places on earth. ‡

They are carrying the P. R. interest to such a preposterous height, that I begin to doubt the propriety of inserting " Collars." All depends, of course, upon the treatment. The noble C. has not yet " entered an appearance " with his copy. We adopt that legal phraseology, at our Sporting Houses.

---

* Occasional papers, entitled "Our Eye Witness" at this or the other place or spectacle, began to appear in the first volume of *All the Year Round.* Charles Collins was the author. He was then engaged to be married to Dickens's younger daughter.
† *All the Year Round,* May 5th.
‡ I suppose Wills was in Paris.

With kind regard to Mrs. Wills, in which all at home join.

Ever faithfully,
C. D.

Gad's Hill Place,
Higham by Rochester, Kent,
Thursday, Twelfth July, 1860.

My Dear Wills:—My active and intelligent mind has reverted twice or thrice to the close of that Spirit-article of Mrs. Linton's, and is not quite easy about it. If you will look back to the last paragraph of the paper, you will find it said that after deduction for imposition, lies, and so forth, there remains a "large residuum" of something to be accounted for. I think this wants qualifying. At all events I would take out "large," and let her know it.

In haste,
Ever faithfully,
C. D.

26, Wellington Street, W.C.
OFFICE OF *ALL THE YEAR ROUND.*
A *Weekly Journal conducted by Charles Dickens.*
Late
No. 11, Wellington Street North,
Strand, London, W.C.,
Tuesday, Fourth September, 1860.

My Dear Wills:—Your description of your sea-castle* makes your room here look uncommonly dusty. Likewise the Costermongers in the street outside, and the one Customer (drunk with his head on the table) in the Crown Coffee House over the way in York

---

* Wills was away—at Llandudno, I think.

Street, have an earthy and, as I may say, a Landlubberly aspect. Cape Horn to the best of *my* belief is a tremendous way off; and there are more bricks and cabbage leaves between this office and that dismal point of land than *you* can possibly imagine.

Some demon sprite will somehow have informed you before I write this letter, that Mr. —— has poisoned himself. Frederick Chapman wrote me last night that he had done it " in his father's house." A gloomy professional purchaser of Nos., with a dirty face, whom Johnson presented to me in the shop today as " this young man who is always down in Whitefriars," at ½ past 11 a.m. of this day offered to make oath " wot he dun it in Cre-morne in a bottle o' Soda Water. It wos last Sunday, wot he knowed Mr. Simpson well, and he dun it there." I cannot say which account is correct—probably neither—but the wretched creature is doubtless dead. And when I came along just now from Haverstock Hill the house looked grim and dry, with all the blinds down, brooding in a hot, dusty, tearless, frozen kind of way, at the unsympathetic street. Nothing having appeared in the papers, I suppose strong influence to have been used in that wise, to keep the dismal story quiet. Holdsworth (in a cracked voice and with a great deal more hair on his head than he can possibly govern) said that he, the deceased, " had been laying it at Miss ——'s door for her getting married." God knows whether any blurred vision of that most undesirable female with the brass-headed eyes, ever crossed his drunken mind. Frederick Chapman seemed to think it an extraordinarily unpolite thing that he hadn't waited over tomorrow, " when he knew his brother was going to be married." And that's all I know of the ghastly story.

Coming here from the Station this morning, I met, coming from the Execution of the Walworth Murderer, such a tide of ruffians as never could have flowed from any point but the Gallows. Without any figure of speech, it turned one white and sick to behold them.

Tavistock House is cleared today, and possession delivered up to the new tenant. I must say that in all things the purchaser has behaved thoroughly well, and that I cannot call to mind any occasion when I have had money-dealings with any one that have been so satisfactory, considerate, and trusting.

I am ornamented at present with one of my most intensely preposterous and utterly indescribable colds. If you were to make a Voyage from Cape Horn to Wellington Street, you would scarcely recognise in the bowed form, weeping eyes, rasped nose, and snivelling wretch whom you would encounter here, the once gay and sparkling &c., &c.

Everything else here is as quiet as possible. Business reports you receive from Holdsworth. Wilkie looked in today, going to Gloucestershire for a week. The office is full of discarded curtains and coverings from Tavistock House, which Georgina is coming up this evening to select from and banish. Mary is in raptures with the beauties of Dunkeld, but is not very well in health. The Admiral (Sydney)* goes up for his examination tomorrow. If he fails to pass with credit, I will never believe in anybody again—so in that case look out for your own reputation with me.

This is really all the news I have—except that I am lazy, and that Wilkie dines here next Tuesday in

---

* Sydney Smith Haldimand Dickens, the fifth son. He was born in 1847, entered the Royal Navy, and died at sea in 1872.

order that we may have a talk about the Christmas Number!

I beg to send my kind regards to Mrs. Wills, and to inquire how she likes wearing a hat, which of course she does. I also want to know from her, in confidence, whether

Crwllm festidiniog llynythll y wodd?

Yesterday I burnt, in the field at Gad's Hill, the accumulated letters and papers of twenty years. They sent up a smoke like the Genie when he got out of the casket on the sea-shore; and as it was an exquisite day when I began, and rained very heavily when I finished, I suspect my correspondence of having overcast the face of the Heavens.

Ever faithfully,
C. D.

Kind regard to Mr. and Mrs. Novelli.
I have just sent out for the *Globe*. No news.

Wednesday, Twenty-sixth September, 1860.

MY DEAR WILLS:—Many thanks for your news of Mary, received here this morning. (I mean that illegible proper name for Mary.)

I have both heard from Reade[*] and seen him. There is only one obstacle, and that is a treaty he has with Ticknor and Fields. It is possible the obstacle may be overcome. We must have a talk about it. I have engaged him to dine here *on Saturday in next week at* 6. Will you book it? I write by this post to Wilkie, in order that notice of the Feast may reach him on his coming to town.

---

[*] Charles Reade. I think this is an allusion to a suggestion that Reade should write a novel for *All the Year Round* or join the staff. It was revived later (see letter of January 5th, 1862, *post*).

The Times of this morning having a mention of Ingram's death in the leader, I suppose there is little or no doubt of the fact.

The No. is made up, and the "Uncommercial" is in, and all is right. Will you mention to Mrs. Wills with my kind regard, that I ought to have been born at Peebles,* but (owing to the constitutional perversity of my mother) was not?

Ever faithfully,
C. D.

LISKEARD,
Saturday, Third November, 1860.

MY DEAR WILLS:—We have had two days posting from Bideford here, and have arrived (at a quarter past 3) about half an hour before the going out of the Post. I have not written sooner, because of our having been in inaccessible places. We have now struck the Railway, and, making a little posting expedition from here tomorrow, will be safe in town, I hope, on Monday evening.

We have got everything we want, I think, and have arranged and parcelled out the Xmas No. †

On Tuesday we will make up as usual.

So no more at present from

Yours ever faithfully,
C. D.

Wilkie sends kind regard.

---

* Mrs. Wills, like her brothers, William and Robert Chabmers, was born at Peebles.
† "A Message from The Sea."

1861.

Dickens's second series of public readings occupied most of his time and attention this year. He read in London, at St. James's Hall, during the season, took a short summer holiday at Gad's Hill, and read in the provinces and Scotland in the autumn, the tour being prematurely interrupted owing to the death of the Prince Consort.

3, HANOVER TERRACE,
Monday, Eleventh March, 1861.

MY DEAR WILLS:—I have had a begging letter from that Robert Barrow—a very bad one by the way—with an awful affectation of Christian piety in it—a pretence of having known me and offended me, which is altogether a Lie—and the usual blaring assumption (of which I shall die at last) that I am immensely rich.

If you would not object to see him, I shall be very much obliged to you if you will do so once more, at that same wretched lodging hard by Holborn. He seems to have no idea of my having already relieved him. I wish you would tell him that you have already given him £2 and that you have £3 more in hand; but that you must impress upon him in the strongest manner that he has no hope in making any further appeal to me—that it is quite impossible and monstrous —that I am quite weighed down and loaded and chained in life, by the enormous drags upon me which are already added to the charges of my own large family—and that he must not deceive himself with the notion of my assisting him further. It is very important indeed that he should be got to understand this, quite apart from the question of his own necessities.

I declare to you that what with my mother—and Alfred's family—and my wife—and a Saunders or so—I seem to stop sometimes like a steamer in a storm, and deliberate whether I shall go on whirling, or go down.

Ever faithfully,
C. D.

LORD WARDEN, DOVER,
Sunday, Twenty-sixth May, 1861.

MY DEAR WILLS:—Many thanks for your report of Wilkie, which amused and interested me very much. His quality of taking pains, united to natural quickness, will always get him on. He was delighted with the success, and wrote to me that night before going to bed.

I hope I am really and permanently better. I work here, like a Steam Engine, and walk like Captain Barclay.*

Enclosed, a letter forwarded here this morning.

Ever faithfully,
C. D.

GAD'S HILL PLACE,
HIGHAM BY ROCHESTER, KENT,
Saturday, Thirty-first August, 1861.

MY DEAR WILLS:—I have received your letter this morning, and—not to lose a post—write to you before

---

* Robert Barclay-Allardice (1779—1854) was famed for his powers as a pedestrian. His greatest feat took place in 1809, when he walked 1,000 miles in 1,000 consecutive hours at Newmarket. *Chambers's Encyclopædia* says of him that he "devoted himself to agriculture, cattle-breeding, and the claiming of earldoms."

going to Sheerness for the day with Miss Boyle, Charley Collins, Marcus Stone, and the rest of them.

You will, doubtless, hear from Holdsworth the Brilliant that the Sale keeps up well, and that Bulwer seems so far to succeed capitally. In the making-up, I find Morley very helpful indeed—always there early on the Wednesdays, always ready with his proofs and scheme, and always prepared for any kind of alterations on my part. The two Nos. we have made up since you left are very good indeed. In last Wednesday's make-up, is a paper which I have called " Four Stories,"[*] by Gleig's fair friend. They are Ghost Stories. The first (by far the best) is a remarkably good and original one. I nearly rewrote them all. In the same making-up, we had the " Cinque Ports." But I was so disgusted by the preposterous homage to the Palmerston nonsense in *The Times*, and with the base flunkeyship of *Punch*, that I told Morley to take the article out again and for ever cancel the same. The Solicitor employed by the Minister for Saxony in that suspected Murder case, has written me a very intelligent letter, to say that it was an exceedingly curious case of circumstantial evidence, where there was always a destructive and more or less quashing circumstance to oppose to the suspicious circumstance; and that he believes he could write an interesting picture narrative of it. I have replied that with fictitious names, and with no assumption of the prisoner's innocence, and no championing of either side, I shall be glad to have it. Sala has offered a heap of rubbish by some brother of his at Southampton, which I have declined. Spicer writes to know whether his " Polly " is Burked or is to appear? I have

[*] *All the Year Round*, September 14th.

replied, Is to appear 'twixt this and Christmas. He also mentions (his letter is addressed to you) that he has not been paid for " The First of April."* I have paid him therefore. All else goes on regularly and well—perfectly well.

From Frederick Chapman concerning "Great Expectations," I have a note this very morning. There are only 90 copies left of the Third Edition, and we are going to Press with the Fourth.

I work every day for two or three hours on my Readings. Have a very considerable hope that "Copperfield" will do a great deal in London. Am hopeful of seeing Arthur [Smith] soon; who has been ill at Worthing, but is better. Charley † has been here, and is going to start in business for himself on the First of October. He stayed here a week, and looked very much the better for it. Cricket came off, and the " Governor " your present correspondent got a hit high over the apple tree, for which he scored three, and which covered him with glory. C.H.O.R.L.E.Y. ‡ was here before starting for Spain, and walked—with me at my pace—two and twenty miles, without appearing in the least the worse for it. At which I stood amazed, and have ever since remained in that attitude.

The weather here is perfect, the beauty of the country marvellous, and the harvest abundant. My old enemy, that infernal bushel of wheat, will have a great deal to say for himself in the Money Market shortly, I suppose.

* *All the Year Round*, March 30th, where the title is " A Very Likely Story."
 † His eldest son.
 ‡ Henry Fothergill Chorley, musical critic of the *Athenæum*, writer of novels and libretti for operas.

I stick to my prediction that the people of the North (in America) will neither raise the money nor the men required by the Government; and that an ignoble and contemptible compromise will be made soon.

I wish you were in some hostelry, with more *comfort* about you. My belief in the efficacy of comfort is very great. I am rather disappointed that you didn't go to Chamounix from Geneva, and come down to Martigny, and then go to the great St. Bernard, and then over one of the great Passes. But I know that "Our Bore" always found the places his friends had omitted to visit, to be the best places in the Universe.

You don't mention how many ancient cripples are in Miss Coutts's party. I can imagine —— and Co. toddling sinuously up and down the ten thousand stairs of the Gibbon—which the natives pronounce Jibbone—and corkscrewing themselves down the stony-hearted ways to the Lake.

Frank* shall have your remembrance when he comes home to-night. His holiday dates from Monday next I believe.

This is all my news, and little enough. Mary, Katie, Georgina, and all, unite with me in kind regard to Mrs. Wills and to you.

     Ever, My Dear Wills,
      Faithfully yours,
       C. D.

GAD'S HILL PLACE,
 HIGHAM BY ROCHESTER, KENT,
  Friday, Twenty-fifth October, 1861.

MY DEAR WILLS:—Bulwer, in a note I meant to have enclosed herein but have inadvertently destroyed,

---

* Francis Jeffrey Dickens, his third son.

asks, " Would it be very inconvenient to set up and print off the whole of 'Strange Story' * from No. 20 to the End. In that case I could give the final revises up to No. 19. But the revise of No. 20 necessitates the survey of all the numbers that have gone before." I have told him that I think we can do it—that I write to you—and that you will stir up the printer and tell him about and when he may expect. He writes from Marine Parade, Ventnor.

Ever faithfully,
C. D.

Miss Power is going to Alexandria, and no doubt wants all the money she has earned, or can earn.

Was she paid for "Things I Can't Stand"?

And was she paid for the poem now in type? I forget its name.

Will you let her have a cheque, at once, for anything we may owe her. She is here.

ANGEL HOTEL, BURY ST. EDMUNDS,
Wednesday, Thirtieth October, 1861.

MY DEAR WILLS :—I do not remember accurately (though I have a general impression) what was done at the office before, concerning John, when he was away with me. But I wish whatever was done before to be done now. His salary from the Readings is paid by Headland.

It may save some discomfort hereafter if I beg you not to allow my old servant to be the subject of any kind of officiousness on the part of Holdsworth or Johnson. I have lately observed a little thing or two

---

* Lytton's "A Strange Story" began in *All the Year Round*, August 10th, 1861, and ended in the issue of March 8th, 1862.

in that direction, not at all consistent with my notion of my supremacy. And I have not noticed it, because I could possibly take no notice of it but one final and conclusive one.

We opened ill at Norwich. (There had been great mismanagement, but perhaps poor Arthur's illness* may have had to do with it.) We had not a good hall, and the audience were heavy, and put me out of sorts. Last night was brilliant, and I think "Nickleby" tops all the readings in its astounding Go.

We are full here for tonight.

Ever faithfully,
C. D.

Gad's Hill Place,
Higham by Rochester, Kent,
Sunday, Third November, 1861.

My Dear Wills :—Excellent work both at Ipswich and Colchester. I start again tomorrow morning from here.

It is "Copperfield" at Brighton on Thursday evening. Let me know whether I am to expect you. Dinner hour, 4. We hear of a great Let at Hastings, but know nothing yet of Brighton. Probably we shall find this time, as poor Arthur and I did last, that the first reading in a place where there are more readings than one, is invariably the poorest Let.

I was amused by a letter in *The Times* yesterday (though it was unnecessary and ill-natured) about Bulwer. When I looked over the proceedings in Fenwick's first examination and subsequent release (which were very wrong), I particularly wrote to him:

---

* Arthur Smith died early in this month. Dickens had had a last interview with him on September 28th.

"Whatever you do, remember that under the English criminal law, nothing can be done without the accused. The accused *must be* present." He wrote back, saying that he quite understood that, and would not forget it.

There was a rush at Colchester, in which John was nearly swept into space. The rest were obliged to dive at him, and drag him out of the crowd.

Ever faithfully,
C. D.

Lord Warden Hotel, Dover,
Wednesday, Sixth November, 1861.

My Dear Wills :—I have received your letter here this morning, and the satisfactory account, but *not* the proof. What have you done with Robert Lytton's "Dead Pope"? There can be no doubt, you know, of its being far better than any make-weight.

The Brighton "fixture" stands thus :

Thursday evening,	"Copperfield."
Friday evening,	"Nickleby" and "Trial."
Saturday afternoon,	"Copperfield."

There was a tremendous storm here yesterday, so that all that side of this house which fronted the gale had to be emptied of guests. The sea was prodigiously high, and the uproar deafening. Between 4 and 5 in the afternoon, the wind shifted to the north, and it became fine. We had a great squeeze at night, and turned away money. Room small, but not ill-constructed. Audience, most capital — faultless! There was a ditto audience at Canterbury, where they took "Copperfield" most delightfully.

From Hastings we have a telegram that they have

sold for tonight nearly 300 stalls ! We go over there, at noon.

Ever faithfully,
C. D.

Queen's Head, Newcastle-on-Tyne,
Friday, Twenty-second November, 1861.

My Dear Wills:—I am horribly afraid that Headland* has broken down, and I want you to take the trouble to go round to St. Martin's Lane—see Johnson the Printer—and ascertain if you can, how this state of things that I am going to describe has been brought about.

Observe first of all, that the posting bills, shop-bills, &c., sent off by Johnson for this place, all in one parcel—and (necessarily) *to* this place, were for days and days "lost." At last they were found to have been sent by Johnson to the place of reading—the hall—instead of to the local agent, where they had been lying in some vault or other, and might have lain there until Doomsday. This had previously occurred at some other place—I forget which—I think Ipswich—but it is not material; at some place, indubitably.

When I come here, I find, to my astonishment that I am announced on Saturday to read " Little Dombey " and the " Trial "—which I had no notion of doing, having given directions to Headland to put up " Copperfield " for Saturday : well knowing that " Copperfield " of last night would make Saturday's—" Johnson's mistake," he says.

I begin to read at Edinburgh on *Wednesday.* This

---

* His manager for the readings.

morning comes a letter from the agent there, with the dismal news that he has not got the bills, tickets, and so forth—in a parcel from Johnson again—known to have been sent somewhere!—and that whereas all Edinburgh ought to be now acquainted with everything that is going to be done, nothing whatever is known. Conceive this, and I beginning on Wednesday! Moreover, he has one of our printed cards of the Edinburgh course in his possession, and on that printed card there is *no morning reading of " Little Dombey "*—which I had given out to Headland and knew would be very valuable. Again he says, " Johnson's mistake." But I cannot readily make out how Johnson can be always making mistakes now and never made them before. This is what I want you kindly to ascertain from him.

I do not know what is to be done. It is too plain that the business is most awfully mismanaged, and I cannot see my way to putting it right. I am so perfectly helpless in the matter: having my own hard work in it to do, and having of course supposed all these things to be done already. I have detached Berry to Edinburgh—he is off directly—but I do not believe that anything he can do, can now make that place what it ought to have been. I have instructed him to go on to Glasgow, and put everything right there. I have scarcely a doubt that everything is wrong.

Here, the local Agent of course complains that he was absolutely powerless when he ought to have been busiest—that when Jenny Lind was here, and he was sending her circulars out, and ought to have been sending mine he had none to send, had no notion what I was going to do, could answer no enquiry. We had a most enthusiastic audience last night for

"Copperfield"—but in numbers they were about half what they should have been and would have been.

If all these rooms at all these places in the List were not taken, I would not go on. But the mischief is, that I *must* go on.

Bulwer's proof enclosed.

Ever faithfully,
C. D.

King's Arms Hotel, Berwick-on-Tweed,
Sunday, Twenty-fourth November, 1861.

My Dear Wills :—Just a line to say that I received yours here this morning, and thank you for it. We have done extremely well at Newcastle, and made a very remarkable impression beyond all doubt. Berry telegraphed from Edinburgh that he had got the bills and was issuing them in all proper directions—afterwards from Glasgow, ditto, ditto. Gordon writes from Edinburgh that he "thinks no harm has been done." This must of course be taken with a qualification; but he had been to Wood's, and seemed to have earnestly looked about him. Of course he is waiting for me as a comrade.

This is a dull place for a long Sunday, and as I have no book (no, *not one*—I forgot to buy one yesterday, through going to look at the Pitmen as they came from work), I think I shall learn your account of the "Octoroon." Before beginning to learn it, I send you on the other side my list for the Xmas No. as well as I can remember it.*

Will you write to the enclosed man in confidence, saying that I am away in Scotland?

* This has been torn off.

This seems a most extraordinary place to read in, and one would think it contained nobody to read to; but I believe the sale of tickets is quite surprising, considering the town. I don't know the details yet, and don't want to know them ; for I was up at 5, and have exerted myself very much, at Newcastle. I mean, please God, to do the same in Edinburgh—where I begin with "Copperfield," and hope to make a great effect—in the beginning, intellectually—in the end, pecuniarily.

Ever faithfully,
C. D.

WATERLOO HOTEL, EDINBURGH,
Thursday, Twenty-eighth November, 1861.

MY DEAR WILLS :—A brief report, for I was not well in the night and am out of sorts today.

We had in the hall last night exactly double what we had on the first night last time. "Copperfield," beyond all possibility of doubt, a wonderful success here. The impression on the audience, without precedent in the reading chronicles. Four rounds when I went in—laughing and crying and thundering all the time—and a great burst of cheering at last. They lost nothing—not the minutest detail —and I almost think it would have been better to have done "Copperfield" every night.

I do not return the proofs of the No. as I doubt my ability to get through them today. I will try fresh air instead. Bulwer's proofs enclosed, are (he says) "not for press, but for final revision—to be sent to me and then returned for press."

Ever faithfully,
C. D.

WATERLOO HOTEL, EDINBURGH,
Sunday, First December, 1861.

MY DEAR WILLS:—Blazes of triumph! Immense turn-away. Cram yesterday morning (almost unprecedented in the morning), and general Go of Readings really indescribable.

They write from Glasgow this morning for "more tickets."

In your last, when you write of Mrs. Linton, you say nothing of the book on the American Union in Morley's hands. I hope and trust his article will be ready for the next No. made up. There will not be the least objection to having two American papers in it.*

I am rather tired. For I read twice yesterday and took unusual pains.

Ever faithfully,
C. D.

CARRICK'S ROYAL HOTEL, GLASGOW,
Tuesday, Third December, 1861.

MY DEAR WILLS:—From a paragraph, a letter, and an advertisement in a *Scotsman* I send you with this, you may form some dim guess at the scene we had in Edinburgh last night. I think I may say that I never saw a crowd before.

As I was quietly dressing, I heard the people (when the doors were opened) come in with a most unusual crash; and I was very much struck by the place's obviously filling to the throat within five minutes. But I thought no more of it, dressed placidly, and

---

* In *All the Year Round* of December 21st there were two American papers:—"American Disunion" and "An English-American Sea Duel," the latter being an account of the fight between the *Shannon* and the *Chesapeake*. The former was, evidently, by Morley. It was followed up by another, entitled "The Morrill Tariff," in the next issue.

went in at the usual time. I then found that there was a tearing mad crowd in all the passages and in the street, and that they were forcing a great turbid stream of people into the already crammed hall. The moment I appeared, 50 frantic men addressed me at once, and 50 other frantic men got upon ledges and cornices, and tried to find private audiences of their own. Meantime the crowd outside still forced the turbid stream in, and I began to have some general idea that the platform would be driven through the wall behind it, and the wall into the street. You know that your Respected Chief has a spice of coolness in him, and is not altogether unaccustomed to public speaking. Without the exercise of the two qualities, I think we should all have been there now. But when the uproarious spirits (who, as we strongly suspect, didn't pay at all) saw that it was quite impossible to disturb me, they gave in, and there was a dead silence. Then I told them, of course in the best way I could think of, that I was heartily sorry, but that this was the fault of their own townsman (it was decidedly the fault of Wood's people, with maybe a trifle of preliminary assistance from Headland); that I would do anything to set it right; that I would at once adjourn to the Music Hall, if they thought it best; or that I would alter my arrangements and come back and read to all Edinburgh if they would. (Meantime Gordon, if you please, is softening the crowd outside, and dim reverberations of his stentorian roars are audible.) At this there is great cheering, and they cry, "Go on, Mr. Dickens. Everybody will be quiet now." Uproarious spirit exclaims, "We *won't* be quiet. We won't let the reading be heard. We're ill-treated." Respected

Chief says, "There's plenty of time, and you may rely upon it that the reading is in no danger of being heard until we are agreed." Thereupon good-humouredly shuts up book. Laugh turned against uproarious spirit, and uproarious spirit shouldered out. Respected Chief prepares, amidst calm, to begin, when gentleman (with full dressed lady torn to ribbons on his arm) cries out: "Mr. Dickens!"— "Sir."—"Couldn't some people, at all events ladies, be accommodated on your platform?" "Most certainly." Loud cheering. "Which way can they come to the platform, Mr. Dickens?" "Round here to my left." In a minute the platform was crowded. Everybody who came up, laughed, and said it was nothing when I told them in a low voice how sorry I was; but the moment they were there, the sides began to roar, because they couldn't see! At least half the people were ladies, and I then proposed to them to sit down or lie down. Instantly they all dropped into recumbent groups, with Respected Chief standing up in the centre. I don't know what it looked like most — a battle field — an impossible tableau — a gigantic picnic. There was one very pretty girl in full dress lying down on her side all night, and holding on to one leg of my table. So I read "Nickleby" and the "Trial." From the beginning to the end they didn't lose one point, and they ended with a great burst of cheering.

Very glad to hear that Morley's American article is done. Rather fagged today, but not very. So no more at present. Ever faithfully,
C. D.

Will you reply to enclosed letter.
200 Stalls let here for tonight.

CARRICK'S ROYAL, GLASGOW,
Friday, Sixth December, 1861.

MY DEAR WILLS:—I enclose three letters. On two I have endorsed the kind of reply I want sent. The third is in your way and speaks for itself.

It rained last night—and came on at 6 o'clock too—sheets of water. Under which adverse circumstances you will be concerned to hear that we had only one thousand eight hundred and sixteen persons in the Hall, and that the night's receipts were only one hundred and eighty-six pounds, nine shillings!!!

Ever faithfully,
C. D.

WATERLOO HOTEL, EDINBURGH,
Sunday, Eighth December, 1861.

MY DEAR WILLS :—Before I can answer or consider Bulwer's letter that you enclosed me this morning, I must have proofs of the rest of his story. Will you send them on to me when ready?

Glasgow finished nobly, and last night here was signally successful and positively splendid.

Mary and Georgina arrived punctual to the minute, and send you their kindest regard.

Will you give my small Admiral, on his personal application, one Sovereign? I have told him to come to you for that recognition of his meritorious services.

Ever faithfully,
C. D.

CARLISLE,
Wednesday, Eleventh December, 1861.

MY DEAR WILLS:—No to the Poem. There is no good in it; it is conceited and morbid; directly counter to the spirit of the Xmas No. The man who talks of himself as "the poet" is really not to be endured in this age—especially when he isn't one.

I don't like —— either. Exactly for the reason which has led to our leaving Xmas alone in the Xmas No. we should avoid it—if we can—in the regular No. I put in that saving clause, because you *may* have nothing else by you. But I don't like it, and would rather have something else.

It is scarcely possible to make less of Mr. Spence's book than Morley has done.*

Costello very amusing. Lever extremely dangerous in places. I have taken out the most dangerous—and really unfair—bits. Look to it again in the Revise.

Carlisle has done its best, and crammed its room (a sort of cellar, and very mouldy) twice. One would not have expected it in this place, but it is indisputable that they took "Copperfield" last night as well as the Edinburgh people. We go on to Lancaster at 1 today.

    Kindest regard,
      Ever faithfully,
        C. D.

The Proofs returned separately.

   VICTORIA HOTEL, PRESTON,
    Friday, Thirteenth December, 1861.

MY DEAR WILLS:—The news of the Xmas No.† is indeed Glorious, and nothing can look brighter or

---

* Mr. Spence's book on the American Union is mentioned in the last paragraph of the article entitled "American Disunion," *All the Year Round*, December 21st.

† "Tom Tiddler's Ground," to which Dickens contributed the first, sixth and seventh chapters.

better than the prospects of the Illustrious Publication.

Both Carlisle and Lancaster have come out admirably, though I doubted both, as you did. But, unlike you, I always doubted this place. I do so still. We have a hundred stalls let, but it is a poor place at the best (you remember?) and the Mills are working half-time, and trade is very bad. The expenses however will be a mere nothing. The accounts from Manchester for to-morrow, and from Liverpool for the Readings generally, very cheery indeed.

The young lady who sells the papers at the Station is just the same as ever. Has orders for tonight, and is coming, "with a person." "*The* person?" said I. "Never *you* mind," said she.

I was so charmed with Robert Chambers's "Traditions of Edinburgh" (which I read *in* Edinburgh), that I was obliged to write to him and say so.

Kindest regard from the Ladies.

Ever faithfully,
C. D.

Adelphi Hotel, Liverpool,
Sunday, Fifteenth December, 1861.

My Dear Wills:—I sent you a Telegram today, and I write before the answer has come to hand.

I have been very doubtful what to do here. We have a great Let for tomorrow night. The Mayor recommends closing tomorrow, and going on on Tuesday and Wednesday; so does the Town Clerk; so do the Agents. But I have a misgiving that they hardly understand what the public general sympathy with the Queen will be.[*] Further, I feel personally

---

[*] The Prince Consort had died on the previous day.

that the Queen has always been very considerate and gracious to me, and I would on no account do anything that might seem unfeeling or disrespectful. I shall attach great weight, in this state of indecision, to your Telegram.

A capital audience at Preston. Not a capacious room, but full. Great appreciation.

The scene at Manchester last night was really magnificent. I had had the platform carried forward to our "Frozen Deep" point, and my table and screen built in with a Proscenium and room Scenery. When I went in (there was a very fine hall), they applauded in the most tremendous manner; and the extent to which they were taken aback and taken by storm, by "Copperfield," was really a thing to see. It was a most signal and remarkable success.

The Post closes early here on a Sunday, and I shall close this also, without further reference to " a message from the "—W. H. W.—being probably on the road.

Radley is ill, and supposed to be fast declining, poor fellow. This House is crammed. The assizes on. And Troops perpetually embarking for Canada, and their officers passing through the Hotel.

Kindest regard.

Ever faithfully,
C. D.

1862.

At the beginning of the year Dickens resumed his interrupted readings and continued them until February, when he came to London. From March until June he gave a series of readings in St. James's Hall.

At the end of October he went to Paris, taking with him his sister-in-law, Miss Hogarth, and his elder daughter, Mamie. In the middle of November Wills joined them there for a short visit. He had been charged by Miss Coutts to carry a box of flowers to the Empress Eugénie at Compiègne—Dickens refers to this as "your Imperial charge" in a letter of November 7th—and in a letter to Mrs. Wills, which I printed in "Memories of Half a Century," he gives an account of how he accomplished his mission, and adds, "here I am in the middle of the Christmas number, writing this between whiles as Dick goes over his proofs." My father and mother joined the Dickens party in Paris. I have a memento of their visit in the shape of a *carte* of the "Café Voisin," on which are written in pencil these words, "19th Nov. 1862.—In grateful memory of a wonderful dinner at the "Café Voisin," from [here follow the signatures] Nina Lehmann, Charles Dickens, Georgina Hogarth, Frederick Lehmann, W. H. Wills, Mamie Dickens." This was sent to Mrs. Wills in London. This was, no doubt, the "Restaurant Dinner," for which Wills, in the letter of November 11th, was requested to "bring treasure" with him.

[To the second paragraph of this letter Wills has appended the following note in pencil:—"It would gratify me to see this passage in print. The whole is worth publishing, I think."]

AT THE BIRMINGHAM STATION,
Thursday, Second January, 1862.

MY DEAR WILLS:—Being stranded here for an hour, on my way from Leamington to Cheltenham, I write to you.

Firstly to reciprocate all your cordial and affectionate wishes for the New Year, and to express my earnest hope that we may go on through many years to come, as we have gone on through many years that are gone. And I think we can say that we doubt whether any two men can have gone on more happily and smoothly, or with greater trust and confidence in one another.*

Secondly: As the Proofs reached me yesterday at Leamington, where I had a double day, I was not able to look at them. I have eyed them on the Railway today, but necessarily in a cursory way. Look to the Russian paper for clearness. In Robert Lytton's poem —at the end—the word "both" is used as applied to several things. The word "all," with a slight alteration in the pointing, will express what he means.

Keep articles which *will* have the first person singular, inveterately, as wide asunder as you can.

Birmingham is in a very depressed state, with very few of its trades at work. Nevertheless we did extremely well here. At Leamington yesterday, immense. "Copperfield" in the morning absolutely stunned the people: and at "Nickleby" and the "Trial" at night, they roared and roared until I think they must have shaken all the air in Warwickshire.

Faithfully ever,
C. D.

ROYAL HOTEL, PLYMOUTH,
Sunday, Fifth January, 1862.

MY DEAR WILLS:—I couldn't answer your letter about Reade † until I had it. *Could* I now?

He seems to me, to be the best man to be got for our purpose. But I think his terms will be rather

---

* The first two paragraphs of this letter are printed in "Letters," II., 171; but the rest of the letter there printed is made up of a letter dated April 5th of this year (see *post*).

† This refers, I think, to the suggestion that Charles Reade should join the staff of *All the Year Round*. His novel, "Very Hard Cash," began to appear in the issue of March 28th of the following year.

higher than yours. Seeing that we shall not be paying Wilkie's salary then, I think you might at once (if you saw it to be necessary) go up to five and twenty pounds a week. But he *may not* be used to such receipts as I suppose. I would decidedly pursue the idea, with the intention of getting him, as the best man to be got. No doubt he would be glad to work with me. I believe he has a respect for me.

I shall be here until after post time on Wednesday morning, and at Torquay until after post time on Friday morning. Any word from you concerning Reade, by letter or telegram, shall be answered immediately.

(His singing, I know. Very innocent and harmless.)

Your heavy debt here shall be paid in full. I doubt the judiciousness of Frank's taking a ticket for a month, because, unless I am mistaken, he will be a week of the time in London. But I suppose three weeks' single tickets might have cost him as much too. I ought to have written to him about it. Will you tell him with my love, that I have been too busy.

Macready's amazement at "Copperfield" really was something to see. He told me, with the tears running down his face, that "as a piece of art it—-er—laid him on his—er—back; and that as a piece of passion and pathos and playfulness, it—er—well!—there was nothing to be said about it. N—no, Dickens, Nothing!"   Ever faithfully,
C. D.

Torquay,
Wednesday, Eighth January, 1862.

My Dear Wills:—First, as to the No. I return all the proofs in which I have made marks—pencil marks, because done on the Railway. There is only one in Murray's (poor) and all the rest are in the American story. I conclude "John Ray" to be out, as I see so much matter over. I hope he is out, because he is the dreariest of the dreary.

Your account of the wretched business (which I have sent to Forster) made me roar with laughter at Plymouth this morning and then inspired me with a sort of pity—though the fellow is as poor and mean a Hound as lives.

I think you remember that I did not approve of your townsmen when I was last there?* We had one good night, and one bad one. The bad one was last night. But I perfectly bowled them over and over and over too:—it was "Copperfield." Plymouth is a bad place for any such purpose, with a room I hate, in a perfectly inaccessible position.

Good Lets here, but a very small room. The room at Exeter also, is small.

Delighted to find that we start fair with *All the Year Round* again.

Reade, good. I would give him what he asks, holding him to a certain space within which the story shall be comprised. Ever faithfully,
C. D.

OFFICE OF *ALL THE YEAR ROUND*.
A Weekly Journal conducted by Charles Dickens.

No. 11, WELLINGTON STREET NORTH,
STRAND, LONDON, W.C.,
Wednesday, Twenty-second January, 1862.

Dick bets Stanny that "Masaniello" was produced, AS AN OPERA, at Drury Lane Theatre thirty years ago;

* Plymouth.

reference is supposed to be had to the date of the year, without reference to months.

The bet is, a dinner for four at Greenwich, Richmond, or elsewhere, for the party present, that is to say:

>Stanfield.
>Dickens.
>Wilkie Collins.
>Wills.

Witnesses:
Wilkie Collins. C. STANFIELD.
W. H. Wills. CHARLES DICKENS.

[Wills has added in pencil, "I think C. D. lost, for 'Masaniello' was produced as a *ballet*."]

RADLEY'S ADELPHI HOTEL, LIVERPOOL,
Wednesday, Twenty-ninth January, 1862.

MY DEAR WILLS:—I have gone over the Proofs. In the 1st Vol. of *Household Words*, Morley did a paper (from my books and suggestions), or two papers, concerning Pirates. As I see in Spicer's article, several cases that I know to be in the same books, just glance back at Morley and see that there is no repetition.

The longer Charley Collins's paper is, if it be really good, the better. I was going to telegraph to you by all means to keep the No. open for it, if I had not had the information contained in your note of this morning. It would be quite thrown away and lost, if it were delayed.

I think you had best pay B. and E's cheque at once to my account at Coutts's.

I come up from Chester in the night tomorrow.

Another tremendous cram here last night; and everything let, out and out, for tonight.

Ever faithfully,
C. D.

Adelphi Hotel, Liverpool,
Tuesday, Twenty-eighth January, 1862.

My Dear Wills :—The 12th of February will suit me perfectly.

A tremendous cram here last night, and a great turn-away.

My suggestions to Wilkie * as to altering what he has done, were very slight indeed; because he *cannot* alter it in any essential particular. They went mainly to the warning that it must inevitably come to pass that the more severely and persistently he tells the story, unrelieved by whimsical playing about it, the more he will detract from the steadiness and inflexibility of purpose in the girl. Contrast in that wise is most essential. She cannot possibly be brought out as he wants to bring her out, without it.

"Under a Cloud" was one of my names on my list, but I did not send it to Wilkie because it has a semi-slang-acceptation that is dead against it and makes it small.

Ever faithfully,
C. D.

16, Hyde Park Gate, South,
Kensington Gore, W.,
Saturday, Fifth April, 1862.

My Dear Wills :—A little packet will come to you to-day from Hunt and Roskell's : almost at the same time, I think, as this note.

---

* Wilkie Collins's novel, "No Name," began in *All the Year Round,* March 15th, this year.

The packet will contain a Claret Jug.* I hope it is a pretty thing in itself for your table, and I know that you and Mrs. Wills will like it none the worse because it comes from me.

It is not made of a perishable material, and is so far expressive of our friendship. I have had your name and mine set upon it, in token of our many years of mutual reliance and trustfulness. It will never be so full of wine, as it is to-day of affectionate regard.†

Ever faithfully yours,
CHARLES DICKENS.

GAD'S HILL PLACE,
HIGHAM BY ROCHESTER, KENT,
Sunday, Fourteenth September, 1862.

MY DEAR WILLS :—I have received yours from the shores of Lethe, and expect you to come back in the fat and rank condition of the Weed that rots upon the Wharf there.

It will be a convenience to me to make up 2 Nos. on Thursday (subject, of course, to any substitution in the second, of a better or more appropriate paper, if any should come in), and towards this end, I shall appear with a host of proofs.

Trollope's story is *exceedingly good;* highly picturesque and full of interest. But he mars the end by over-anticipating it, and I have changed it there, a good deal.

I think Lever will be fair:—at any rate I will take

---

* This claret jug, fashioned in silver after the model of an Etruscan jug, is now in my possession, having been bequeathed to me by Mrs. Wills.

† This letter is printed in "Letters," II., 171; but it is there given as forming part of a letter dated January 2nd of this year (see *ante*).

good care that he is not foul. Have ready for me, all that is come of his narrative.

You will be perhaps a little surprised (and not disagreeably) to learn that I have done the opening and end of the Xmas No. (!) * and that I mean soon to be at work on a pretty story for it. I think what I have done is exceedingly droll, and new. Circular letter to contributors, for said No. enclosed.

After the astounding and brilliant intelligence of "Somebody's Luggage" being already on and off the anvil, I leave you to take breath—if you can, in your (necessarily) breathless admiration of

Yours,
Ever Illustriously,
C. D.

GAD'S HILL PLACE,
 HIGHAM BY ROCHESTER, KENT,
  Wednesday Night, Fifteenth October, 1862.

MY DEAR WILLS:—I am to be at Boulogne on Sunday to meet Mary and Georgina, and I hope to post you from thence my corrections in the proofs for next Wednesday's make-up.

Wilkie has been thrown into a state of inexpressible enthusiasm by "His Boots." † He is rather knocked up by the bye. Don't seem to know it, for he is nervous. I have told him to have no fear of failure, for if he should break down, I would go on with his story so that nobody should be any the wiser!

Poole's receipt enclosed.

What on earth *can* you be going to Skibbereen for?

---

 * "Somebody's Luggage." Dickens wrote for it four chapters and a portion of another.
 † One of Dickens's chapters in "Somebody's Luggage."

I am glad you put in Morley's waste-article.* I thought it very good. Is he getting on with the Laboratory one?† It would be well-timed soon after this poisoning case.

      Faithfully always,
        CHARLES DICKENS.

HAZEBROUCKE, FRANCE,
Friday, Seventeenth October, 1862.

MY DEAR WILLS:—Without waiting until I get to Boulogne, I make up my parcel of corrections here *en route*, and will post it somewhere or other, when I have got the last proofs in.

I find "Princely Travel in America" and "An Old Country Town" among my proofs. I presume you returned them to me in mistake? It is because I find them, that I write to you sooner than I intended. They are enclosed.

Both the enclosed printer's lists are wrong. Each of them contains an article—"What's the use of that" —which is already used. If the list be not kept correctly while I am away, we shall get into great difficulty.

It is absolutely impossible to put in "Our Last Attempt"‡ until Lever has corrected the proofs. I have spent a couple of hours on it, but there is scarcely one single name accurately printed. And I am not sufficiently acquainted with some of the names to know even what is meant. It must positively stand over until you have got corrections back from Lever, or we shall be ridiculous. In its place, insert

---

* I think this is "Victoria's Ironsides" (October 11th), an impeachment of the waste caused by our dockyard system.
† "The Modern Alchemist," December 22nd.
‡ "Our Last Attempt," in *All the Year Round*, November 8th and 15th.

"Only One Room"*—cut down from my corrected proof (I corrected the paper some time ago) to the length you want.

The Poem is very good. I can see nothing at all in the Persian paper. I hope its successors may be better.

As I have leisure for adventure before meeting Mary and Georgina, I am now going to have a look at Dunquerque—in the "Uncommercial" † interest. And by the bye I must say that I find the French fortified town in "His Boots" to be amazingly accurate. I have been lazily checking it off at two old Vauban-defended towns since I came over yesterday.

Ever faithfully,
C. D.

Paris, Rue du Faubourg St. Honoré, 27,
Friday, Twenty-fourth October, 1862.

My Dear Wills:—First as to Miss Parr's story. It is very pretty, and *decidedly accepted*—but whether for the Xmas No. or no, I cannot yet positively say. Because the best of the papers that come in must be taken for that, and some *may* come in that would fit better both to the *general* idea and the demand for variety in the contents.

I don't much like the scheme for the next No., it looks so excessively patch-worky. But I will go carefully over it and the printer's list, in good time for Wednesday.

The "Foray in the Ballad Country," I think may be distributed.

---

* November 29th.
† "The Uncommercial Traveller" papers which Dickens was writing in *All the Year Round.*

Pay Miss Power, and also for her sister's "At Home at Panama."

I find the enclosed two *A.Y.R.* papers among my letters brought away from England. I have nothing else.

We have a most elegant little apartment here; the lively street in front, and a splendid courtyard of great private hotels behind, between us and the Champs Elysées. I have never seen anything in Paris, so pretty, airy, and light. But house rent is fearfully and wonderfully dear.

High upon the Boulevard, the old group of Theatres that used to be so characteristic is knocked to pieces, and preparations for some amazing new street are in rapid progress. I couldn't find my way yesterday to the Poste Restante, without looking at a Map!—I suppose I have been there, at least 50 times before. Wherever I turn, I see some astounding new work, doing or done. When you come over here for the Xmas No. (as I think you must!) you shall see sights.

Ever faithfully,
C. D.

Love to Frank.*

PARIS, RUE DU FAUBOURG ST. HONORÉ, 27,
Tuesday, Fourth November, 1862.

MY DEAR WILLS:—I find that my means of suggesting the contents of the next No.† are extremely limited, for I have proofs only of "Windbags"—"Under the Black and Yellow"—"The Shamrock," and some of the "Persian Papers."

---

* His third son.

† The number of November 22nd.

"Windbags" may go in; but call it
"Critical Bulls
In Historical China-Shops."

"The Shamrock" is just nothing at all, and really not worth inserting. "Under the Black and Yellow" will just do, but will not more than just do, because the writer always does the same thing and rides somewhere to save somebody. When it goes in, observe (besides looking it well over for the pointing) that "vetturi*no*" in the fourth paragraph, ought to be "vetturi*ni*"; and that "Ingleseo" at the bottom of the same slip, ought to be "Inglesi." But I think that for this No. Sala's "Bleeding Diamond" (out of the question for the Xmas No.) may be better than "Under the Black and Yellow." I would put it last.

I should like a Natural History sort of article in the middle of the No. Unless I am mistaken, "Down from the Clouds" has not yet gone in? That would do very well. If you have Morley's Laboratory paper in connection with the Poisoning question, by all means get *that* in, and don't delay it. (I wrote to Morley last Wednesday, telling him to hold over the "English Convict's Progress," because I have never seen the paper, and it is a subject on which I have written strongly.)

Therefore you have in hand

    "No Name."
    "Down from the Clouds."
    "Critical Bulls in Historical China-Shops."
    Perhaps Morley's article on the Poison-Test Laboratory.
    "Legend of the Bleeding Diamond."
    "Persian Papers."

Taking "No Name" for the beginning, and "The Legend of the Bleeding Diamond" for the end, and following "No Name" with "Critical Bulls"—or, if the varying of foreign subjects with English should render it more advisable, with "Persian Papers" (not overmuch of them)—take Morley (if you have him), or "Down from the Clouds" for the middle, and so make up. On no consideration put in any Poem that I have not seen. When I come upon a strange Poem in print and publication, my distress is abject.

According to my Diary, Monday the 17th is the day for making up the Xmas No. As soon as you know for certain when you will come over, let *me* know. It will be a very difficult making-up, because I have written 20 pages (I suppose), and already there must be no end of Xmas Nos. got and getting, into type, and generally the things run long. But I read every paper as soon as it comes here, and keep myself well primed about them all, to make selection easier by and bye.

Will you ask whether my watch has come to the office from Hunt and Roskell's? And if not, will you send there for it? It went to have a new spring, and in the meantime they lent me one which goes like the Clown's in a Pantomime.

Ever faithfully,
C. D.

Paris, Rue du Faubourg St. Honoré, 27,
Friday, Seventh November, 1862.

My Dear Wills:—We certainly are getting the columns up, to an amazing extent! But I cannot release any of the matter until you come, because the Xmas No. can only be made up, on a careful comparison of the relative merits and possibilities of the best things we have.

Let me know whether, when you arrive, you propose to come straight *here*. If so, we will try to get you a bedroom close at hand, and I think we can do it without difficulty at a clean little hotel over the way. But if your Imperial charge should involve your going to any other Hotel at first, then let me know as much, so that we may not provide for you in vain. I will ask you to bring my watch, and perhaps a pair of trousers; but on this head, more in due course.

I saw the advertisement yesterday, at the top of Olliffe's *Times*.

(— And I am again revolving restlessly, Australia in my head!)

Ever faithfully,
C. D.

PARIS,
Tuesday, Eleventh November, 1862.

MY DEAR WILLS:—Will you tell Mrs. Linton that, in looking over her admirable account (most admirable) of Mrs. Gordon's book, I have taken out the references to Lockhart, not because I in the least doubt their justice, but because I knew him and he liked me. And because, one bright day in Rome, I walked about with him for some hours when he was dying fast, and all the old faults had faded out of him, and the mere ghost of the handsome man I had first known when Scott's daughter was at the head of his house had little more to do with this world than she in her grave, or Scott in his, or small Hugh Littlejohn in his. Lockhart had been anxious to see me all the previous day (when I was away on the Campagna), and as we walked about I knew very well that *he* knew very well, why. He talked of getting better, but I never saw him again. This makes me stay Mrs. Linton's hand, gentle as it is.*

Next as to your coming. In order that you may be over the way, just opposite (an immense convenience compared with having to go round to the Rue de Rivoli or elsewhere) I have taken you a room for a week from next Thursday. On Saturday morning, unless you advise me to the contrary, you will find it ready for you, and a good fire there. We will breakfast here at half past 9. Observe: *Your* number is 38 Rue du Faubourg St. Honoré; *ours* is 27. The No. of your room itself is 7. Your house is called "The Hôtel St. Honoré."

Bring treasure with you, because I think *A.Y.R.* must stand a Restaurant Dinner, and a Box at the Play.

Also will you bring me, if you conveniently can, the following articles:

1. Cash for the enclosed cheque, in gold.
2. My watch.
3. The Nos. of *A.Y.R.* from No. 182 inclusive.
4. A pair of new trousers from Skinners my Tailors, if John has received such a parcel since I left.

Your idea of our title being taken hold of by "sharks and pirates" (see "Larboard Fin"†) had also come into my head, and when you wrote to me, I was going to write to you!! I wonder the reeling brain of Holdsworth bears all this pressure. But its weakness (excessive) is probably its strength.

* This paragraph is printed in "Letters," II., 207, as part of a letter of December 20th, 1863.
† Another allusion to the imaginary drama, the authorship of which was imputed by Dickens to Wills.

I write all that concerns tomorrow's make-up on the other side, in order that you may have it by itself for reference.

For your guidance when you come over, I enclose a list of the Xmas No. papers, received from Birtles this morning. I have put a mark X against *all the papers that have come to me.*

Faithfully ever,
C. D.

[This is part of the preceding letter.]

Concerning No. 188.

I cannot take your make-up as it stands, because two of the papers included in it, are perfectly unknown to me; and at least one of them—"A French Soldier"—is on a very important subject indeed. Because I have convinced myself in my French wanderings this summer, that the French Soldier is being improved, in a most alarming manner, every day, and that ours is at least a century behind him.

You will understand from the foregoing, that I have no proof of "A French Soldier," or of "A Clear Title to Land." If the latter be a useful article (as I suppose), some such make-up as this, would be the best.

"No Name"	14¾
"John Wilson"	9
"A Clear Title to Land" or "At Home at Teheran" } say	5
"Small Beer Chronicles"	9½
One of Mr. Harwood's stories, reduced to the cols. wanting.	

I think "A Cheap Passage Home" is the best of his Stories. I have no corrections to make in "Virgilius the Enchanter," so that too is available.

Paris,
> *Friday, Twenty-first November,* 1862.

My Dear Wills:—I see that Mrs. Gaskell *has* put a name to her story—at the end, instead of the beginning—which is characteristic. The addition of one word will make it a striking name. Call the story

"A Dark Night's Work."

—and don't confound it with a cold night's work: which you must have had last night.

You got to London safe and sound, and found Mrs. Wills ditto ditto? All send kindest regard. The breakfast-corner looked quite unfurnished this morning when I went in, without you and *Galignani*.

Ever faithfully,
C. D.

Paris,
> *Tuesday, Twenty-fifth November,* 1862.

My Dear Wills:—With the alteration I am going to mention, I prefer the enclosed make-up.

It is not a No. strong enough for Ollier's Poem (which is maudlin), if anything can be put into its place. What I should like best, would be to get in some reasonably good *prose* article, after Murray; getting the excess it would occasion, out of the "Cotton" paper.* I see no such article in the List, but perhaps you may have one in MS. Something light and pleasant in that place—and no poem—would be a great improvement.

It is not worth while my posting the proofs this time; I go on to add all I have to say respecting them.

* "State and Prospects of Cotton," December 13th.

Take out of Murray anything "swell"—such as the word "shindy," or any similar yaw-yawdom. Take out his last paragraph, touching his gallant steed, altogether.

In cutting the "Cotton" paper to such dimensions as you can find room for, take nothing out of the first slip. Because the Manchester School deserves all the schooling it can get, touching its reduction to the grossest absurdity of the supply-and-demand dogmatism, and its pig-headed reliance on men's not going to war against their interest. As if the vices and passions of men had not been running counter to their interests since the Creation of the World!

Miss Edwards I have done.

"Fire" had best be distributed—paid for, of course. It is a mere dilution—and a very dry one—of a very well-known paper in *H. W.*

If Spicer is in town, couldn't he do a droll paper representing himself, a Londoner, as having—say seven—quiet visitors from the country (Rule Britannia Britons every one of them, regarding other Empires and States as in mere outer darkness); and giving the particulars of their all being knocked down, garrotted, choked, robbed, and half murdered, in one day? Or Mr. Halliday might do such a thing.

The more I think of "Never Say Die," the less I like it. There is no weight in it, and it is weakly open to all kinds of joking. Something more expressive of No Surrender would be better. Something like "Thorough"—"True to the Death"—"Onward"—"Firm as a Rock"—"Perseverance"—"Nailed to the Mast"—"True to the Colours"—would be more like it, if I understand the intention.

I mean to cross over on Friday afternoon, so as to

get all Saturday in town. I want to see about Frank's* prospects and other things. Will you tell John to have ready for my dinner, at 6 on Friday, a bit of fish and a nice *little* joint of mutton, and will you tell him that Edmund Yates will probably dine with me. I shall expect the honor of Frank's company, of course (please tell him), unless he is otherwise engaged.

Ever faithfully,
C. D.

PARIS,
    Thursday, Fourth December, 1862.

MY DEAR WILLS:—I am so apprehensive of some pervading mistake (which may involve other things) having been made at the office about the Xmas No. that I send you another letter today, to let you know *that no presentation Xmas No. has arrived here.* We have none, Lady Molesworth has none, Lady Olliffe has none. I have sent round this morning to make sure of the fact. It has made me rather ridiculous, as they besieged me for the No. on my return, and I had brought none, in order that I might not confuse the office arrangements. But this is nothing: the grave thing is the break-down of three packets—which suggests thirty—or three hundred—or three thousand.

Ever faithfully,
C. D.

Since writing the above, I have seen Lehmann. He too has none.

* His third son.

GAD'S HILL PLACE,
　　HIGHAM BY ROCHESTER, KENT,
　　　　Saturday, Twenty-seventh December, 1862.

MY DEAR WILLS:—I should very much like to help Miss Power to publish her "Pictures from Egypt," if I could. As well as I can make out, it will form a good octavo volume about 6/- or 7/-. Will you mind asking Sampson Low if he would treat for it? He can see the MS. of course, and I shall have it on Monday. I would give him a good title for it, if he bought it. Miss Power wants to set her mind at rest about the book as soon as she can. Of course Low may know that I am interested in it.*
　　　　　　　　　　Faithfully always,
　　　　　　　　　　　　C. D.

1863.

At the beginning of this year Dickens again went to Paris for the purpose of giving readings at the British Embassy on behalf of a charity. He left Paris on February 5th, and after a ten days' tour went home. Later on he gave another series of readings in London at the Hanover Square Rooms.

　　　　HOTEL DU HELDER, PARIS,
　　　　　　Sunday, Eighteenth January, 1863.

MY DEAR WILLS:—Your Thursday's letter did not arrive here until after post time on Friday night. Therefore I could not answer it until today.

I am in a mess with "A Dark Night's Work,"† for

---

* Writing to Miss Power on February 26th, 1863 ("Letters," II., 194), Dickens tells her he has found a "first-rate title" for her book:—"Arabian Days and Nights."

† Mrs. Gaskell's story. It began in *All the Year Round,* January 24th.

I find it difficult to understand where we are. Follow me with the eye of your mind.

The 3rd portion—consists of chapters 7 and 8.

The 4th portion begins with the printed slip, numbered 27. Turn the slips over, until you come to the one numbered 32. At the end of the first paragraph, after the words "happened at a sadder time," insert *Chapter X.*—which will then begin, "Before the June roses were in full bloom." Turn on again until you come to slip numbered 34, and stop that portion at the end of the first paragraph on it, after the words "except Dixon, could have gone straight to her grave."

The 5th portion will begin, "Chapter XI. In a few days Miss Monroe obtained." The story must be altogether, in 6 portions, and I will send you the dividing of the two last, tomorrow.

The Reading here last night was a most tremendous and brilliant success, paling all——*

PARIS,
Monday, Nineteenth January, 1863.

MY DEAR WILLS:—Looking at your letter again and finding a Make Up in it, I think it best to confine my today's attention to the Proofs you want. You will find them enclosed and corrected. In another letter you will find Robert Lytton's Poem, to which I say decidedly Yes, as being novel and picturesque.

I cannot bear the notion of the "Academy for Cooks" going next to "Illiberal Doctors."† Lytton's Poem would be far better there, or the article (not returned,

---
* The rest of this letter is missing.
† *All the Year Round*, February 7th.

for I see nothing to change in it) called "Giving Up."*

"A Dark Night's Work," concluding portions, I also sound [send].

Horne *could not*—no, even Horne could not—have chosen a more wonderful subject for his Lecture.

The Reading here so stuns and oversets the Parisians, that I shall have to do it again. Blazes of Triumph!

All proofs on hand here shall follow presently. (Take out the "Academy for Cooks"; don't forget.)

Ever faithfully,
C. D.

PARIS,
Wednesday, Twenty-first [January], 1863.

MY DEAR WILLS:—As I shall have an opportunity of sending over what proofs I have, by hand, so that you may get them about Saturday, I put them up now. I am chased out of Paris by enthusiasm, and shall not come back for some five days.

"How we began the War" I keep back, because *it won't do*: it is so dismally out of date. Nor can I point "Rule Britannia"† better than I have done. In all our years of work, I never saw such an intolerably slovenly paper, as "Our Village on the Mediterranean."‡ Look well to the revise, for I have made more correction than there is proof. The more I think of Reade's story the more I think that "Very Hard Cash," or "As Safe as the Bank"—one of the two—would be a capital title.

---
* *All the Year Round*, February 7th.
† This was rechristened "Very Free and Very Easy," and appeared in the issue of February 21st (see letter of February 4th, *post*).
‡ *All the Year Round*, January 31st.

I have no more important news than the astounding intelligence that John * has *no British prejudices!*

Ever faithfully,

C. D.

How were the Surrey Hounds when last heard of?

PARIS, HOTEL DU HELDER,
Thursday, Twenty-ninth January, 1863.

MY DEAR WILLS:—I knew—and I think I mentioned in the letter accompanying them—that you would not get these proofs until after an interval. But as they did not press, I thought it useless to forego the safe and slow opportunity. I am very sorry that "Our Village on the Mediterranean" went in *without* my corrections. It was so horribly in need of them.

You did beyond all question perfectly right in Harper's matter. For my part, I think the gain at the best, not equal to the loss. The perpetual sliding away of temporary subjects at which I could dash with effect, is a *great* loss.

From —— (not one of the wise men of the East, or any other quarter of the compass), I have a letter about what could be done for us in the printing way, at what low charges, by—if I remember the name right—Harrison's house. It will keep till I come back. It is curiously appropriate to your uneasiness in that regard.

I will turn to at the proofs as soon as the Readings are over. The first at 10 francs is tonight; the second, tomorrow night. I believe everything is let out. Imagine my being so entirely out of "Dombey," that I

---

* John was his servant.

have been obliged to go down this morning and rehearse it in the room!

Many thanks for your consideration in the matter of the boys' fares. But Alfred's will be a short spell, and I hope the money is well spent.

The rise, I take to be consequent on the Xmas No. So no more at present from

Yours ever faithfully,
C. D.

P.S.—*Except* that you had best do with "A Dark Night's Work," the best you can—always trying to begin a chapter where I have begun one, and subdividing afterwards, *if you can*. Write me a line by tomorrow (Friday) night's post, if you have anything you think it necessary to suggest or ask, respecting the said "Dark Night's Work."

The title for Reade is decidedly a good one.

HOTEL DU HELDER, PARIS,
Sunday, First February, 1863.

MY DEAR WILLS:—As to the No.*—"Street Terrors" I have already seen. Do., "Before the Trial by Combat." "From the Life of Horace Vernet" all right, except that "I said," should be "I have said," towards the bottom of slip 2. "Small Beer Chronicles" I return herewith corrected. "A Cheap Passage Home" I corrected long ago. Herewith I return all slips of "A Dark Night's Work" that have marks of mine upon them. The rest I retain and destroy, to save postage.

John will be back in London next Thursday night. He shall bring with him, corrected ready for use, all the proofs I have, or may have, here.

* *All the Year Round*, February 14th.

Then observe my movements,—which involve the necessity of Gad's Hill impatience (if it be impatient) being curbed yet a little while. I too shall leave here on Thursday, and shall take about a ten days' tour. Then I shall return for good, and come straight to the office. As I don't want to fix myself to any particular place during the ten days, I do not know that I can give you any reasonable idea where to address me. Therefore will you write to me *here* concerning the next No. *so that I may get your letter before John leaves me, and answer it per John aforesaid.*

Never was anything like the last Reading here. Never, Never, Never!

Murmurs of Kinglake's book * have crossed the water. If he ever comes to Paris, he will have a trifle of fighting on his hands.

Ever faithfully,
C. D.

Please report how we are going.

Hotel du Helder, Paris,
Wednesday, Fourth February, 1863.

Ourselves and *A. Y. R.*

My Dear Wills:—I send by John, with this, all the miscellaneous proofs I have. To wit, "Skin Deep,"† (called originally, "Sontorio and His Theories)," "Small Beer Chronicles," "Some Curious Lights," ‡ (called originally "Light-Bearing"), "Dress in Paris,"‡ (done with great fidelity from a book I have been reading here, and which everybody here reads, because it has been

---

* "The Invasion of the Crimea," the first portion of which, containing severe criticisms of Napoleon III., appeared this year.
† Appeared February 21st.
‡ Appeared February 28th.

suppressed), "Fur Hunters,"* and "What a Bad Hand"; the last named article to be remorselessly distributed, and given to any of the four winds of Heaven that will accept it. I have omitted to mention "Voltaire's Heart," † but that I also send.

For the most part, I think these articles are better than those you mention in your letter received this morning; excepting "Rule Britannia."—which you call by its old name, forgetting that I have rechristened it, "Very Free and Very Easy."‡

Make the last No. of the Volume and the first No. of the Volume as strong as you can.

A most noble month's balance certainly!!!

In re Frank.

Perhaps it would be a damaging thing, suddenly to withhold from him money that he expects. Therefore I would give him his month's three pounds—with a caution that the Settling Day is near at hand, and that I shall soon be home.

Myself and Paris.

It is really the general Parisian impression that such a hit was never made here. The curiosity and interest and general buzz about it are quite indescribable. They are so extraordinarily quick to understand a face and gesture, going together, that one of the remarkable points is, that people who don't understand English, positively understand the Readings! I suppose that such an audience for a piece of Art is not to be found in the world. I wish you could have seen them—firstly, for my effect upon them—secondly,

---

* Appeared March 14th.
† Appeared March 21st.
‡ Appeared February 21st.

for their effect upon me. You have no idea what they made of me. I got things out of the old "Carol"— effects I mean—so entirely new and so very strong, that I quite amazed myself and wondered where I was going next. I really listened to Mr. Peggotty's narrative in "Copperfield," with admiration. When Little Emily's letter was read, a low murmur of irrepressible emotion went about like a sort of sea. When Steerforth made a pause in shaking hands with Ham, they all lighted up as if the notion fired an electric chain. When David proposed to Dora, gorgeous beauties all radiant with diamonds, clasped their fans between their two hands, and rolled about in ecstasy. They took the storm as if they were in it. As to the "Trial," their perception of the Witnesses, and particularly of Mr. Winkle, was quite extraordinary. And whenever they saw the old Judge coming in, they tapped one another and laughed with that amazing relish that I could hardly help laughing as much myself. All this culminated on the last night, when they positively applauded and called out expressions of delight, out of the room into the cloak room, out of the cloak room into their carriages, and in their carriages away down the Faubourg.

Of course, if I had gone on, I could have made a great deal of money. But I thought the dignified course was to stop. I could not reconcile myself to the notion of making the charitable help, the stepping-stone. So, for the present, I have done here.

Does it strike you, however, that there is nothing against taking advantage of the general notoriety of this unusual success, in London? Would you, if you were I, go on at St. James's Hall as of yore? If you should be *quite satisfied* on this head—not otherwise—

would you write for me to Blockheadland* (Sussex Hotel, Eastbourne) telling him that I shall be back for good, within a fortnight, and that I want him to be prepared with six or nine evenings for choice, about once a week, or two within eight days, and holding to the old Thursdays, if possible? Beginning about the end of the month. Of course he is to understand that he commits me to nothing until he has seen me at the office.

I leave here tomorrow morning long before post time.

Ever, My Dear Wills,
Faithfully yours,
C. D.

GAD'S-HILL PLACE,
HIGHAM BY ROCHESTER, KENT,
Monday, Fourteenth September, 1863.

MY DEAR WILLS:—As I am sending over to Rochester tonight, and as I got your note before dinner, and as you will perhaps be glad to have a line from me, and as the local post will probably let you have it in the course of a week or so, I send these lines:

To report that Charley Collins sends assurance of his "Mechanical Horse" † arriving in a hand-gallop, and that I jobbed up an "Uncommercial" and sent *Revise* to Birtles today per messenger, and that I have begun the Xmas No., and that the title is:

"MRS. LIRRIPER'S LODGINGS."

—I am going to do "Mrs. Lirriper," and hope to

---

* See letter of November 22nd, 1861, note.
† *All the Year Round*, October 3rd.

make something of her. I think the title is a good one?

Kind regard to Mrs. Wills.

Ever affectionately,
C. D.

My poor mother died quite suddenly at last. Her condition was frightful.

GAD's HILL PLACE,
HIGHAM BY ROCHESTER, KENT,
Sunday, Twentieth December, 1863.

MY DEAR WILLS :—I am clear that you took my cold. Why didn't you do the thing completely, and take it away from me? For it hangs by me still.

I have restored Spicer's incident (sending the proof and insertion straight to Birtles), and have also written to Spicer and told him what is curious to me —that he does not in the least suspect why I took it out. I did so, *because it tells his story.* His main incident is gone—disclosed to any sharp reader—the moment that passage is read. It occurs in the first portion.

Mrs. Lirriper is indeed a most brilliant old lady. God bless her!*

I am glad to hear of your being "haunted," and hope to increase your stock of such Ghosts pretty liberally.*

Ever faithfully,
C. D.

I shall be at the office on Wednesday morning from ¼ before 11 to 12.

---

* These two paragraphs are printed in "Letters," II., 207, with an interpolated paragraph taken from a letter of November 11th, 1862.

1864.

During this year Dickens was at work on "Our Mutual Friend," the first monthly number of which appeared on May 1st. Mr. Marcus Stone was the illustrator.

From February to June he was in London, at 57, Gloucester Place, Hyde Park, after that at Gad's Hill.

Gad's Hill Place,
Higham by Rochester, Kent,
Friday, Eighteenth March, 1864.
57, Gloster Place.

My Dear Wills :—I hope you won't send the price of Brandy up, for I want to buy a cask.

Yesterday I went to the office and wrote to Morley, about the No. begging him to send me the Proofs here. For I have given a meeting to Forster today, who wants to see me. All is right and straight, no doubt. We will take counsel together (I can come to you any day in the afternoon, mind) when Lilie's estimate comes in. The office at present is simply hideous.

I send you the first 3 Nos. of " Our Mutual Friend." When you have done with them let me have them again, as they contain my marks for the Printer.

Edmund [Yates] wrote to ask me what I thought of his going to the Volunteer night attack and defence in Kent. I told him he might try it*

Ever faithfully,
C. D.

---

* The original of this letter is written on black-edged paper. Dickens's second son, Walter Landor, a lieutenant in the 42nd Highlanders, had died in India on December 31st of the previous year. The news reached Dickens only on February 7th.

OFFICE OF *ALL THE YEAR ROUND.*
A Weekly Journal conducted by Charles Dickens.

No. 26, Wellington Street,
Strand, London, W.C.,
Saturday, Second April, 1864.

My Dear Wills:—I hope you are deriving benefit from the sea—and the shore—and the young ladies on horseback—and the Jews—and the riding masters—and the schools—and the gallant seamen who never do what England expects of them, in the least.

As next week will not be my working-time at "Our Mutual Friend," I shall devote the day of Friday (*not* the evening) to making up here. Therefore I write to say that if you would rather stay where you are, than come to London, *don't come.* I shall throw my hat into the ring at 11, and shall receive all the punishment that can be administered by two Nos. on end, like a British glutton.*

Ever,
C. D.

Gad's Hill Place,
Higham by Rochester, Kent,
Friday, Fifteenth April, 1864.

My Dear Wills:—By all means. Any time after 3 on Wednesday afternoon. But don't you think you had best come and dine here, and make up the No.? The office is the Abode of Desolation.

There was no letter of mine to Thackeray about the

---

* This paragraph is printed in "Letters," III., 218, but is wrongly incorporated in a letter dated October 16th, 1864.

Yates matter (that I can remember), but one—and *that* was published at the time, in Yates's pamphlet.*

I hope John will get his voice on the margin of the sounding deep.

— But Lord bless you, you have no idea of what I said, from those wretched accounts. I hate the thought of anybody's reading them.

Kindest regards to the Ladies.

Ever faithfully,
C. D.

We'll have a bet on " Our Mutual Friend," when we meet.

GAD'S HILL PLACE,
HIGHAM BY ROCHESTER, KENT.
57, GLOSTER PLACE, HYDE PARK GARDENS,
Sunday Evening, Eighth May, 1864.

MY DEAR WILLS:—You have heard, I daresay, of the deplorable condition of poor John. His life still hangs on a hair, but there seemed a shade of hope this afternoon. I am going out to him again tonight. Beard is really a Guardian Angel to him.

But it is not to say this, that I write; but to tell you that that diabolical wife *and her sister*, being left last night to watch him, got blind drunk together on Gin—omitted everything they had undertaken to do—dropped Gin and God knows what over his poor dying figure—and pitched into the landlady and attendant

---

* A reference to his controversy with Thackeray about Edmund Yates's expulsion from the Garrick Club. Yates had in a published article commented on Thackeray—both were members of the Garrick—in a manner which the latter resented. Thackeray brought the matter before the committee of the club, who expelled Yates. Dickens, thinking expulsion too severe a penalty, took Yates's part, and Thackeray was annoyed at his interference. There was a reconciliation between them before Thackeray's death.

gossips when with natural indignation they found them this morning and took their gin away. John was then doubled up, his knees to his head, sinking out of life. And so Beard found him. Of course we take care that he is not left to those amicable mercies any more.

Pray have this made known in its fullest atrocity to everybody at the office, and let everybody be strictly charged never on any pretence to let the woman into the house. If she wants anything out of the house, the children must come for it, or she must go without it; but she is never to be let in. And pray let them understand that we would immediately discharge anybody who—even in mistaken compassion, or for any other mistakenly good reason—disobeyed this injunction. I tumbled her out of the sick chamber just now, and will at least (John lost or saved) have done with that abominable wretch.

I find that she has been perpetually drunk ever since they have been to Kentish Town. I hope to deposit her (with the Lord's help) in Kentish Town Station House yet!

Ever,
C. D.

GAD'S HILL PLACE,
HIGHAM BY ROCHESTER, KENT,
Friday, Twentieth May, 1864.
57, GLOSTER PLACE.

MY DEAR WILLS:—The statement is indeed astounding, and no doubt expresses in every figure that goes to make up every result, your incessant vigilance and care in every department of *A. Y. R.* business. This I feel strongly, and am thoroughly well assured of.

When we get into our places again, and often meet at the office, we must dive into that question of the falling-off. Of course we have to consider that Sala's is not a good name, and that he is accustomed to address a lower audience. I am inclined to believe that an anonymous story depending on its own merits would be better for us than he.

We must drink a glass of wine together tomorrow, to the next balance sheet.

Ever faithfully,
C. D.

Gad's Hill Place,
Higham by Rochester, Kent,
Sunday, Twenty-sixth June, 1864.

My Dear Wills:—I have carefully gone over all the Proofs, and here they are. The No. as it stands is a very fair one indeed.

I have complied with all the necessary forms about Mrs. Austin's* pension, and am Circumlocutionally apprised that on application at the Paymaster General's Department I shall "receive the necessary instructions as to obtaining the first payment." Will you instruct whosoever goes about Poole's pension *after the 1st of July*, to make enquiries? I hope there may be arrears to receive.

You will get proof of "Our Mutual Friend," No. VI., in a note from Townshend. As I shall want it on my return, please have it ready for me in an envelope on my table. I expect to be at the office on Thursday the 7th or Friday the 8th at latest.

I have been working desperately hard to get away. It has occurred to me that the next "Mrs. Lirriper"

---

* Dickens's sister, widow of Henry Austin.

might have a mixing in it of Paris and London—she and the Major, and the boy, all working out the little story in the two places. As my present Mysterious Disappearance is in that direction, I will turn this over on French ground with great ease. I seem to have a sort of inspiration that may blend the undiminished attractions of Mrs. Lirriper with those of the Babelle life in Paris.

                                   Ever,
                                   C. D.

[To Mrs. Wills.]
        GAD'S HILL PLACE,
            HIGHAM BY ROCHESTER, KENT,
                Sunday, Seventh August, 1864.

MY DEAR MRS. WILLS:—I am exceedingly relieved by your account of the invalid which came to hand this morning. I read it aloud at breakfast, to the great gratification of an attentive audience, and it made so great a sensation that you really might have thought him rather a popular personage! Yesterday I had it in my mind, somehow, that he was not so well, and was in two minds whether to stay quiet here, or come or send.

Will you tell him with my love that I shall *try* to work at my book (for I can't do it in this heat, though I make believe every day) until well on in the week —say Friday, when I shall of course be ready to do all office needful. Also, that I am producible there, at any time, day or hour. Also, that I have gone over Mrs. Sartoris's* story carefully, and sent her

---

* Adelaide Kemble, younger daughter of Charles Kemble, married Edward John Sartoris in 1843. She was famous as a singer. Her "A Week in a French Country House" appeared in the *Cornhill,* and was published in book-form in 1867.

for correction my marked proofs. Lastly, will you congratulate him on his nurse, and tell him that like the Americans I " defy cre-ation " to produce a better.
Believe me always,
Faithfully yours,
CHARLES DICKENS.

GAD'S HILL PLACE,
HIGHAM BY ROCHESTER, KENT,
Saturday, First October, 1864.

MY DEAR WILLS :—I wrote to Holdsworth yesterday about the fire, saying that I hoped you would not go up to town and that I would be at the office on Monday morning. However you went, and did all. It is much to be regretted that we could not take —— to Bow Street. In the case of so nefarious an offence there really is a duty to be done to Society—though I am almost afraid to use the phrase : it is so horribly abused. It is curious that I anticipated the facts here, on receiving the news.

I don't like "Bees" as a subject: having had my honey turned into Gall by "Bee Masters" in *The Times.* I think I have a better paper—a musical one—of Chorley's. I will see to it the first thing on Monday and will see Morley. All next week (except Thursday) I expect to be at the office.

"Mrs. Lirriper" is again in hand. I have flown off from the finish of No. IX. of "Our Mutual," to perch upon her cap. I hope to make way apace with her at the office.

You asked me for Plorn's address. Here it is :
The Rev. W. C. Sawyer,
Cambridge House,
Tunbridge Wells.

I hope and trust you are by this time getting better. Set yourself up for the Xmas No. campaign, and don't come back too soon.

Kind regard to Mrs. Wills,
Ever yours,
C. D.

OFFICE OF *ALL THE YEAR ROUND*.
A Weekly Journal conducted by Charles Dickens.
No. 26, WELLINGTON STREET,
STRAND, LONDON, W.C.,
Saturday, Eighth October, 1864.

MY DEAR WILLS:—Pray let me know how the leg comes out. I am very anxious to be informed that it's " only " a boil !

I have gone through the No. carefully, and have been down upon Chorley's paper* in particular, which was " a little bit " too personal. It is all right now, and good, and them's my sentiments too of " The Music of the Future."

" Mrs. Lirriper " † will be in your arms, I trust two or three days hence. I have enjoined Birtles to the greatest caution in setting it up, and have told him to lock up the type and pull no proof but on a written instruction from me. I have done the opening paper (longer than the last, I fancy), and am now knocking off the couple of pages or so for the end. I am something the worse for work, and have an idea of going to the sea for a day or two about Friday next. But I shall be here until further notice.

Ever faithfully,
C. D.

* Presumably " Old, New, and No Music," in *All the Year Round*, October 22nd and November 5th.

† " Mrs. Lirriper's Legacy," the Christmas number.

LORD WARDEN HOTEL, DOVER,
Sunday, Sixteenth October, 1864.

MY DEAR WILLS:—I was unspeakably relieved and most agreeably surprised to get your letter this morning. I had pictured you as lying there waiting, full another week. Whereas Please God you will now come up with a wet sheet and a flowing sail,—as we say in these parts.

My expectations of "Mrs. Lirriper's" sale, are not so mighty as yours. But I am heartily glad and grateful to be honestly able to believe that she is nothing but a good 'un. It is the condensation of a quantity of subject and the very greatest pains.

George Russell knew nothing whatever of the slightest doubt of your being elected at The Garrick. Rely on my probing the matter to the bottom, and ascertaining everything about it, and giving you the fullest information in ample time to decide what shall be done. Don't bother yourself about it. I have spoken. On my eyes be it.

Wilkie sends kindest regard. Ditto Georgina. Mrs. Wills included in all remembrances.*

Ever, My Dear Wills,
Affectionately yours,
C. D.

GAD'S HILL PLACE,
HIGHAM BY ROCHESTER, KENT,
Wednesday, Thirtieth November, 1864.

MY DEAR WILLS:—I found the beautiful and perfect brougham† awaiting me in triumph at the

---

* This letter is printed in "Letters," III., 218, but in place of the last paragraph it has a paragraph transferred from a letter of April 2nd, 1864.
† A present from Wills.

station when I came down yesterday afternoon; Georgina and Marsh both highly mortified that it had fallen dark, and the beauties of the carriage were obscured. But of course I had it out in the yard the first thing this morning, and got in and out at both doors, and let down and pulled up the windows, and checked an imaginary coachman, and leaned back in a state of placid contemplation.

It is the lightest and prettiest and best carriage of the class, ever made. But you know that I value it for higher reasons than these. It will always be dear to me—far dearer than anything on wheels could ever be for its own sake—as a proof of your ever generous friendship and appreciation, and a memorial of a happy intercourse and a perfect confidence that have never had a break, and that surely never can have any break now (after all these years) but one.

Ever your faithful,
CHARLES DICKENS.

1865.

Dickens was in London from March to the end of May, when he went to France for a short holiday. On his way home, on June 9th, he was in the railway accident at Staplehurst. He refers to this in the letter of June 13th. At the end of August he took another trip to France.

During a great part of the year he was working at "Our Mutual Friend," the last number of which was issued in November. The Christmas number of *All the Year Round* was "Dr. Marigold's Prescriptions," Dickens contributing to it three portions and part of another.

The letter of March 17th refers to Wills's nonelection to the Garrick Club. He had been proposed by Dickens and seconded by Wilkie Collins. On Wills's rejection they both resigned membership of the club, and were followed by Fechter, the actor.

Gad's Hill Place,
 Higham by Rochester, Kent,
  Sunday, Twenty-ninth January, 1865.

My Dear Wills:—Birtles is too cavalier in his posting of the proofs. To send them to me on a Sunday morning, when you want them posted back on Sunday night, and when our post goes out at noon, is something like impertinence. Not to mention our being snowed up.

I am excessively doubtful about Vauxhall Illuminations.* It is fully as long again as it ought to be. However estimable these Clergymen are, it is quite out of the question for us to go on spinning out dry catalogues of what they do. I have as much real interest in such deeds as anyone *can* have, I think; but my soul is weary of this sort of paper. Ever the same, ever the same. Paganini's one string, and no Paganini. From the time when we did "What a London Curate Can Do if He Tries," it is but one perpetual drowsy repetition, generally with anything good in the original treatment left out. Pray hold this paper over, and remind Morley of the great number of similar papers that we have had, and the necessity, if they be still pursued, of more grace of handling and less statement of sums of money, and what an income was and is at a dozen periods, and

---

* "Through Lambeth to Vauxhall," an account of the district and of Church work in it appeared in *All the Year Round*, April 15th, 1865.

what is wanted for a Church Tower, and what was got from this Church Aid Society, and what from the other. All, like a Tract, like the *Saturday Magazine*, like speeches at Exeter Hall, like the Ecclesiastical-Tackle Shops in Southampton Street, like Mrs. Brown.

If you are so driven for matter as that you want this paper in a sort of famine, then please re-read it with an eye to my objections, and put the whole of the second slip and half the third into a column.

I will order dinner at 5 on Tuesday.

Never have I seen such a thing as the cutting from the Sheffield paper!

Ever,
C. D.

GAD'S HILL,
Sunday, Twelfth February, 1865.

MY DEAR WILLS:—Miss Power's little story is so much more meritorious than anything else in the No. that I propose to alter the No. as I have marked on your making up. But as that will probably not be matter enough, you can substitute "The Danes" for "Coaching." I think highly of Miss Power's story.*

Bowring scrambles in the strangest way. I will try to put the paper together in some endurable manner, at the office on Tuesday morning.

I am exceedingly doubtful about Edmund's paper on the Crystal Palace. It is so mechanically done, and in the old *Household Words* days we did that class of papers so well (when you and I did them, and

---

* "The Danes at Home, by a Frenchman Abroad" appeared in *All the Year Round*, February 25th, 1865. The only "story" in this number is "In the Untrodden Ways." "Coaching" appeared in the next number.

when Horne did them), that I think it suggests to our public, falling off. I wish you would tell this to Edmund when you see him, and say that unless that sort of article has some fancy and literary merit, I am against it.

To Halliday's "Poetry of the Pantomimes"—No. Pay him for it, of course. But the game is really not worth the candle. If the East end part of it could be quite separated, by himself, from the rest, it might just possibly be worth using. I have an idea, however, that it would spoil an excellent subject for me a year hence. *On the whole therefore,* distribute it.

Ever faithfully,
C. D.

16, SOMERS PLACE, HYDE PARK, W.,
Friday, Seventeenth March, 1865.

MY DEAR WILLS :—You ought to know that Fechter has done a very manly thing in a very delicate way.

I discovered last night, quite incidentally, that he heard of your being blackballed and of my having resigned with Wilkie, a week ago. He instantly sent in his resignation. It caused some consternation in the Club, and Palgrave Simpson was deputed to ask him what his offence was. He requested Simpson to reply for him that he resigned "because they had blackballed Mr. Wills, and he would trust himself to no community of men in which such things were done."

Ever faithfully,
C. D.

16, Somers Place.
Sunday, Twenty-sixth March, 1865.

My Dear Wills :—I am rather at sea about the No. because I only assume that you propose to put in half of the "Lottery Dreamer,"* and because the printers have (of course) not put the quantity on your "Forty Years in London"†—which is very good indeed.

But such a list as the enclosed is the best. "My Idea"† could come out, if there were not room. Or, "The Lottery Dreamer" could be cut anywhere to make room.

I return all the proofs corrected. You will see that I have taken a quantity out of "Talk."‡

In your "Forty Years," you have got the maiden name of Mrs. Kelly wrong. I have put it right. If you refer to Gale Jones, he kept a little chemist's shop, and sold Ginger Beer Powders, then rather a crack sort of novelty. The shop was very like the apothecary's in "Romeo and Juliet," and (I suppose in consequence of the masters being politically occupied) always had the door locked. An old woman appeared on a bell being rung, and if you wanted Ginger Beer Powders, and could point them out in the window, and didn't want change, she would sometimes sell them. He was a lean, polite, inoffensive, much-enduring Radical of the peacefullest sort. Ever yours,
C. D.

P.S. I hope to get away on Friday or Saturday, and should like to see you before I go. Shall we dine

---

* *All the Year Round,* April 8th, 15th and 22nd.
† *All the Year Round,* April 8th.
‡ *All the Year Round,* April 15th.

at the office, Wednesday or Thursday? If so, appoint day and hour.

P.P.S. You anticipated me about the '34 Port. I had put aside a dozen to ask you to put in your cellar. It is on its way from Gad's—much shaken, of course. Keep the bottles lying down; but stand one up for 3 or 4 days before using. Decant with great care through a strainer, and a quantity of crust and bee's wing will remain in the bottle. I am assured that the wine is unapproachable.

16, Somers Place,
Twenty-second April, 1865.

My Dear Wills:—Cheque enclosed, with thanks.

You want to bid for something at poor Leech's sale.* I ditto. Forster (as he writes to me from Bath this morning) ditto. Let us three go into one boat, and charter Schloss accordingly. I take it we each want a good pencil or water colour drawing. What maximum shall we go to? Twenty pounds, Thirty pounds, what? If you will settle that, according to your lights on the subject rely (in this as in all other matters) on the staunchness of the undersigned.

C. D.

Tell Mrs. Wills that I have undergone great unhappiness on the subject of the Port, but am more cheerful—as I hope she is.

Gad's Hill Place,
Higham by Rochester, Kent,
Tuesday, Thirteenth June, 1865.

My Dear Wills:—I feel it rather more in my head to-day than I have done yet. Quiet is the

---

* John Leech, the *Punch* artist, a great friend of Dickens, had died on October 29th of the previous year.

main thing. I write two or three notes and turn faint and sick.*

Ever heartily,
C. D.

Gad's Hill Place,
  Higham by Rochester, Kent,
    Sunday Night, Twenty-seventh August, 1865.

My Dear Wills:—No news,—except that I am working like a Dragon,† and that I hope something near a week may bring me through it. In the course of this next week, I will appoint a day (probably Monday, 4th September, or Tuesday, 5th) for our Meeting at the office, before I decamp for about one fortnight. But observe. *If you should want to go away before either of those days,* then try to come down here on a little visit, and we will Do, after my day's work, what we may have to do.

I am already buckling myself up for *A. Y. R.*

Enclosed is the MS. story that I did not send the other day.

Ever,
C. D.

Mary Boyle's "Madeira"‡ may go; it must be throughout either "I" or "We." And the *Fortnightly* needn't be called "one of our leading *Reviews*" but one of the *Reviews.*"

---

* Dickens was a passenger in the train which was wrecked at Staplehurst on June 9th. He escaped without injury, and displayed great presence of mind and energy in rescue-work.

† At "Our Mutual Friend," the last number of which appeared in November of this year.

‡ "Will You Take Madeira," *All the Year Round,* September 16th. It was "I."

[To Mrs. Wills.]
GAD'S HILL PLACE,
HIGHAM BY ROCHESTER, KENT,
Thursday, Twenty-eighth December, 1865.

MY DEAR MRS. WILLS:—I am very sorry indeed to receive this poor account of Wills, and am truly grieved to know that he is again enduring pain.

Will you kindly tell him with my love, that when I have made up the No. at the office tomorrow, I shall come to Regents Park Terrace to enquire about him of you. But pray add that I shall not in the least expect or want to see him, if he prefer (as he very likely will) to remain undisturbed. Do impress this upon him, as being sincerely meant.

Faithfully yours always,
CHARLES DICKENS.

1866.

After some negotiations Dickens came to an agreement with Messrs. Chappell for a series of readings in England, Scotland and Ireland. I gather that Wills went with him during part of the time (letter of April 20th to Mrs. Wills). His manager during these readings, and afterwards in America, was Mr. George Dolby.

OFFICE OF *ALL THE YEAR ROUND.*
A Weekly Journal conducted by Charles Dickens.

No. 26, WELLINGTON STREET,
STRAND, LONDON, W.C.,
Monday, Fifteenth January, 1866.

MY DEAR WILLS:—Coming here this afternoon, and finding your letter dated yesterday, I suppose the railroads to have recovered, and the British Post to have asserted itself triumphantly.

As soon as I read yours, I sent for Birtles and the making up. The latter was all right and even (wonderful to relate!) and stood in no need of change whatever. Sala has sent a paper on the Havannah,* which has duly gone to Beaufort House† the Sprightly. All things else, official, are *in statu quo.*

In the matter of Beale, it occurs to me that he *may*, perhaps, ask for 30 readings instead of 25. I should not be indisposed (for I should not think it unfair) to let him have 30 for 2,000 *Guineas*. Perhaps he may not come near the mark at all. In such case I think I will resolve to keep quiet and not read at all.

I send my kindest regard to Miss Coutts and am ever,

Heartily yours,
C. D.

Gad's Hill Place,
Higham by Rochester, Kent,
Sunday, Twenty-eighth January, 1866.

My Dear Wills:—After we parted yesterday I chance-lighted on the information that Mitchell, having of yore burnt his fingers a good deal, speculates very little now, yet likes to be considered as doing much in that way.

This is worth bearing in mind. Also, that he may have some dread of giving offence to Fanny Kemble.

Proceeding on your own judgment and observation, of course you will more than satisfy me. I suggest

---

* Probably "The Humours of Havana," *All the Year Round,* February 10th.

† Beaufort House, Strand, the printing office of *All the Year Round.*

that perhaps it would be best to keep our figures back,—always, if you approve. I would take up the ground thus: There is Mr. Dickens, whose position you understand probably at least as well as I do, constantly entreated to read, and proposed to in all manner of ways. He is enough at leisure to undertake in town and country (suggesting the country places) 30 readings, or 20, or 15. The business of such things is not in our way since the death of Mr. Arthur Smith. He is willing to undertake them for a sum of money. Are you willing to enter into a negotiation with me for buying him?

Questions of detail to be agreed upon, if terms agreed upon. They are chiefly, avoidance of morning readings as much as possible, both as distasteful to me, and as not addressing my large miscellaneous following, which is limited to no class—limitation of country places to those first-class ones which I have proved to be the best for me—and agreement beforehand, between us, on the rooms to be engaged, according as I have also proved them.

I would lead him to an offer, if he should be disposed to make one; but I would throw the terms of it, in money, upon him.

Ever faithfully,
C. D.

[To Mrs. Wills.]

EDINBURGH,
Friday, Twentieth April, 1866.

MY DEAR MRS. WILLS:—As a reminder of my having deprived you of your husband (not that you are likely to need any!) I bring you from Edinburgh a shepherd's plaid silk dress, which I shall entrust to his care. When you wear it, forgive me as nearly as you can.

There are 20 yards of the dress, in order that there may be something in the nature of a jacket superadded. At least, I believe that is the intention, but your excellent housewifery will know all about it.

Faithfully yours ever,
CHARLES DICKENS.

GAD'S HILL PLACE,
HIGHAM BY ROCHESTER, KENT,
Monday, Thirtieth July, 1866.

MY DEAR WILLS:—Forster, being here yesterday, asked me what there was amiss between him and you? I said that I did not know from you that anything was amiss. He rejoined that he had made such and such approaches to you, which you had avoided, and that if there were something wrong between you, it was quite unconsciously on his part. I repeated what I had already said. He then asked me if I would let you know that he had spoken to me? I replied, Most willingly. Hence this note.

I shall look in at the office at one on Wednesday (in case any Writer of transcendent genius should have turned up since Saturday).

Ever faithfully,
C. D.

GAD'S HILL PLACE,
HIGHAM BY ROCHESTER, KENT,
Tuesday, Eleventh August, 1866.

MY DEAR WILLS:—Many thanks for the information concerning that loose fish. Ouvry held it best to wait until the half year's accounts come in next month, before taking action. I think he must already have paid the balance due upon them, if not more. He has been paying £300 *per month* on account, since the last settlement.

The picture of the Tinsley fête, magnificent!

I don't think I shall come to town (there being things to look after here) until Thursday; but I may, if I can get away, look in at the office to-morrow evening. Will you leave the proofs for me? If I come on Thursday, it will be soon after 11 A.M. to remain until after lunch.

The Xmas No. continues to reside in the Limbo of the Unborn—as Tinsley's friend Tom Carlyle would say.*

Ever,
C. D.

Gad's Hill Place,
Higham by Rochester, Kent,
Sunday, Twenty-first October, 1866.

My Dear Wills:—I have mislaid the proof of the Xmas No. advertisement. But it was wrong, I remember. The important word "stories" was omitted altogether. Let it stand in this way—"*will continue, in addition to other stories to be announced shortly*" and then my list.

I read "The Boy"† to Miss Boyle, my two girls, and Georgina, last night, with such extraordinary peals and tears of laughter, that I think I foresee

---

* It was born as "Mugby Junction." Dickens contributed four parts to it. Some 265,000 copies of it were sold (see letter of January 24th, 1867, *post*).

† "The Boy at Mugby," one of the four parts written by Dickens for the Christmas number, "Mugby Junction."

a great success. I don't think I ever saw people laugh so much under the prosiest of circumstances.

Mr. Horace Wigan so presses me about Wilkie's play,* that I must come up on Tuesday, and go to rehearsal at 12. I will call at the office about ½ past 11, in case you would care to go with me. Will you tell Birtles to have two things ready for me. First, the exact cast-off in pages of what I have done for Xmas No. Second, a complete proof of "Kätchen's Caprices."†

Many thanks for the Ouvry and Farrer report. It will not do to bear this kind of insolence, as a consequence of a perfectly independent and moderate piece of criticism. He must apologise in the papers, or we positively must go on with our action for libel. It is nothing to say that the man is insignificant. The precedent is dangerous and compromising. I wish you would impress this on Lincoln's Inn Fields.

The secret concerning our Vestiges friend remains a secret.‡

Ever faithfully,
C. D.

GAD'S HILL PLACE,
HIGHAM BY ROCHESTER, KENT,
Tuesday, Thirteenth November, 1866.

MY DEAR WILLS :—It is curious I should not have noticed that mistake. The substitution of "today" for "yesterday" makes all right. I have sent the correction to Birtles in a parcel.

* "Armadale."
† *All the Year Round*, November 24th.
‡ Probably an allusion to the approaching second marriage of Robert Chambers, Wills's brother-in-law. In an introduction to the 12th edition of the "Vestiges of Creation," published in 1884, Alexander Ireland has explained how Robert Chambers wrote the book and how and why the name of the author was concealed.

Ellen* has been here. She has "very nice furniture," she says, for her own rooms. I told her that she would find the Kitchen furnished for her. I think it better not to summon her before Saturday. I will be at the office that day, to make it easier for her. Let us make up the No. at the same time. There is not a doubt, I hope, of her being exactly the person we want.

Tomorrow (Wednesday) I am due at the office at half past eleven, and am to sit to Mason in Bond Street (for some tattoo'd staring monster to be displayed in the Paris Exhibition) at 12. At 1, I go with Chappell to explain a notion I have for improving the acoustics of St. James's Hall. After that, I shall look in at the office again.

Tell Miss Coutts with my kindest regards and remembrance, that I shall be delighted to try my hand promptly at the inscription.

What do you mean by this passage in one of your notes received this morning? "I sent a despatch last night, one Xmas No." Do you mean sent it to me? I have never had it.

Ever faithfully,
C. D.

1867.

Dickens continued his English reading tour during the early part of the year. Proposals more and more tempting from a pecuniary point of view were now made to him for a tour in America, and it is evident

---

* The servant engaged to look after the rooms at the office.

that before the year was half through his mind had become engrossed by the idea. In answer to Wills's strong remonstrance he wrote the letter of June 6th, setting out the reasons that moved him to undertake such a venture. Dolby was sent out to make preliminary enquiries. His report was favourable, and on September 30th Dickens made up his mind and telegraphed his acceptance to America.

On Saturday, November 2nd, Dickens was entertained by his friends at a farewell dinner at the Freemasons' Tavern. A week afterwards he sailed, and landed in Boston, after an unadventurous voyage, on Tuesday, November 19th.

In "Letters," II., 301, there is published a letter from Dickens to Wills, which I cannot find in my collection. It was written on the morning after the dinner at the Freemasons' Tavern, and throws so pleasant a light on the relations between the two men that I venture to transcribe it here :—

26, WELLINGTON STREET,
Sunday, November 3rd, 1867.

MY DEAR WILLS :—If you were to write me many such warm-hearted letters as you sent this morning, my heart would fail me! There is nothing that so breaks down my determination, or shows me what an iron force I put upon myself, and how weak it is, as a touch of true affection from a tried friend.

All that you so earnestly say about the goodwill and devotion of all engaged, I perceived and deeply felt last night. It moved me even more than the demonstration itself, though I do suppose it was the most brilliant ever seen. When I got up to speak, but for taking a desperate hold of myself, I should have lost my sight and voice and sat down again.

God bless you, my dear fellow. I am ever and ever,

      Your affectionate.

———

   Adelphi Hotel, Liverpool,
    Sunday, Twentieth January, 1867.

My Dear Wills:—The second and third readings here have gone with such wonderful enthusiasm and have so astonished the natives, that we are coming back here for two more in the middle of next month. The weather continues so severe, and the suburban roads are so heavy, that we feel it in the stalls, but the half-crowns and ones (who don't come in from distances, with horses) crowd their places splendidly.

We have been over to Rock Ferry today, to see the Great Eastern lying high and dry there for repairs. She looks hideous, and (strange to say) not very big, so situated! A very large and strong pack of Ice is on that side of the river, and the general appearance of things is Arctic.

Will you kindly read the enclosed letter? Is it hopeless? Or can any reasonable thing be done? I am afraid it is a weary and intangible case.

Dolby is always talking about you, and said to me on Friday night (when I did exactly one million one hundred thousand and one new things with "Marigold," which the audience seized each with exactly one million one hundred thousand and one rounds), "Why isn't Wills here?" I told him he reminded me of Collingwood and Nelson. In terms disrespectful to both of those great English Worthies, he rejoined: "Neither of them was Wills, and I want Wills!"

      Ever faithfully,
        C. D.

HEN AND CHICKENS, BIRMINGHAM,
Thursday, Twenty-fourth January, 1867.

MY DEAR WILLS :—We shall evidently sell our 265,000.* Expect me at the office on Monday afternoon, say at 4 o'clock. Also on Tuesday.

We have been reading in snow-storms, and downpourings of sheets of solid ice. At Chester it was such a night as one sees once in half a century. Nevertheless we had close upon £70, and the people were enchanted. Last night at Wolverhampton the thaw had set in thoroughly, and it rained heavily. There we had close upon £80. The Mersey was like the Channel on a bad day, between England and France, when we came across. The cold was stupendous. To-day is pleasant here, and quite warm. I have been fainter of a night, after leaving off, than I like. This, on two occasions.

The *Ci-devant* Miss Marryat's letter, I shall not answer. Concerning the letter of the lady who referred to Halliday, what is to be done? I am very much afraid, from its terms, that it is quite beyond my reasonable reach. Would you mind writing to her *with that express caution*, and telling her that you will see her at the office at such or such a time?

Dolby's legs stand as they did. His right eye becomes inflamed of a morning, only when he goes out, after I go to bed, to treat the local agent. He appeared at breakfast one morning at Liverpool, with three glasses of gin and water and two cigars distinctly to be seen under his right eye-lid. Our pervading joke is "Schloss's Solicitor." We recognize him in

---

* Of "Mugby Junction," the Christmas number of *All the Year Round* (see "Letters," II., 265).

all sorts of shabby genteel people at stations and elsewhere. This mild recreation keeps us going.

Ever faithfully,
C. D.

[At the top of the following letter Wills has written in pencil :—" This letter, so illustrative of one of the strong sides of C. D.'s character—powerful will—I think ought *decidedly* to be published in justice to Forster and myself, who dissuaded him from America —which killed him eventually.—W. H. W."]

Thursday, Sixth June, 1867.

My Dear Wills :—I cannot tell you how warmly I feel your letter, or how deeply I appreciate the affection and regard in which it originates. I thank you for it with all my heart.

You will not suppose that I make light of any of your misgivings if I present the other side of the question. Every objection that you make, strongly impresses me, and will be revolved in my mind again and again.

When I went to America in '42, I was so much younger, but (I think) very much weaker, too. I had had a painful surgical operation performed, shortly before going out, and had had the labour from week to week of "Master Humphrey's Clock." My life in the States was a life of continual speech-making (quite as laborious as Reading), and I was less patient and more irritable then, than I am now. My idea of a course of Readings in America, is, that it would involve far less travelling than you suppose—that the large first class towns would absorb the whole course—and that the receipts would be very much larger than your Estimate. Unless the demand for the Readings is *enormously exaggerated on all hands*, there is considerable reason for this view of the case. And I can hardly think that all the Speculators who beset me, and all the private correspondents who urge me, are in a conspiracy or under a common delusion.

I also believe that an immense impulse would be given to the C. D. Edition by my going out.

If you were to work out the question of Reading profits here, with Dolby, you would find that it would take years to get £10,000.* To get that sum in a heap so soon is an immense consideration to me.

I shall never rest much while my faculties last, and (if I know myself) have a certain something in me that would still be active in rusting and corroding me, if I flattered myself that it was in repose. On the other hand, I think that my habit of easy self-abstraction and withdrawal into fancies, has always refreshed and strengthened me in short intervals wonderfully. I always seem to myself to have rested far more than I have worked, and I do really believe that I have some exceptional faculty of accumulating young feelings in short pauses, which obliterates a quantity of wear and tear.

My worldly circumstances (such a family considered) are very good. I don't want money. All my possessions are free, and in the best order. Still, at 55 or 56, the likelihood of making a very great addition to one's capital in half a year, is an immense consideration. I repeat the phrase because there *should* be something large, to set against the objections.

I dine with Forster today to talk it over. I have

---

* His profit in America was eventually within a hundred or so of £20,000 ("Life," III., 410).

no doubt he will urge most of your objections, and particularly the last—though American friends and correspondents he has, have undoubtedly staggered him more than I ever knew him to be staggered, on the money question. Be assured that no one can present any argument to me, which will weigh more heavily with me than your kind words, and that, whatever comes of my present state of abeyance, I shall never forget your letter or cease to be grateful for it.

Ever, My Dear Wills,
Faithfully,
C. D.

[In "Letters" II., 295, the second paragraph of the following letter is printed as the concluding paragraph of a letter of September 2nd.]

OFFICE OF ALL THE YEAR ROUND.
A Weekly Journal conducted by Charles Dickens.
No. 26, WELLINGTON STREET,
STRAND, LONDON, W.C.,
Friday, Twenty-eighth June, 1867.

MY DEAR WILLS:—No doubt "Eliza Fenning"* will come down to Gad's. I will return her by post to you. I did not mean to negative her. Merely raised my eyebrows at a subject so well known.

I am glad you see a certain unlikeness to anything, in the American story†; and I hope that when you

---

* This appeared in *All the Year Round*, July 13th, 1867, being one of a series of papers under the general title of "Old Stories Re-told," written by Walter Thornbury. Eliza Fenning was executed in 1815 for poisoning her employers. Thornbury argues strongly for her innocence.

† "George Silverman's Explanation," which, together with "A Holiday Romance," Dickens wrote for first publication in America.

see it complete, you will think still better of it. Upon myself, it has made the strangest impression of reality and originality!! And I feel as if I had read something (by somebody else) which I should never get out of my head!! The main idea of the narrator's position towards the other people, was the idea I *had* for my next novel in *A. Y. R.* But it is very curious that I did not in the least see how to begin his state of mind, until I walked into Hoghton Towers one bright April day with Dolby.

Faithfully ever,
C. D.

[The following letter is wrongly dated June 13th in "Letters," II., 292. Parts of this letter only are there printed, and it closes with a paragraph taken from a letter of August 3rd, 1869.]

Gad's Hill Place,
Higham by Rochester, Kent,
Sunday, Thirtieth June, 1867.

My Dear Wills:—I have heard read the first 3 Nos. of Wilkie's story* this morning, and have gone minutely through the plot of the rest to the last line. Of course it is a series of "Narratives," and of course such and so many modes of action are open to such and such people; but it is a very curious story —wild, and yet domestic—with excellent character in it, great mystery, and nothing belonging to disguised women or the like. It is prepared with extraordinary care, and has every chance of being a hit. It is in many respects much better than anything he has done.

We have talked over the time of beginning to

---

* "The Moonstone." It began its appearance in *All the Year Round*, January 4th, 1868.

publish, and it is evidently desirable not to begin, if we can possibly help it, until the Xmas No. is out—say, the middle of December. The question then is, how shall we fill up the blank between "Mabel"* and Wilkie? What do you think of proposing to Fitzgerald† to do a story three months long? I dare say he has some unfinished or projected something by him.

I have an impression that it was not Silvester who tried Eliza Fenning,‡ but Knowles can hardly suppose Thornbury to make such a mistake, but I wish you would look into the "Annual Register." I have added a final paragraph about the unfairness of the Judge, whoever he was. I distinctly recollect to have read of his "putting down" of Eliza Fenning's father when the old man made some miserable suggestion in his daughter's behalf (this is not noticed by Thornbury),§ and he also stopped some suggestion that a knife thrust into a loaf adulterated with alum, would present the appearance that these knives presented. But I may have got both these points from looking up some pamphlets in Upcott's collection. Which I once did.

If you would not object to take my packet to Brown and Shipley's on Tuesday, I should be very much obliged to you if you would do so. I shall be at the office at 5 tomorrow (Monday), or will meet you there if you leave a note to me to that effect, at 11 on Tuesday. I have told Birtles to send you complete revise, thinking Mrs. Wills may like to see it.

Ever faithfully,
C. D.

---

* "Mabel's Progress" ended in *All the Year Round*, November 2nd, 1867.
† Mr. Percy Fitzgerald, a frequent and valued contributor.
‡ She was tried by the Recorder, Silvester.
§ This is in the paper as printed.

Gad's Hill Place,
    Higham by Rochester, Kent,
        Monday, Second September, 1867.

My Dear Wills:—Like you, I was shocked when this new discovery burst upon me on Friday—though, unlike you, I never could believe in —— —solely (I think) because, often as I have tried him, I never found him standing by my desk, when I was writing a letter, without trying to read it.

I fear there is no doubt that, since John's discharge, he (——) has stolen money at the Readings. A case of an abstracted shilling seems to have been clearly brought home to him by Chappell's people, and they know very well what *that* means. I supposed a very clear keeping off from Anne's husband (whom I recommended for employment to Chappell) to have been referable only to John; but now I see how hopeless and unjust it would be to expect belief from him with two such cases within his knowledge.

But don't let the thing spoil your holiday. If we try to do our duty by people we employ; by exacting their proper service from them on the one hand, and treating them with all possible consistency, gentleness, and consideration, on the other; we know that we do right. Their doing wrong cannot change our doing right, and that should be enough for us.

So I have given *my* feathers a shake, and am all right again. Give *your* feathers a shake, and take a cheery flutter into the air of Hertfordshire.

Great reports from Dolby,* and also from Fields.† But I keep myself quite calm, and hold my decision in abeyance, until I shall have book, chapter, and verse,

---

* Dolby had gone to America to investigate matters on the spot.
† Mr. James T. Fields, the publisher, of Boston, an old friend of Dickens.

before me. Dolby hoped he could leave Uncle Sam on the 11th of this month.

Sydney* has passed as a Lieutenant and appeared at home yesterday, all of a sudden, with the consequent golden garniture on his sleeve. Which I, God forgive me, stared at, without the least idea that it meant promotion.

Ever faithfully,
C. D.

Gad's Hill Place,
Higham by Rochester, Kent,
Tuesday, Third September, 1867.

My Dear Wills :—I am glad that the misconduct of —— has given us the opportunity of advancing people whose conduct has been good. May we have got at the bottom and the end of it at last!

So overwhelmed am I by letters concerning this absurd newspaper paragraph about my being out of health—which has now swelled out into my being recommended by "eminent surgeons" to go to America for "cessation from literary labour"(!) that I have deemed it necessary to write a line to *The Times.* I have also written to the *Sunday Gazette,* the oftenest-quoted authority, and I *think* I will have a few words ready for Thursday to go in before "Mabel."†

The best answer to your U.S. enquiry, is the enclosed from Fields this very morning. Preserve it for return, please.

Ever faithfully,
C. D.

---

* Dickens's fifth son. He died at sea in May, 1872.
† No such words were printed.

GAD'S HILL PLACE,
  HIGHAM BY ROCHESTER, KENT,
   Tuesday, Twenty-fourth September, 1867.

MY DEAR WILLS :—I send you, enclosed, a plain statement of the American question, deduced from a mass of notes and figures. Give me your opinion on it. To go, or not to go?

I have sent it to Forster in exactly the same way, with exactly the same request, and no hint of my own tending either way.

On Saturday I will call at the office sometime in the day, for a letter from you. I would rather make up on *Monday morning*, as on that day I must be in town to send off the decisive Telegram to Boston.

Ever faithfully,
C. D.

[I cannot find the draft of this plain statement;* but there is in Wills's "Letter Book" a copy of a letter written by him in answer to the above, under date September 27th. In this Wills makes another strong effort to dissuade Dickens from the American enterprise. He argues against the accuracy of Dickens's figures, warns him that, in the present condition of American feeling about England, he may not be so well received as he anticipates, and ends thus:—"Now is it worth £10,000 to face such a state of things—although they may be out of the pale of possibility, yet, being possible, they have to be dreaded. Is it worth £10,000 to risk not only your bodily health but your mental comfort in a country where success will be a penance; for the more excitement you occasion the more you will be bored. Is it worth going to America for four months when you can ensure in double the time quite as large a sum at home. However, until Monday, when, all well, I shall meet you at the office."]

* It is printed in "Life," III., 290, note.

OFFICE OF *ALL THE YEAR ROUND.*
No. 26, Wellington Street,
Strand, London, W.C.,
Saturday, Twenty-eighth September, 1867.

My Dear Wills:—There are two respects (worth mentioning perhaps), in which you are wrong. 1. If I were to go to America, the Reading months would be December, January, February, March, April—five in all. 2. Extra payments on reserved seats, does not mean run-up prices and jobbery, but simply this:— There will be two prices: a dollar and a half, and (for reserved seat) two dollars. The calculation is always made at one price only, and that the lowest. It is made on the assumption that all places let, are places of the lowest price. You understand?

I am off to Ross, to see Forster and Dolby together. Forster notices the absence of margin that *you* notice, in the calculation. I will return to the office, Monday forenoon. Final telegraph to America, Yes or No, that day!

Ever faithfully,
C. D.

[This paper is in Dickens's handwriting.]

Memoranda.

A. Y. R.

Remember that no reference, however slight is to be made to America in any article whatever, unless by myself.

Remember that the same remark applies to the subject of the Fenians.

Remember that a Poem by Mrs. Cowden Clarke is

accepted for the ordinary current No. at Christmas time.*

Remember that a narrative from official documents of the Webster Murder case, is to come in from Sir James Emerson Tennent.†

JOHN POOLE.

His address is 8, Fitzroy Place, Kentish Town. He will be very thankful if you will sometimes give him a call as you go by on Holly Lodge‡ affairs. He has six envelopes addressed to you at the office, in my writing, with "John Poole" in the corner. This is in case of his wanting any looking after. He is to have £25 sent to him on the 24th of December, and £25 on the 25th of March. *In case of his death I have £25 of his money in my hands for funeral expenses.*

LETTERS.

Any that may come to Gad's Hill will be forwarded to you to open and dispose of. Similarly, open all letters addressed to me that may come here.

PLORN §

After the Christmas Holidays is to go to a Sheep-Farmer for a few months. He, or his tutor, or Mary, or Georgina, will ask you to settle that matter. I suppose that through Sidney and his Agricultural Hall connexion we can know reasonably well whether any suggested person and terms would be likely to act well; or could find out the right person and terms, if none were suggested.

---

* Presumably "The Yule Log," December 27th.
† "The Killing of Dr. Parkman," December 7th.
‡ Miss Coutts's residence at Highgate.
§ His youngest son, Edward Bulwer Lytton Dickens.

MRS. SCOTT AND MRS. KELLY AND MRS. ALLISON.

Mrs. Scott is to be paid One Pound every Saturday, down in the office; beginning this next Saturday, the day of my leaving Liverpool. Mrs. Mary Kelly, 21 Leigh Street, Charles Street, Manchester, is to have a P.O. order for £1 every Saturday. Mrs. Allison, at Mrs. Spreights, Kirkgate, Wakefield, Ditto.

FORSTER

Has an ample Power of Attorney from me, in case you should want any legal authority to act in my name.

MY PRIVATE ACCOUNT AT COUTTS'S

Is subject, in my absence, to the joint cheques of Mary and Georgina.

THE ELECTRIC AND INTERNATIONAL TELEGRAPH COMPANY.

The following Message has been received at G. D. Station.

22. 11. 1867.

From

DICKENS,

To

WILLS, Twenty-six Wellington Street, Strand, London.

Safe and well expect good letter full of hope.

PARKER HOUSE, BOSTON,
Thursday, Twenty-first November, 1867.

MY DEAR WILLS:—A winter passage out here is, under the best circumstances (not to put too fine a point upon it) odious. But I had, in the *Cuba*, a fine run—was not sick for a moment—was highly popular on board—made no end of speeches after the last dinner of the voyage—sang no end of duets with the Captain (never known to come out before) and came over the side into the arms of Dolby (in a steam tug) illuminated with a blaze of triumph.

The Pilot brought the news on board that the people had stood with the greatest good temper in the freezing street, 12 hours, to buy tickets for the first four readings here (the only Readings announced), and that every ticket for every night was sold. I found it to be literally true. The gross receipts of those 4 nights are £250 beyond our calculation. New York tickets are not on sale until next week, but there are signs of the same excitement there. The Hall here is charming—I never saw a better. If I can only hit them hard with the Carol and Trial, I think our expectations may be far overpassed. Longfellow, Emerson, Holmes, Agassiz, and all Cambridge—Professors and Students—are booked in a phalanx for the body of the Hall on the 1st night, Monday, December the Second. Nothing can exceed the interest and heartiness of these men.

Boston, as a City, is enormously changed since I was here, and is far more mercantile. I do not yet notice any special difference in manners and customs between my old time and this time—except that there is more of New York in this fine City than there was of yore. The Hotel* I stayed at in my first visit has now become contemptible. This is an establishment like one of our Termini Hotels, with the addition of an immense quantity of white marble floors. I live on the third storey—our three rooms together—and

* The Tremont House.

have hot and cold water laid on in a bath in my bedroom, and other comforts not known in my former experience. The cuisine is very good. The cost of living is enormous. Ten Pounds sterling a day for Dolby and me is by no means a large estimate. (It was our original calculation.) Happily, Dolby has seen reason to make up his mind that the less I am shown—for nothing—the better for the Readings! So I am fended off and kept—so far—unexpectedly quiet. In addition to which I must say that I have experienced—so far—not the slightest intrusiveness, and everywhere the greatest respect and consideration. There is the utmost curiosity about the Readings, and I should not wonder if they proved to be a great surprise, seeing that the general notion stops at a mere "Reading," book in hand.

Even you, I think, will find it difficult to believe that at this moment —— has not sent out the pamphlet with the Dinner Speeches ! ! ! !* Of course when it does come, it will be waste paper. The American journals all over the country have taken the account from the English Journals, and I am assured that my speech has given the highest satisfaction to the American people.

This is all my news at present—except that I am so well and so free of the ship, that I am worried by not having arranged to begin reading next Monday—for I yearn to begin to check the Readings off, and feel myself tending towards Home.

My love to Mrs. Wills, and my love to the personal and official Wilkie.† Fields does not begin to publish the Holiday Romance until January. I will advise

---

* The farewell dinner to Dickens which had been given at the Freemasons' Tavern, under the chairmanship of Lord Lytton, on November 2nd.
† Wilkie Collins was helping Wills in the work of *All the Year Round*.

you in good time, when you can begin with it in *A. Y. R.* Take all my confidence and trust now and ever,

    And Believe me,
      Affectionately Yours always,
        C. D.

   PARKER HOUSE, BOSTON,
    Tuesday, Twenty-sixth November, 1867.

MY DEAR WILLS :—This morning I got yours of the 14th, just in time to send you an answer by the Cunard Steamer. Our prospects here are MOST BRILLIANT—all people, public and private, seem in the best frame of mind for the Readings and the Reader—and I am so well, thank God, after the voyage, that I am continually chafing at not having begun last Monday instead of next. Will you write Townshend a line giving him my best love, and telling him that I will write to him on the day after my first Reading here. My love to Wilkie. Your account of your getting on together is delightful to me, though I never doubted it.

    Ever, my Dear fellow,
      Yours faithfully,
        C. D.

THE ELECTRIC AND INTERNATIONAL TELEGRAPH COMPANY.

The following Message has been received at Strand Station.
          Dec. 4th, 1867.
     From
DICKENS,
     To
WILLS, *All the Year Round* Office, London.
  Tremendous success greatest enthusiasm all well.

Parker House, Boston,
Tuesday, Third December, 1867.

My Dear Wills:—I cannot convey to you an adequate idea of last night's tremendous success. The City is absolutely mad about it. The reception was magnificent, and the "go" of the Reading without any approach to a precedent in these parts. Nothing that we could have imagined or hoped for, could have surpassed the reality. There was (at the reduced rate of money even) £450 in the house. And the New York House (which is also sold out for every announced night) holds fully 500 people more!

Write to me in future at the Westminster Hotel, Irving Place, New York City. It is a more central address than this, and we shall probably be much oftener there. My present intention is to keep rooms there, and I have also started a Brougham beforehand.

We shall not be able to begin the children* or George Silverman before March, as Fields does not begin either until January. This will come to you by my ship, the *Cuba*, returning home. I am very well indeed, and in great voice and force. You may be absolutely certain that the success here COULD NOT be greater.

Ever, My Dear fellow,
Your affectionate,
C. D.

Parker House, Boston, U.S.,
Friday, Sixth December, 1867.

My Dear Wills:—I am going on (between ourselves) at a *clear profit* of £1,300 per week! And it

---

* "A Holiday Romance" was written for "Our Young Folks," a children's magazine published in Boston.

is quite upon the cards that an occasional morning in New York will raise even these figures. Nickleby and Boots made a tremendous hit here last night, and certainly topped my favourite Copperfield—which may perhaps be a thought too delicate for them, though it went finely too. We had £500 in the House—£500 English at the handsome rate of 7 Dollars to the pound!

I have received 3 Nos. of *A. Y. R.* all good, and Murray very good. Be extremely chary of using those Mugby Junction stories.

To-morrow at 11 we start for New York, being due there at 8 in the evening. On Monday I open there, with Carol and Trial. Tickets at a premium, and we cannot by any means keep out the speculators or prevent their making large profits.

With kind love to Mrs. Wills, Ever, My Dear boy,
Your faithful and affectionate,
C. D.

Address me until further notice:
Westminster Hotel,
Irving Place,
New York City.

Westminster Hotel, Irving Place,
New York City,
Tuesday Evening, Tenth December, 1867.

My Dear Wills:—It is absolutely impossible that we could have made a more brilliant success than we made here last night. The reception was splendid, the audience bright and perceptive. I believe that I never read so well since I began, and the general delight was most enthusiastic. And *now* I may tell you that before I came away, I received at the office by two or three mails from here, various letters about Danger, Anti-Dickens feeling, Anti-English feeling, New York rowdyism, and I don't know what else. As I was in for coming, I resolved to say no word about it to anyone. Nor did I, until I came off from the " Trial " last night, when I told Dolby.

This Hotel is quieter than Mivart's in Brook Street! It is quite as comfortable, and the French cuisine is immensely better. I go in and out by a side door and a little staircase that leads straight to my bedroom. The platform absorbs my individuality, and I am very little troubled. We have on the first floor, a pretty drawing-room, my bedroom, bathroom, and Scott's bedroom. Dolby has his bedroom and another room in which to see his clients, on the floor above. There are Hotels (on the American principle) very near, with 500 bedrooms and I don't know how many boarders. This Hotel (on the Eurōpian principle) is almost faultless, and is as singularly unlike your idea of an American Hotel as unlike can be. New York has grown out of my knowledge, and is enormous. Everything in it looks as if the order of nature were reversed, and everything grew newer every day, instead of older. The Room—very much larger than its capacity of holding people—is about as trying as St. James's Hall. I am in capital health and voice.

It has been intensely cold. But to-day it has thawed, after a fall of snow. Nothing more to report at present, except my love to Mrs. Wills, and my affectionate and faithful regard to you.
C. D.
Wednesday Morning.

Copperfield and Bob even a greater success last night than Carol and Trial on the night before.

"Mr. Digguns," said the German Janitor (the invariable name for the Hall Keeper), "you are gread, meinherr. There is no ent to you!" That was his parting salutation as he locked me out into a hard frost. "Bedder and bedder," he re-opened the door to add, "Wot negst!"

> WESTMINSTER HOTEL, IRVING PLACE,
> NEW YORK CITY,
> *Tuesday, Seventeenth December*, 1867.

MY DEAR WILLS :—No news, except that this house was on fire last Sunday night (a matter scarcely worth mentioning in New York), and that we turned out and packed up. But the fire was happily got under. The meeting of all the inmates, in the most extraordinary dresses, and with their most precious possessions under their arms or imperfectly crammed into their pockets, was very ridiculous. Everybody talked to everybody else, and it was on the whole convivial.

Everything unchanged. Everybody sleighing. Everybody coming to the Readings. There were at least ten thousand sleighs in the Park last Sunday. Your illustrious chief—in a red sleigh covered with furs, and drawn by a pair of fine horses covered with bells, and tearing up 14 miles of snow an hour —made an imposing appearance.

Tell Wilkie with my love that I have received his work * (admirably done) to the first scene of the 4th Act inclusive, and that I hope to bring the thing to terms with Wallack. But he seems a little shy

---

* Presumably the dramatic version of "No Thoroughfare."

(or I fancy it) touching the 10 per cent. I hope to report finally by the next mail.

Ever, My Dear fellow,
Your affectionate,
C. D.

BOSTON,
Christmas Eve, 1867.

MY DEAR WILLS:—Many, many merry Christmases and Happy New Years to you and yours, and to all of us! *We* spend our Christmas Day this year on the Railway between this place and New York.

The same success always.

Ticknor and Fields publish the first part of "Holiday Romance" on the 1st of January. They publish it in 4 parts. Each part on the 1st of the month. Make your calculation so that you will not jostle them (remembering that we are weekly and they monthly), and accordingly announce and publish. Follow up—perhaps after a short interval—with George Silverman's "Explanation." They publish that in 3 monthly parts, beginning on the 1st of January.

Dolby's best regard. He is incessantly abused, for no reason on earth but that he is not an American agent. Think of a low newspaper (which had been refused our advertisements) in Boston, the Hub of the Universe as they call it (Hub being the nave of a wheel), having this article of news last Sunday morning:—"The chap calling himself Dolby got drunk last night down town, and was locked up in the Police Station for fighting an Irishman"!

I have a dismal cold, but beat it down at 8 p.m.

In making up *A. Y. R.* try to bring the matter

closer down to the foot of the last page of the No.
And for the love of Heaven no more of those Xmas
Railway stories. Parkinson* very good.

Ever, My Dear Wills,
Affectionately yours,
C. D.

Mrs. Wills not forgotten.

Remark of a Western Agent (we mean to go out West) to Dolby this morning; Western Agent having been present at "Copperfield" and "Bob" last night.

"Wa'al, Mas'r Dolby, I tell yew this, Sir. He has a 'tarnal tall name, but he don't want it. The man as can *do that*—never was so skeared, I tell you, in all my life, and thought I should ha' burst!—might just go out West, never been heard of—and Damn me if he couldn't draw 'em across the plains if he chiz, till they hit their foreheads 'gain the Rocky Mountens."

Additional Memorandum. My New York landlord makes me a drink melodiously called "A Rocky Mountain Sneezer."

WESTMINSTER HOTEL, IRVING PLACE,
NEW YORK,
Monday, Thirtieth December, 1867.

MY DEAR WILLS:—Yours dated on the publishing day, gives glorious tidings of the Xmas No.† But somehow I am not sanguine about the play. I don't see it, as I read it. It may be my mood, or my anxiety, or I know not what else; but I don't see it rush on to its end in a spirited manner.

---

* J. C. Parkinson, a contributor. A letter from Dickens warmly commending his services and his ability is printed in "Letters," II., 401.

† "No Thoroughfare."

I have not been well, and have been obliged to call in a doctor; but am very greatly better—all right, in fact. A tonic seems to do me a deal of good.

All right about Plorn.* By the Lord, he ought to be a first-rate settler after all his cramming!

Blazing away here, after more tremendous blazing in Boston (where they went absolutely mad with "Copperfield"), and previous to blazing in Philadelphia, Brooklyn, and Baltimore. Those places, this, and Boston for another 2 nights, will occupy this coming month of January. At Brooklyn I read in Mister Ward Beecher's Church (wonderfully seated for 2,000) with the audience in veritable pews! I went to look at it the other day, and, found myself in a comically incongruous position. It is the only building suitable to the purpose in the town.

Many happy New Years to you, old fellow. And to Mrs. Wills with my love.

Ever affectionately,
C. D.

1868.

The final American Farewell Reading took place in New York on Monday, April 20th, and on the 22nd Dickens sailed for home on the *Russia*. His health towards the end of his tour had given cause for great anxiety, for he had suffered from a violent catarrh, and his foot had been in great pain. The voyage, however, seemed to restore him in a wonderful way. He arrived at home early in May.

In October he began another reading tour in England and Scotland. On November 14th he gave

---

* His youngest son was preparing to go to Australia.

a private reading of the *Sikes* and *Nancy* scenes from "Oliver Twist," but it was not until early in the following year that he added them to his public repertory. Wills had an accident in the hunting field during Dickens's absence in America, and was laid up for a long time.

PROVIDENCE,
Friday, Twenty-first February, 1868.

MY DEAR WILLS:—In case you should not have discovered Lytton's Grosvenor Square No. I send you this second note by tomorrow's mail, to let you know that it is *12*.

I have your letter about "Holiday Romance," this morning. You will know before you get this, that it is all right.

—— has proved untrustworthy, and the instant he comes back from a mission he is now upon at Buffalo, I shall peremptorily and finally discharge him. That will probably be tomorrow. Dolby will write to you as soon as the man is displaced telling you when the weekly payment made by the office on his account is to cease and determine. Here is another Paragon found out! The fellow (speculating himself) is at the bottom of all the trouble we have had, and has not only made me appear in this town the most grasping and sordid scoundrel going, but has cost me in this one place £300.

It is curious that I conceived a great dislike towards this man, aboard the *Cuba* coming out. He was ill all the voyage, and I only saw him two or three times, staggering about the lower deck; but I underwent a change of feeling towards him, as if I had taken it in at the pores of the skin. Dolby had great confidence in him, and I have never suspected him until within the last few days; but an inscrutable item of complaint about the sale here, being brought in yesterday afternoon by Osgood, it suddenly fired a whole train in my mind and blew up the scheme. It became as intelligible to all three of us, after a few minutes, as to the concoctor himself.

Ever, My Dear Boy,
Affectionately yours,
C. D.

BOSTON,
Tuesday, Twenty-fifth February, 1868.

MY DEAR WILLS:—It is especially lucky that I made so much money at first, for this Impeachment of the President [*] which you will have known of long before you get this (the vote was taken at five yesterday afternoon), will for the time, probably over-ride and overthrow everything in this country. It instantly emptied our great gallery here last night, and paralyzed the Theatres in the midst of a rush of good business.

I think of striking out next week's Readings here (not yet announced), and giving the political uproar and excitement that much time to take a distinct direction and be intelligible to a foreigner. This business of the War Secretary is the result of a deliberate plan on the part of the President, to bring the question between him and Congress to an issue.

---

[*] President Andrew Johnson had, in defiance of the Tenure of Office Act, removed the Secretary of War (Edwin M. Stanton) from office without the consent of the Senate. The House of Representatives thereupon voted to impeach him before the Senate for high crimes and misdemeanours. In the following May he was acquitted, the majority of votes against him being one less than the two-thirds required for conviction.

I was confidentially forewarned of it at Washington 18 days ago.

Love to Mrs. Wills,

    Ever, My Dear Boy,

      Your affectionate,

        C. D.

[This list is in Dickens's handwriting.]

REMAINING LIST OF READINGS.

Monday, March 1st [2nd] to 6th		Second Week of Boston Fortnight		Marigold and Gamp. Copperfield and Boots. Carol and Bob. Dombey and Gamp. Marigold and Trial.
Monday,	March	9th.	Syracuse	Carol and Trial.
Tuesday,	,,	10th.	Rochester (first)	Carol and Trial.
Wednesday,	,,	11th.	Off Night.	
Thursday,	,,	12th.	Buffalo	Carol and Trial.
Friday,	,,	13th.	Do.	Marigold and Bob.

(To the Falls of Niagara, 2 hours railway.)

Monday,	,,	16th.	Rochester (second)	Marigold and Bob.
Tuesday,	,,	17th.	Off Night for travelling.	
Wednesday,	,,	18th.	Albany	Carol and Trial.
Thursday,	,,	19th.	Do.	Marigold and Bob.
Friday,	,,	20th.	Springfield	Carol and Trial.
Monday,	,,	23rd.	Worcester	Carol and Trial.
Tuesday,	,,	24th.	Newhaven (second)	Marigold and Bob.
Wednesday,	,,	25th.	Hartford (second)	Marigold and Bob.
Thursday,	,,	26th.	Off Night.	
Friday,	,,	27th.	New Bedford	Carol and Trial.
Monday,	,,	30th.	Portland	Carol and Trial.
Tuesday,	,,	31st.	Off Night for travelling.	
Wednesday,	April	1st.	1st Boston Farewell	The subjects of the remaining Readings not yet fixed.
Thursday,	,,	2nd.	2nd Do.	
Friday,	,,	3rd.	3rd Do.	
Monday,	,,	6th.	4th Do.	
Tuesday,	,,	7th.	5th Do.	
Wednesday,	,,	8th.	Final Boston Farewell	
Thursday,	,,	9th.	Off Night.	
Good Friday	,,	10th.	Do.	
Monday,	,,	13th.	1st New York Farewell	
Tuesday,	,,	14th.	2nd Do.	
Wednesday,	,,	15th.	Off Night.	
Thursday,	,,	16th.	3rd New York Farewell	
Friday,	,,	17th.	4th Do.	
Monday,	,,	20th.	Final American Farewell, in New York. And last Reading of the Series! Wednesday, 22nd April, Cuba.	

Boston,
Friday, Twenty-eighth February, 1868.

My Dear Wills :—I enclose a curious article (written for the *Atlantic Monthly*) on the "Poison of the Rattlesnake." * You may publish it in *A. Y. R.* any day after the 20*th of March.*

As Dolby was uneasy about ——'s dismissal, I have consented to keep him on, within narrower limits, until we come back.

I have decided to give myself a holiday next week. My next week's readings here were not announced when the Impeachment broke out again, and caused great excitement. As I am coming back here on the 1st of April for 6 Farewells, I thought it best (under the exceptional circumstances of the time) to abolish next week's nights. We had a fine house last night for Carol and Trial, and a tremendous call between the two. I responded to it, and when I came in again they had covered my table with lovely flowers.

Very sorry to hear of Wilkie's having been so ill. Pray give him my love, and tell him that I earnestly hope he is much better.

Our tickets at Rochester and Buffalo were sold this week. People came out of Canada, struggling on foot across the frozen river and climbing over great ice-blocks, to buy some!

With love to Mrs. Wills,

Ever affectionately,

C. D.

Rochester,
Monday, Sixteenth March, 1868.

My Dear Wills :—The pony an immense—a prodigious — a rapturous — success ! The photograph

* *All the Year Round*, March 28th, 1868.

didn't come, either in your letter or in Mrs. Dolby's; but I was present, alone with Dolby, when he opened her letter last night, and the surprise and delight were marvellous to behold!

Enclosed:
1. Another letter.
2. 2 Documents to compare with Coutts's receipts, as usual.
3. Receipt for a small box from Niagara that is to come to the office addressed to me. Please pay all charges on it, and put it (unopened) in my office bedroom to await *my* coming.

You will know from another letter of mine before you get this, that I have always purposed doing *something* for our new Series,* though I don't yet know what. I have positively resolved to write no American sketches whatever.

Very extraordinary about poor Townshend! He told me, and he told Henri, that he had left the latter £50 a year. I wonder did he alter his will in that wise, after the discovery of the missing prints.

I don't agree with you about the Farewell Readings, but think £8,000 quite as much as they will reasonably bear. It is indisputable that Chappell's profits in the last Series was very small. There is no doubt of it, because Dolby kept the accounts.

We have had two bright brilliant days at Niagara, and the scene was splendid beyond all description.

With love to Mrs. Wills,
Ever my Dear Boy,
Your affectionate,
C. D.

* The first number of a "New Series" of *All the Year Round* appeared on December 5th of this year.

NEW YORK,
Friday, Seventeenth April, 1868.

MY DEAR WILLS:—We have notice to be on board on Wednesday at half-past one, and shall probably sail at half-past two. The Farewells are going finely here. I am very weary, but no worse. Your last letter gives me the hope that I may find you quite restored. I have discharged —— and he goes home tomorrow.

Ever affectionately,
C. D.

[To Mrs. Wills.]

OFFICE OF *ALL THE YEAR ROUND*.
A Weekly Journal conducted by Charles Dickens.

No. 26, WELLINGTON STREET, STRAND,
LONDON, W.C.,
Monday, Twenty-fifth May, 1868.

MY DEAR MRS. WILLS:—As I am the man who is not going to the Derby, I will come down on Wednesday by the 11.55 train you tell me of, returning to town by any good train in the early evening. My love to Wills, whom I hope to find coming round the corner (figuratively) at a steady pace.

Faithfully yours always,
CHARLES DICKENS.

[To Mrs. Wills.]

A. Y. R.,
Friday, Twenty-sixth June, 1868.

MY DEAR MRS. WILLS:—I should have answered your letter yesterday, but for an unusual amount of drudgery in setting Proofs right for the No.

Your tidings of Wills I think good. That he must

have time, we knew from the first. He has not had a long time yet; and I cannot help thinking that even to be no worse is to be better. The bracing place I am strongly in favour of. I am very hopeful that it will make a great change in him.

I had seen that letter about the Ladies' College, and will be prepared to pursue the subject should the opportunity be presented. Do you know that some rather ugly disclosures are afloat about ——? I know of others, hushed up a few years ago. It is my belief that some men will come to the Guild meeting, expressly to prevent his having that advance of money. I think I know of two, who are influencing more. And as I cannot conscientiously propose it, or support it, I don't think he'll get it.

Will you tell Wills at some time or other, that his old Mare has not done a week's work since she came to Gad's, and is totally unfit for any sort of usefulness. Shall I have her shot?

Everything at the office is quiet and straight. With my love to Wills, believe me ever,

Faithfully yours,
CHARLES DICKENS.

GAD'S HILL PLACE,
HIGHAM BY ROCHESTER, KENT,
Tuesday, Thirtieth June, 1868.

MY DEAR WILLS:—Of course the Mare shall roll in the lap of luxury (which is very much dried up by the bye, for want of water) until you send for her.

I don't think Mr. Robertson would do. There is no literature in that kind of Drama, and I feel convinced that the short notice and the necessity of compression would be too much for him, with no experience of that kind of writing—our kind, I mean. Of the Miss Mulholland idea, I think much better. I will write to her on Thursday.

Fitzgerald's "Boy's Biography"* is "servilely founded" (he writes) on me. But it goes on well enough, and I was to have the whole of it this week. If I get it, and it continues up to the mark, we shall be none the worse for having two strings to our bow.

I don't like Mrs. Linton for a story.

The fly-swallowing Holdsworth asking me with open eyes t'other day what was to be done about Mr. Yates's story and the volume, I thought it best to maintain the fiction that we were going straight on from Wilkie to Edmund. If we do not keep the fiction up as long as possible, we shall not get the copy that ought to be written. Grave and gloomy resolve therefore sits upon my lofty brow.

I will write to you again about the Guild, on Thursday or Friday. I shall be very glad when you change your air again, and try a new and a bracing place. Never mind the singing. If you feel that your head is better, rely upon it you are right, howsoever vaguely you may feel it.

For the soul of me, I cannot (hammer and think as I will) raise the ghost of an idea for the Xmas No.

       Disconsolately,
        C. D.

 Gad's Hill Place,
  Higham by Rochester, Kent,
   Sunday, Twenty-sixth July, 1868.

My Dear Wills:—I have yours of the 22nd this morning, and am delighted to get it. It has made

---

* "Autobiography of a Small Boy," *All the Year Round*, August 15th and 22nd, 1868.

two journeys between this place and the office before coming to hand.

The "Militia" paper * *is* by Sydney Blanchard. In justice to him I must mention that it has been in type for several weeks, but that I could not get it in sooner. I have taken great pains with the Nos. and have selected carefully. There are two papers by Sala now in type. Not much in them.

I have been, and still am—which is worse—in a positive state of despair about the Xmas No. I cannot get an idea for it which is in the least satisfactory to me, and yet I have been steadily trying all this month. I have invented so many of these Christmas Nos. and they are so profoundly unsatisfactory after all with the introduced stories and their want of cohesion or originality, that I fear I am sick of the thing. I have had serious thoughts of abandoning the Xmas No.! There remain but August and September to give to it (as I begin to read in October), and I CAN NOT see it.†

I quite agree with you about the "Moonstone." The construction is wearisome beyond endurance, and there is a vein of obstinate conceit in it that makes enemies of readers.

My love to Mrs. Wills. All sorts of messages to you.

Ever affectionately,
C. D.

Poor George Cattermole is dead.‡ Very, very, poor. Family quite unprovided for; debt and distress.

---

* "Out With the Militia," *All the Year Round*, July 25th, 1868.
† The Christmas number was abandoned.
‡ He died on July 24th, aged 68. He and "Phiz" illustrated "Master Humphrey's Clock."

Friday, Thirty-first July, 1868.

MY DEAR WILLS:—I had such a hard day at the office yesterday, that I had not time to write to you before I left. So I write to-day.

I am very unwilling to abandon the Xmas No. though even in the case of my little Xmas Books (which were immensely profitable) I let the idea go, when I thought it was wearing out. Ever since I came home, I have hammered at it more or less, and have been uneasy about it. I have begun something which is very droll but it manifestly shapes itself towards a book, and could not in the least admit of even that shadowy approach to a congruous whole on the part of other contributors which they have ever achieved at the best. I have begun something else (aboard the American mail steamer) but I don't like it, because the stories must come limping in after the old fashion—though of course what I *have* done, will be good for *A. Y. R.* In short, I have cast about with the greatest pains and patience, and I have been wholly unable to find what I want.

And yet I cannot quite make up my mind to give in, without another fight for it. I offered £100 reward at Gad's to anybody who could suggest a notion to satisfy me. Charles Collins suggested one yesterday morning, in which there is *something* though not much. I will turn it over and over, and try a few more starts on my own account. Finally I swear I will not give it up until August is out! Vow registered.

I am clear that a No. "by various writers" would not do. If we have not the usual sort of No. we must call the current No. for that date, the Xmas No. and make it as good as possible. The way to that can be paved in the Introduction to the new Series, and we will even make a merit of it.

Charles Collins is, for the time, better. I am buying the freehold of the meadow at Gad's, and of an adjoining arable field, so that I shall now have about eight and twenty freehold acres in a ring fence. No more news.

I made up a very good No. yesterday. You will see in it a very short article that I have called "Now!"* which is a highly remarkable piece of description. It is done by a new man from whom I have accepted another article, but he will never do anything so good, again. Fitzgerald's "Autobiography of a Small Boy" not very original, but still good.

Ever affectionately,
C. D

Gad's,
    Sunday, Twenty-seventh September, 1868.

My Dear Wills:—I want to have a talk with you on Thursday, relative to putting my son Charley into Morley's present place.† I must turn his education to the best account I can until we can hit upon some other start in life, and he can certainly take the bag and report on its contents, and carry on the correspondence. He seems to have an idea himself that he can strike out some notions at the Museum Library, and I have not dissuaded him from trying.

---

* *All the Year Round*, August 15th.

† Henry Morley was at this time, and had been since 1865, Professor of English Literature at King's College. Charles Dickens, junior, eventually came into the office, and, after his father's death, carried on the publication of *All the Year Round*.

Who *is* the New Librarian? I have lost sight of the place since Panizzi's* time, and want to write for a ticket for Charley.

I had a sad parting with poor Plorn † yesterday afternoon, and have not been myself since.

Ever affectionately,
C. D.

[To Mrs. Wills.]

No. 26, WELLINGTON STREET,
STRAND, LONDON, W.C.,
Saturday, Fourteenth November, 1868.

MY DEAR MRS. WILLS:—I am very sorry indeed that I shall not see you and Wills to-night ‡—though I think you will escape a rather horrible business!

Tell Wills with my love that everything is right here, and going like a clock—a great deal more like a clock than this thing he bought me for my room here, which is an utterly unreliable, unreasonable, and incomprehensible Beast.

Ever faithfully,
CHARLES DICKENS.

1869.

In spite of evident signs of illness and exhaustion Dickens continued his provincial reading tour until

---

* Sir Antonio Panizzi, principal librarian of the British Museum from 1856 to 1866.

† His youngest son sailed for Australia, where he settled.

‡ At a private reading of the *Sikes* and *Nancy* scenes from "Oliver Twist."

it was peremptorily brought to an end by his doctor's orders at Preston on April 22nd. Henceforth readings which entailed travel were to be entirely abandoned.

He was at work on " Edwin Drood " in October, though the first monthly number was not published until the following April.

Wills in the course of this year, after having travelled abroad, resigned his position as sub-editor of *All the Year Round* and retired to the house which he had taken near Welwyn in Hertfordshire. His health had for some time past troubled him, and his serious accident had greatly shaken him and had produced what Dickens in the letter of March 30th calls " that Church organ in your head." His place on *All the Year Round* was taken by Charles Dickens, junior.

A letter from Dickens to Wills of June 24th, printed in "Letters," II., 422, is not in my collection.

No. 26, Wellington Street,
Strand, London, W.C.,
Tuesday, Second February, 1869.

My Dear Wills :—In case your cold should keep you at home both to-day and to-morrow (and mind you don't come out, unless in a fit state to do so) I send you this line in reference to Charley.

Don't you think, as he has so much on his hands, that it will be fair to rate him on the ship's books at Six Guineas per week ?

Affectionately ever,
C. D.

Edinburgh,
Thursday, Twenty-fifth February, 1869.

My Dear Wills :—Yours received this morning.

I have been getting on exceedingly well with my foot, so far. Although I feel it a little fatigued by the standing at night, it has caused me no other inconvenience. "Business" here is *tremendous!*

I shall hope to see you at the office on Tuesday. If not, I will write to you from thence, giving you the "fixture" for next day.

Ever affectionately,
C. D.

No. 26, Wellington Street,
Strand, London, W.C.,
Tuesday, Thirtieth March, 1869.

My Dear Wills :—You will be glad to hear that Wilkie's play* went brilliantly last night. It was extremely well played throughout, and I have rarely seen Fechter to greater advantage. It was more like a fiftieth night than a first. Everything was exactly as I left it after four or five hours at it on Saturday. Not a word or a person out of place. I told Fechter that he ought to thank every one concerned, down to the Supers, for their remarkable care and attention, which he did when the curtain fell. There is no doubt that it ought to run, for it has real merit and is most completely and delicately presented.

By this time I hope you will have had a touch or two of warm weather. Bitter east winds, hail, snow, and other ingenious congelations of rain, are the rule

---

* "No Thoroughfare" at the Adelphi.

here. All well and brilliant personally. I have had a great burning of papers in your room—have destroyed everything not wanted—and have laid in a stock of Dictionaries and reference-books.

"Our Mr. C. Greatorex" is in communication with me about a house that promises—but I have not yet been inside it. He seems to be a very fair and honest fellow.

I went to see old Poole* yesterday, who was full of interest about you. He was so dirty, smelt so ill, and scratched himself so horribly, that he turned my stomach. I came back in a Hansom, quite sick, and was revived (by Georgina) with brandy. N.B. I have scratched myself ever since, and am doing so now.

This is all my news, except that I send my love to Mrs. Wills. If that Church Organ in your head will but leave off playing Voluntaries, you have nothing else—that *I* know of—to trouble yourself about; so stick to the mountains and the Spanish border.

Ever affectionately,
C. D.

I am off for Sheffield, Birmingham, and Liverpool, tomorrow morning. "Dombey" tonight.

Monday, Third May, 1869.

MY DEAR WILLS:—This is to send my love to Mrs. Wills and you, and to assure you that I am really *all right*. I had begun suddenly to be so shaken by constant Express travelling, that I might very easily have been ill. Said the Doctors: "Take

---

* See *ante*, p. 28, note.

warning, stop instantly." I made the plunge, and became, please God, well.

Ever affectionately,
C. D.

[The first paragraph of the following letter is printed in " Letters," II., 292, but is there wrongly added to a letter of June 13th, 1867—which letter ought to be dated June 30th.]

26, Wellington Street,
Strand, London, W.C.,
Tuesday, Third August, 1869.

My Dear Wills :—Your account of your journey reminds me of one of the latest American stories :— How a Traveller by Stage Coach said to the driver : "Did you ever see a snail, Sir?"—"Yes, Sir." "Where did you meet him, Sir?"—"I didn't meet him, Sir."—"Waal, Sir, I think you did, if you'll excuse me, for I'm damned if you ever overtook him."

As to Mrs. ——, Lord! If she only knew how ugly I am! I do believe her to be—well—let me be calm—and yet—under that Skimpolian mask of childishness as to money and worldly affairs, what abysses of shallow cunning are discernible!

All goes well here. I have been "at it" considerably. Look at a very remarkable story in 2 chapters, "An Experience,"* which begins next week.

* All the Year Round, August 14th and 21st.

Love to Mrs. Wills. I shall be here on Thursday.

Ever, My Dear Wills,
Your affectionate,
C. D.

GAD'S HILL PLACE,
HIGHAM BY ROCHESTER, KENT,
Friday, Twenty-fourth December, 1869.

MY DEAR WILLS:—I have been so put about by conflicting engagements—readings, writings, editings, Birmingham correspondence and other botherations—that I have not even written to you. And now I must put off my pleasant visit of inspection, until I get a little clear, for everything comes at once. Many Merry Christmases and Happy New Years to Mrs. Wills and you.

Ever yours affectionately,
CHARLES DICKENS.

1870.

From January to March 16th, Dickens gave a series of Farewell Readings in London at St. James's Hall.

When he died on June 8th three numbers of "Edwin Drood" had appeared and he had written enough for three more.

I have no letters, except the two that follow, for this year.

Wills outlived his friend and chief by more than ten years.

5, Hyde Park Place, London, W.,
Sunday, Twenty-third January, 1870.

My Dear Wills:—In the note to hand from you about Nancy and Sikes, you seem to refer to some other note you had written me. Therefore I think it well merely to mention that I have received no other note.

I do not wonder at your not being up to the undertaking* (even if you had had no cough) under the wearing circumstances. It was a very curious scene. The actors and actresses (most of the latter looking very pretty) mustered in extraordinary force, and were a fine audience. I set myself to carrying out of themselves and their observation, those who were bent on watching how the effects were got:—and I believe I succeeded. Coming back to it again, however, I feel it was madness ever to do it continuously. My ordinary pulse is 72, and it runs up under this effort to 112. Besides which, it takes me ten or twelve minutes to get my wind back at all: I being in the meantime like the man who lost the fight:—in fact, his express image. Frank Beard was in attendance to make divers experiments to report to Watson; and although, as you know, he stopped it instantly when he found me at Preston, he was very much astonished by the effects of the "Reading" on the Reader.

So I hope you may be able to come and hear it before it is silent for ever. It is done again on the evenings of the 1st February, 15th February, and 8th March. I hope, now I have got over the mornings, that I may be able to work at my book. But up to this time the great preparation required in

---

* This refers to a morning reading of "Sikes" and "Nancy," mainly attended by actors and actresses.

getting the subjects up again, and the twice a week besides, have almost exclusively occupied me.

I have something the matter with my right thumb, and can't (as you see) write plainly. I sent a word to poor Robert Chambers,* and I send my love to Mrs. Wills.

Ever, my Dear Wills,
Affectionately yours,
C. D.

THE ATHENÆUM,
Saturday, Twenty-sixth February, 1870.

MY DEAR WILLS :—You know that you are expected at a certain small dinner of four, next Thursday, the 3rd March, at Blanchard's in Regent Street at 6 sharp? Don't you? A word in answer to 5, Hyde Park Place, W.

Ever affectionately,
C. D.

---

* Robert Chambers's second wife had died.

INDEX.

ABSOLON, Mr., 44
Ainsworth, Harrison, 3
Albert, Prince Consort, 282, 300, n.
All the Year Round, xi, xiv, 46 ; founding of, 238 ; partnership agreement, 261 ; Charles Dickens, jun., becomes sub-editor of, 390
Allingham, William, 96, 113
Allison, Mrs., 367
Argyll, Duke of, 204
Arnold, Matthew, 47
Athenæum, 101, 286, n.
Atlantic Monthly, 381
Austin, Henry, 49, 56, 181, 187
—— Mrs. Henry (Dickens's sister), 335

BAINES, Mr., 57
Bamford, Mr., 61
Barclay-Allardice, Robert, 284
Barings' Bank, 176
Barnard, Mr., 132, 138, 139
Barrow, Robert, 283—4
Bates, Mr., 175
Beale, Mr., 348
Beard, Frank, 56, 147, 153, 333—4, 395
Beaucourt, M., 97, 129
Beecher, Ward, 377
Bell, Robert, 44
—— Mrs., 123
Bennett, W. C., 91—2
Bentley's Miscellany, 1—5
Berry, Mr., 292—3
Berwick, Miss (*see under* Procter, Adelaide).
Birtles, Mr., 317, 329, 330, 338, 341, 348, 352, 361
Blacker, Mrs., 262, 268—9
Blackwood, publisher, 249, 266

Blanchard, Sydney, 386
Bowring, Mr., 342
Boyle, Hon. Mary, 59, 285, 346, 351
Brackenbury and Wynne, 230
Bradbury, William, 19, 134, 139, 196 223
Bradbury and Evans, 123, 126, 134, 177, 209, 215—6, 236—7, 306 ; and Dickens's separation from his wife, 238 ; Dickens's disagreement with, 252—7 ; founding *Once a Week*, 269, n.
Breach, Mr., 173—4, 176
Brockedon, Mr., 60—1, 102
Brough, Mr., 170
Brown, Commodore, 68
—— Mrs., 180—2
Brown and Shipley, 361
Browne, Mr., 177—8
Brownlow, Mr., 98
Bruce, Downing, 37, 164
Buckingham, Second Duke of, 45
Buckland, Frank, 198
Buckstone, actor, 125, 209, 232
Bulwer Lytton, Sir Edward, 40, 44, 47, 51—2, 59—60, 76, 190, 285—9, 293—4, 298
Bunbury, Miss, 72
Burdett-Coutts, Baroness, xii, 66, 77, 80—1, 95, 98, 181—3, 190, 207, 237, 243, 348, 353, 366 ; Wills becomes secretary to, 157, 185—6, 201—2, 210—11 ; in Switzerland, 287 ; and Empress Eugénie, 302

CALLAGHAN, attendant, 57, 66, 71, 78
Canning, Sir Stratford, 45
Cardale, Mrs., 127

INDEX.

Cardigan, Lord, x
Carleton, Mr., 152—3
Carlisle, Lord, 82
Carlyle, Thomas, 214, 266, 351
Carrington, Lord, 46
Carter, Mr., 223
Cattermole, George, 386
Caudle, Mr., 95
Chadwick, Mr., 72
Chambers, Mr., 51, 53
—— Janet (*see under* Wills, Mrs. W. H.).
—— Robert, xi, 282, n. ; "Traditions of Edinburgh," 300 ; "Vestiges of Creation," 352 ; death of his second wife, 396
—— William, x, xi, 282, n.
Chambers's Journal, x, xiii, 195, 250
Chapman, Mr., 88
—— Frederick, 279, 286
Chapman and Hall, 286, 289
Chappell & Co., 347, 353, 362, 382
"Charter House Charity, The," 177 184
Chesterton, Mr., 51
Chisholm, Mrs., 24, n.
Chorley, Henry Fothergill, 286, 337 —8
Chute, Mr., 69
Civil Service Gazette, 162—166
Clarke, Mrs. Cowden, 365
Cleopatra's Needle, 373, n.
Coe, Mr., 69, 86
—— Mrs., 69
Collins, Charles Allston, 238, 242, 251, 285, 306, 329 ; engagement, 277 ; illness, 388
—— Mrs. C. A., 238 (*see also under* Dickens, Catherine).
—— Wilkie, 44, 97, 135, 157, 160, 192, 203, 206, 213—18, 242—4, 247—9, 256, 264—5, 270, 275— 6, 280—2, 304—5, 309, 339—41, 374, 385 ; "The Frozen Deep," 223—31, 240 ; engaged on *Household Words* staff, 221—3, 238 ; "The Dead Secret," 223, n. ; "The Idle Apprentice," 226— 36 ; " No Name," 307 ; and the

Collins, Wilkie—*continued*.
Garrick Club, 341—3 ; "Armadale," play, 352 ; "The Moonstone," 360, 386 ; assists at *All the Year Round* office, 369—70 ; illness, 381 ; " No Thoroughfare," play, 391
Cooper, Mr., 127, 133, 142
—— Thomas, 15
Coote, Mr., 80, 83
Cornhill Magazine, 195, 336, n.
Costello, Miss, 114
—— Dudley, xv, 44, 62, 82, 103 147—9, 299
Coutts, Miss (*see under* Burdett-Coutts, Baroness).
Coutts' Bank, 108, 124, 144, 199— 202, 206, 220, 237, 272, 306, 367, 382
Covent Garden Theatre, 216, n.
Craik, Georgina M., 93
Crowe, Mrs. Catherine, 23
Cruikshank, George, 110
Cuba, steamer, 367, 371, 378
Cunningham, Peter, 44, 71, 107, 172

Daily News, xi, 4, 7—16, 165, 250
—— *Telegraph*, 46
Davey, Mr., 130
Davis, Mr., 276
Devonshire, Duke of, 44, 62, n., 72
Dickens, Mrs. (*mother*), 276, 284 ; death, 330
—— Mrs. (*wife*), 35, 45, 53, 78, 103, 107, 120, 123, 128, 155, 189, 198, 215, 228 ; ill-health, 231 ; separation, 238
—— Alfred (*brother*), 178, 180—1, 275, 284
—— Augustus (*youngest brother*), 147, 215
—— Catherine (*Katey*), 179, 219, 274, 287, 351 (*see also under* Collins, Mrs. C. A.)
—— Charles, his restless energy, vi, 358 ; appreciation of Wills, xi ; edits *Daily News*, xi, 7— 11 ; edits *Bentley's Miscellany*,

INDEX. 399

Dickens, Charles—*continued.*
3—5 ; joint proprietor and editor of *Household Words,* 19 ; its scope and aims, 20 ; his suggestions for its title, 21 ; in Paris, 27—8 ; obtains a pension for John Poole, 28, 108; birth of his daughter Dora Annie, 35 ; and the Guild of Literature and Art, 44, 45 ; death of his daughter and father, 45, 54 ; on advertising, 59, 61 ; on G. A. Sala, 65, 70 ; on the deficiencies of *Household Words,* 73 ; on the loss of a friend, 81 ; an imitator of, 93 ; tour in Switzerland, 97 ; takes a château at Boulogne, 102, 129 ; his courier, 118—9 ; his "Hard Times" doubles the circulation of *Household Words,* 121 ; completes "Hard Times," 131—3 ; purchase of Gad's Hill, 157, 180—1, 187, 192, 210, 216, 217, 388 ; on Wills and the *Civil Service Gazette,* 162—6 ; on a story by Holme Lee, 168, 169 ; begins "Little Dorrit," 169—73 ; adventures in Paris, 177—82 ; and Miss Martineau's charges, 192—4, 198—200 ; and Forster's share in *Household Words,* 195—7 ; and Wilkie Collins's "The Frozen Deep," 219, 223—31 ; removes to Gad's Hill, 226 ; "The Idle Apprentices" Tour, 226—36 ; separation from his wife, 238 ; "reading" tour, 1858...239 *seq.;* on his impressionable mind, 247 ; disagreement with Bradbury and Evans, 252—7 ; founds *All the Year Round,* 261 ; partnership agreement, 261, 271 ; ill-health, 270 ; sells Tavistock House, 276, 280 ; destroys his papers, 281 ; his heavy bur-

Dickens, Charles—*continued.*
dens, 284 ; success of "Great Expectations," 286 ; on the American War, 287 ; scene at Glasgow "reading," 295—7 ; Macready on Dickens's reading, 304 ; loses a bet, 304—5 ; gift to Wills, 307, 308 ; in Paris, 311 ; on J. G. Lockhart, 315—6 ; readings in Paris for charity, 326—8 ; "Mrs. Lirriper's Lodgings," 329—39 ; death of his mother, 330 ; death of his son Sydney, 331, n. ; in a railway accident, 340, 345—6 ; resigns membership of Garrick Club, 341, 343 ; the "Chappell" reading tour, 347—9 ; American reading tour, 353 *seq.*; on the farewell dinner to him, 354—5 ; circulation of his Christmas number, "Mugby Junction," 356 ; profit of American tour, 358 ; on his own restless activity, 358 ; on Wilkie Collins's "The Moonstone," 360, 386 ; illness, 377 ; list of American readings, 380 ; returns to England, 383 ; buys land at Gadshill, 388 ; parting with his youngest son, 389 ; illness, 389—91 ; death, 394 ; effect on himself of his readings, 395

—— Charley (*eldest son*), 158, 175—6, 217, 286, 388—9 ; sub-editor of *All the Year Round,* 390

—— Dora Annie (*daughter*), 35, n. ; death, 45

—— Edward B. L. ('Plornishghenter,' *youngest son*), 78, 123, 337, 366, 377 ; departure for Australia, 389

—— Francis Jeffrey (*third son*), 287, 304, 312, 320, 327

—— Frederick (*second brother*), 228

—— H. F., K.C. (*son*), v, 76, n.

400   INDEX.

Dickens, John (*father*), 24, 49, 57;
  death, 45, 54
—— Mary (Mamie, *daughter*), v.,
  xiv., 147, 219, 280, 287, 298,
  302, 309, 311, 351, 366
—— Sydney S. H. ("the Admiral,"
  fifth son), 280, 298, 363
—— Walter Landor (*son*), 216, 230;
  death, 331, n.
Dixon, W. Hepworth, 101, n., 109,
  139, 174, 185, 204
Dodd, Mr., 102
Dolby, George (Dickens's agent for
  the "Readings"), 347, 354
  —5, 360—5, 368—9, 373—8,
  381—2
—— Mrs., 382
Dulcamara, Dr., 255
Dumas *fils*, 50

EDMUND, Mr., 343, 385
Edwards, Miss, 319
Egg, Augustus, 43—4, 97, 153
Eliot, George, 266
Ellen, *servant*, 353
Elliotson, Dr. 109—10, 223
Eugénie, ex-Empress, 302
Evans, Frederick M. (joint proprietor
  of *Household Words*), 19, 56, 59,
  80, 138—9, 144, 150, 167, 237,
  271, 273; and *Household Words*
  accounts, 252—4

FARRER, Mr., 352
Featherstone, Miss, 125
Fechter, *actor*, 341, 343, 391
Fenning, Eliza, 359, 361
Field, Inspector, 41—2, 80
Fields, James T., 362—3, 369, 371
Fillonneau, Mrs., 201
FitzGerald, Percy, 361, 385, 388
Fitzwilliam, Mrs., 125
Foote, Samuel, 112, n.
Ford, Rev. Mr., 237
Forster, John, 25—7, 30, 38, 44,
  48, 59, 69, 76, n., 98, 103,
  111, 116, 123—7, 140, 145—8,
  151, 156—8, 175, 188, 195, 200,
  203, 217, 229, 274—5, 305,

Forster, John—*continued*.
  331; *quoted*, xi; "Life of
  Charles Dickens," xiv, 121,
  226—7; joint proprietor
  Household Words, 19; and the
  Trelawney Ballad, 90; illness,
  109, 110; his share in *Household Words*, 196, 212, 253—5;
  and Tavistock House, 263;
  letter quoted, 264; and the
  Leech sale, 345; relations with
  Wills, 350; and Dickens's
  American tour, 357—9, 364—5
—— Mrs. John, 264, 274—5
Fortnightly Review, 346
Foster, Mr., 55
Franklin, Sir John, 156
—— Lady, 157

GARRICK Club, 262, 332—3, 339,
  341, 343
Gaskell, Mrs., 20, 23, 42—3, 93, 122,
  126, 137, 151, 176, 266; "North
  and South," in *Household
  Words*, 134—5, 141—5, 155;
  "My Lady Ludlow," 242; "A
  Dark Night's Work," 318,
  321—5
—— Rev. Mr., 151
General Theatrical Fund, 9—11
  35, n.
Gillies, Miss, 95
Gleig, Mr., 285
Gordon, Mr., 293, 296
—— Mrs., 315
Great Exhibition (1851), 62, 65
Greatorex, C., 392
Greening, Mr., 24, 26, 64
Grey, Lady, 59
Grieve, Thomas, 44
Guild of Literature and Art, xii, xv,
  44—5, 55, 59, 62, 66, 69, 72, 76, 79,
  80, 84, 88, 97, 109, 131, 133, 140,
  150, 153, 384—5
Guizot, M., 255, n.

HAGHE, Lewis, 45
Hale, Mr., 177

INDEX.

Hall & Co., 218
Halliday, Mr., 319, 343, 356
Hannay, James, 58, 61, 65, 69, n., 85
Harper Bros., 271, 324
Harrisons, *printers*, 324
Harwood, Mr., 317
Hawker, Rev. R. S., 90, n.
Haydn, Mr., 110
Headland, *manager*, 288, 291—2, 296, 329
Henri, *servant*, 135, 382
Henry, Mr., 84
Hill, Rowland, 25
Hobhouse, Mr., 271
Hogarth, Mr., 24, 173
—— Mrs., 202
—— Georgina, v, xiv, 39, 103, 107, 123, 142, 155, 179, 182, 219, 280, 287, 298, 301, n., 302, 309, 311, 339—40, 366, 392
—— Mary, 3
Holdsworth, Mr., 53, 173—4, 188, 241, 285, 288, 316, 337, 385
Hollingshead, John, 236
Hollyer, Mr., 230
Holmes, O. W., 368
Holt, Mr., 160
Hood, Thomas, 88
Horne, Richard H., 20, 33—40, 44, 49, 61—2, 66, n., 68—9, 77—8, 84—5, 113, n., 323, 343; dinner to, 80; in Australia, 94
—— Mrs. R. H., 94, 140
Horner, Mrs., 122
Household Words, xi, xiii; Office Book of, xiv; partnership agreement, 19; scope and aims of, 20; Dickens's suggestions for its title, 21; winding up of, 238; accounts of, 252—3; stock and title sold, 261
Howitt, William, 12, 20, 66, 85, 198
—— Miss, 65
Hullah, John Pyke, 267
Hunt, Leigh, 80, 96, 108, 113, n., 114, 156
Hunt and Roskell, 307, 314

Illustrated London News, 14
Ingram, Herbert, 217, 282

JEPHSON, Mr., 187
Jerrold, Douglas, 9, 44, 71, 105, 232; death, 226
Jewsbury, Geraldine, 71
John, *servant*, 113, 135, 139, 144, 147, 158, 170, 189, 202, 207—8, 216—18, 237, 240—1, 266, 288, 290, 316, 320, 324—6, 362; illness, 333—4
Johnson, President Andrew, 379, n.
Johnson, *printer*, 53—6, 59, 83, 109, 185, 216, 273, 279, 288, 291—2
Jolly, Emily, 167, n.
Jones, Gale, 167, n.

KAMB, Edward, 116—19
Keith, Mr., 72
Kelly, Mrs., 344, 367
Kemble, Adelaide (*see under* Sartoris, Mrs.)
—— Charles, 336, n.
—— Fanny, 348
Kinglake's "Crimea," 326
Kitton, F. J., 262
Knight, Charles, 34, n., 44—6, 53, 57, 61
Knowles, Mr., 361

LAING, Mr., 132
Lamb, Mr., 156
Land, Mr., 56
Landells, Mr., x
Landseer, Sir Edwin, 185, 206
Law, Mr., 75
Lee, Holme (*see under* Parr, Harriett)
Leech, John, xii, 42; at Boulogne, 108; sale of his effects, 345
—— Mrs., 108
Lehmann, Frederick, 302, 320
—— Nina, 302
—— R. C., 308
Lemon, Betty, 130
—— Lally, 130

INDEX.

Lemon, Mark, x, 42—4, 56—7, 66, 69, 94, 120—2, 124—5, 128, 183, 209, 217
Lever, Charles, 272, 299, 308—10
Lewis, Thomas, 50, 275
Lind, Jenny, 292
Linton, W. J., 107, n.
Lock, Mr., 230
Lockhart, J. G., 315—6
Longfellow, H. W., 368
Low, Sampson, 321
Lynn-Linton (*neé* Lynn), Mrs., 107—8, 136, 141, 154, 169—71, 188, 277—8, 295, 315—6, 385; sells Gad's Hill to Dickens, 157
Lytton, Robert, 2nd Lord, 290, 303, 322, 369, n., 378

McCULLOCH, John R., 114
Maclise, Daniel, 28, 227—8
Macready, W. C., 48, 69, 124, 229, 251; on Dickens's reading of "Copperfield," 304
Manley, Mr., 12
Marryat, Miss, 356
Marsh, Mr., 340
Marston, J. Westland, 44
Martell, Mrs., 208
Martineau, Harriet, 20, 26, 36—7, 66, 90—3, 141, 154, 205; charges against Dickens, 192—200; anecdote of, 249
Mason, Mr., 30, 353
Masson, Prof., 266, n.
Matz, B. W., 262
Mayhew, Henry, x
Mazzini, Joseph, 175
Measom, Malcolm R. L., 197
Mendicity Society, 56
Meredith, George, 270
—— Mrs., 252
Meriton, Mr., 170
Mitchell, Mr., 59—60, 348
Molesworth, Lady, 320
Morgan, *apothecary*, 202
Morley, Henry, 20, 42, 57, n., 61, 67 —9, 75, 78, 83, 86, 91, 106, 118, 126, 129, 134, 137, 149, 155, 160, 171, 177, 200—5, 214—5, 221,

Morley, Henry—*continued*.
268, 295, 299, 306, 310—14, 331, 337, 341, 388; his articles on Factory Reform, 192—9; Dickens on, 285
Morning Advertiser, 78
Mortlock, Mrs., 208
Morton, Mr., 86
Mulholland, Miss, 385
Murray, E. C. Grenville, 45—6, 51, 95, 175, 305, 318—9, 372
Mylne, Mr., 150

NATHAN, Mr., 69
National Association of Manufacturers, 193
Newgate Market, 228
Northumberland, Duke of, 204
Novelli, Mr. and Mrs., 281

OLLIER, Mr., 114, 117, 189, 318
Oliffe *family*, 190, 315
—— Lady, 320
Once a Week, 269, 274
Orr, W. S., 32
Osgood, Mr., 379
"Our Young Folks," 371, n.
Ouvry, *solicitor*, 210, 253, 257, 267, 271, 350—2
Oxenford, John, 236

PALMERSTON, Lord, 285
Panizzi, Sir Antonio, 389
Parkinson, J. C., 376
Parr, Harriett ("Holme Lee"), 147, 168, n., 311
Patmore, Coventry, 33, n.
Paxton, Sir Joseph, 40, 56, 62
Payn, James, 21, 205, 225, 248; quoted, 194—5, 249—51
Phillipps, Mr., 84
Pitt, *scene painter*, 49
Poole, John, 159, 198, 206, 219, 272, 309, 335, 366; Dickens obtains a pension for, 28, 108; Dickens visits, 392
Powell, Mr., 15
Power, Miss, 288, 312, 321, 342
Priestley, R. C., v

INDEX. 403

Priestley, Lady, v
Prince, John C., 87
Procter, Adelaide ("Miss Berwick"), 99, 121, 267
Punch, x, 9, 62, 111, 285, 345, n.

"QUEEN'S MESSENGER," 46
Quin, Lord George, 116

RACHEL, Madame, 27, 28
Radley, Mr., 301
Rae, Dr., 156
Reade, Charles, 281, 303—5; his "Hard Cash," 323—5
Rintoul, Robert S., 114, n.
Roberts, David, 9, 56
Robertson, John, 173, 183, 384
Ruffini, Agostino, 266, n.
—— Giovanni, 266
Russell, George, 339
Russia, steamer, 377

SALA, George Augustus, 46, 71, 83, 86—89, 98, 99, 103, 106—109, 113—116, 124, 136, 137, 143, 154, n., 174, 175, 208, 213, 214, 218, 225, 236, 285, 313, 335, 348, 386; Dickens on, 65, 70
Samee, Mrs. Ramo, 207, 208
Sammins, W. L., 3
Sartoris, Mrs., 336
—— Edward John, 336, n.
Saunders, *family*, 185, 284
Sawyer, Rev. W. C., 337
Scheffer, *painter*, 190
Schloss, *dealer*, 345, 356
Scotsman, 295
Scott, Mr., 71, 373
—— Mrs., 367
Shaw, Sir Charles, 155
Sidney, Mr., 136, 188, 366
Simpson, Palgrave, 343
Simpson's, 55
Skinner's, *tailors*, 316
Sloman, Mr., 49, 83, 88
Smart, Mr., 82
Smith, Albert, 208, 226

Smith, Arthur, 226, 234, 243—246, 274, 286; manages Dickens's "reading" tour, 238, 241; death, 289, 349
—— Joseph, 58
Snow, Mr., 214
Spectator, 114, n.
Spence, Mr., 299
Spicer, Mr., 285, 286, 306, 319, 330
Spielmann, Mr. H., xiii
Stacey, Mr., 23, 94
Stanfield, Clarkson, 9, 14, 39, 56, 212, 224, 270, 304, 305
Stanton, Edwin M., 379, n.
Stephen, Sir Leslie, 195
Stone, Dr., 41, n.
—— Mrs., 83
—— Frank, 44, 82, 83, 275, n.
—— Marcus, 275, n., 285, 331
Storrar, Dr., 109
Sunday Gazette, 363
Sydney, Mr., 76, 204

TAUCHNITZ, Baron, 84, 86
Telbin, Mr., 45
Temple Bar, 47
Tennent, Sir James E., 366
Tenniel, John, 44
Tennyson, Lord, 189
Thackeray, W. M., 177, 226; and Yates, 262, 332, 333
Thomas, William Moy, 83, 88, 92, 103, 128, 197, 205
Thornbury, George Walter, 268, 269, 359
Thornton, Mr., 53
Ticknor and Fields, 281, 375
Times, 137, 236, 250, 274, 282, 285, 289, 337, 363
Tinsley, Mr., 351
Topham, F. W., 44
Topping, *servant*, 70—1
Toussenel, M., 112—3
Townshend, Chauncey Hare, 135—6, 140—1, 184, 335, 370, 382
Train, The, 47, 236
Trollope, Anthony, 266, 308

UPCOTT, Mr., 361

INDEX.

VALE, Mr., 40
Victoria, Queen, 241, 300—1
Von Goetnitz, Mr., 244, n.

WALES, Prince of, 273—4
Wallack, M., 374
Walpole, Miss, 207
Watson, Mr., 395
—— R., 77, 81
—— Hon. Mrs. R., 81, 116, 157, 184, 189—90
Wellington, Duke of, 91—2
Wheatstone, Mr., 184
White, Rev. James, 170, 186, 192, 199, 201, 206, 209, 248
Whitehead, Charles, 191
Whitings, *printers*, 265, 269, 272
Whitly, Mr., 268
Wigan, Alfred, 247, n.
—— Horace, 352
Wills, William Henry, birth, vi; on his journey to London, vii—ix; school and journalism, ix; writes for *Punch*, x; assistant editor *Chambers' Journal*, x; marriage, xi; sub-editor *Daily News*, xi; assistant editor *Household Words*, xi; Dickens's appreciation of, xi; almoner secretary to Miss Coutts, xii, 157, 185—6, 201—2; love of foxhunting, xii; his personality, xii; riding accident, xiii, 378—385; appointed magistrate, xiii; death, xiii; his works, xiii; his letters, xv; joint proprietor *Household Words*, 19; his letters quoted, 30—2, 35—6, 48—9, 73—5; 164—6; and

Wills, William Henry—*continued*.
R. H. Horne, 34—8; secretary to the Guild of Literature and Art, 44—5; ill-health, 121, 267—9, 273, 335—8, 347; his mother's death, 155; offered the editorship of the *Civil Service Gazette*, 162—6; James Payn on, 194—5; his share in *All the Year Round*, 261, 271; at Llandudno, 278; in Switzerland, 287; in Paris, 302; Dickens's gift to, 307—8; his work on *All the Year Round*, 334; presents a brougham to Dickens, 339—40; and Leech's sale, 345; relations with Forster, 350; advice to Dickens on his American tour, 357, 364; retirement, 390.
—— Mrs. W. H., xi, 38, 85, 123, 130 144, 155, 171, 223, 228, 242—9, 269, 275, 278, 281—2, 287, 302, 318, 330, 339, 345, 361, 369, 372 —3, 376—7, 380—2, 386, 392—6; death, xiv; Dickens's letters to, 120—1, 211, 229, 336—7, 347—350, 383—4, 389; legacy to R. C. Lehmann, 308
Wilson, Sir Erasmus, 73
Woods, *agents*, 293, 296
World, 46, 262

YATES, Edmund, 46—7, 236, 265, 268, 320, 331, 385; and Thackeray, 262, 332—3
Young, Mr., 178
—— Miss, 69

76727

THE LIBRARY
ST. MARY'S COLLEGE OF MARYLAND
ST. MARY'S CITY, MARYLAND 20686